DOLLS! DOLLS! DOLLS!

Deep Inside *Valley of the Dolls*, the Most Beloved Bad Book and Movie of All Time

STEPHEN REBELLO

PENGUIN BOOKS

PENGUIN BOOKS

An imprint of Penguin Random House LLC
penguinrandomhouse.com

LIBRARY OF CONGRESS CATALOGING-IN-PUBLICATION DATA

Names: Rebello, Stephen, author.
Title: Dolls! Dolls! Dolls! : deep inside Valley of the dolls, the most
beloved bad book and movie of all time / Stephen Rebello.
Description: [New York] : Penguin Books, [2020] |
Includes bibliographical references and index. |
Identifiers: LCCN 2019053123 (print) | LCCN 2019053124 (ebook) |
ISBN 9780143133506 (paperback) | ISBN 9780525505297 (ebook)
Subjects: LCSH: Susann, Jacqueline. Valley of the dolls. |
Susann, Jacqueline. Valley of the dolls—Film adaptations. | Valley of the dolls
(Motion picture) | Motion pictures—Production and direction—United
States—History—20th century. | Popular literature—United
States—History and criticism.
Classification: LCC PN1997.V264 R43 2020 (print) |
LCC PN1997.V264 (ebook) | DDC 813/.54—dc23
LC record available at https://lccn.loc.gov/2019053123
LC ebook record available at https://lccn.loc.gov/2019053124

Printed in the United States of America
1   3   5   7   9   10   8   6   4   2

Set in Cheltenham ITC Pro
Designed by Sabrina Bowers

For Gary,
who never had to put up with
booze and dope, just *mishegas*

"I'm not the only one who came out of the *Valley of the Dolls* premiere thinking, 'Well, that's the end of my career.'"

—PATTY DUKE

Contents

Author's Note

How do I love thee, *Valley of the Dolls*? Let me count the whys. My magnificent obsession with all things *Valley* began when I secretly rummaged through my mom's dresser for her (carefully hidden between her slips and a hot water bottle) paperback copy of Jacqueline Susann's notorious Hollywood and Broadway roman à clef. Having been a precocious kid and an insatiable reader, I'd already been to the sex/sin/salvation literary rodeo thanks to Harold Robbins's *The Carpetbaggers*, Grace Metalious's *Peyton Place*, and Rona Jaffe's *The Best of Everything*. But from all I had heard, Jacqueline Susann's novel promised to be those novels *squared*. It didn't disappoint. I mean, it had everything. It *was* everything. Boozers! Pill-heads! Lesbians! Sex! Heartbreak! More sex! Homosexuals! Catfights! Incurable diseases! Wig snatching! Handsome caddish and spineless wonders! Still more heartbreak! Still more sex! And, for kicks, hey, aren't those characters pretty transparently based on Judy Garland, Ethel Merman, Marilyn Monroe, and Grace Kelly?

With Susann at the wheel, show business schadenfreude felt alluring, voyeuristic, and deliciously *inside*. No wonder *Valley of the Dolls* became a straight-up pop cultural phenom, the most talked-about, record-breaking bestseller of its era. The book was terrible, irresistible, hokey, hot, and, in its way, transgressive. And for me—a kid aching to bust loose from a leafy, straitlaced, idyllic, Lawrenceville-like New England small town—it was a road map. And a warning. The way people talked back then about *Valley of the Dolls*—on TV and radio, blasting it from church pulpits, whispering about it over the back fence, and sniggering about it at parties for grown-ups—a movie version just had to be inevitable. And so, just in time for Christmas 1967, *Valley of the Dolls*, all glittery and glossy in Panavision and Color by Deluxe, opened, with a hand-painted ticket booth sign screaming "Adolts [*sic*] Only" in our neighboring city's most cavernous, slightly faded movie palace. But that mis-spelled sign meant that the puckered, steely woman sitting in the ticket booth would never let slip past her judgmental gaze the fresh-faced likes of me. Besides, like many locals back in a time when there were such now-quaint notions as shame and when some peo-ple took seriously the finger-wagging and dire warnings of the Cath-olic Church, I'd never want to be caught buying a ticket to the "dirty movie" our parish priest had been warning us about for weeks. So, three pals and I piled into my shimmying, heatless VW bug and drove fifty miles through freezing rain to Boston for a look-see at the notorious film that critics were shredding but audiences were see-ing in droves. My regular worship of moviemaking idols like Fellini, Lean, Hitchcock, Penn, Antonioni, Wilder, Bergman, and Kubrick would have to be put on hold for a bit. *Valley of the Dolls* promised to be a sizzling, steamy, check-your-brains-at-the-door blast.

Outside the opulent Savoy Theatre, opened in 1928 and today the Boston Opera House, my friends and I queued up with several hun-dred other rain-pelted fellow stalwarts and thrill seekers. Gigantic lobby posters blared the hard sell. "The Producers wish to state that any similarity between any person, living or dead, and the characters portrayed in this film is purely coincidental and not in-tended." "Leave the Children Home!" "The Motion Picture That Shows What America's All Time #1 Best Seller First Put Into Words!" Other posters offered teasing glimpses of a half-clad Patty Duke and kit-teny Miss *Peyton Place* Barbara Parkins. Another photo depicted a fully clad Susan Hayward gritting her teeth and flaring her nostrils while leaning backward as if executing some faintly bizarre interpretative dance position. *Hoo boy, this is going to be a weird, hot ride*, we thought.

It was. Just not the way we'd hoped.

Valley of the Dolls arrived in an era that had already brought us such adult fare as *Blow-Up, Alfie, Bonnie and Clyde, Point Blank, Who's Afraid of Virginia Woolf?*, and *Persona*, in a pop culture that had already spewed out such satiric gems as Allan Sherman's 1964 ditty "Pills" and the dark, driving anthem "Mother's Little Helper," the Rolling Stones' finger wag at Valium, the middle-class woman's pill of choice. By comparison, *Valley* turned out to be clumsy, tone-deaf, unhip, quaint, unintentionally hilarious, and strangely unsexy. Aside from a meant-to-be-shocking naughty word dropped here and there, the movie played like a mash-up of dozens of old movies I'd already seen on *The Late, Late Show* starring, oh, say, Doris Day, Ida Lupino, Joan Crawford, Bette Davis, or Susan Hayward. Mesmerizingly hapless as it was, though, its gloriously entertaining badness grabbed me by the collar. The movie was funny and sad. Tacky and noble. Hokey and moving. A lovable, irresistible train wreck. It got under my skin and stayed there. And *Valley of the Dolls* has woven in and out of my life ever since. In 1993 my coauthor Edward Margulies and I vaulted it to the very top of our pantheon in the celebratory book *Bad Movies We Love*. Then, in the mid-2000s, after happening on a script I'd written for a European producer, a film production company brought me in for early meetings to discuss the possibility of my writing a new *Valley of the Dolls* movie. My pitch for the opening images of the film was a riff on Norma Desmond by way of Peg Entwistle. Suicidal and strung out, superstar-on-the-skids Neely O'Hara teeters in high heels to the top of the Hollywood sign. Once there she lets loose with a scathing indictment of the business and the people who did her wrong; below, rabid newscasters live-broadcast her meltdown, jostling and trampling one another to move their cameras into the best position to catch her fall. And that was just the opening. Apparently, my approach was Nathanael West–, Billy Wilder/I. A. L. Diamond–, and Douglas Sirk–esque enough to encourage the company to inform me that they had begun conversations with Carrie Fisher's agents about the possibility of our collaborating. Carrie never showed up for either of two prearranged meetings, but then again, I never knew whether or not the Carrie talk was for real, let alone whether or not the company even had the rights to do anything with the material. The flurry of phone calls and meetings soon stopped. Somehow the whole thing dissolved, as these things can.

Between the publication of *Bad Movies We Love* and Carrie's purported no-shows, though, I had big fun constantly luring new, unsuspecting victims into the *Valley*. At a special showing one 1997 night at the Los Angeles County Museum of Art, among the *Valley* virgins was Sharon Stone. The audience—some, including Courtney Love, in Jacqueline Susann tribute outfits or full-on *Valley of the Dolls* drag—howled, recited the dialogue, wept, cheered, and popped candy "dolls" along with the heroines on-screen. Stone was so fascinated by Sharon Tate's hair and makeup that she adopted the look for her role in the Martin Scorsese–directed *Casino* that same year, and she looked sensational.

Several other of my *Valley* revisits were in the company of a brilliant, caustic fellow writer and friend, who was a second-generation Hollywood brat. These were some of my richest, funniest encounters with the movie—until they became the most painful. With each viewing, I saw this friend, whose favorite *Valley* girl was Neely O'Hara, grow more and more destructively dependent upon prescription drugs. No matter how many of us tried to help in dozens of different ways, our pal became combative, unreliable, and unemployable before eventually spiraling toward an early death.

Jean Cocteau famously called himself "a lie that always speaks the truth." *Valley of the Dolls* embodies Cocteau's credo. I wanted to write about a movie that had so much going for it behind the camera, had so many reputations riding on it, and yet ran deliriously off the rails. The passage of time since my first encounters with the Susann universe and the joyful process of researching, interviewing those who were there (or nearby), and writing this book have revealed more than I ever bargained for. *Valley*—as soapy, gaudy, ridiculous, and gonzo as it is—delivers its payload as a cautionary, prescient tale of the perils of prescription drug use right alongside its melodramatic trappings that make it a mink-and-mascara-lined kitsch milestone. It's rife with clichés, tacky platitudes, and melodrama, yet it still exposes truths about the callousness and cruelty of the Biz, about aging, about how the deck is stacked against women, about losing one's way and struggling to find the road back, and about the steep cost of fame. It also presages the endlessly self-promoting, self-reflexive, celebrity-obsessed culture we have become.

Maybe the next time I'm asked, Why *Valley of the Dolls?* I'll just smile, shrug, and paraphrase a deathless bit of screenwriters Helen Deutsch and Dorothy Kingsley's dialogue: "I know it's a rotten movie—but I love it!"

—Stephen Rebello,
Los Angeles, 2020

Sinking Ship, or Other Than That, How Was the Movie, Ms. Susann?

November 16, 1967
Venice, Italy

Watch the old newsreel footage. Browse the photographs. If you look closely enough and read carefully enough between the lines, some of it's there. The rest, the *good* stuff, trust me, will get filled in. Arriving for the first of seven international seagoing previews of *Valley of the Dolls*, the movie version of her mammoth bestselling novel, Jacqueline Susann swept across the deck of the sparkling new, $20 million, 492-foot *Princess Italia* luxury cruise ship. She looked like a woman convinced she had life by the shorthairs. Crowned by a selection from her arsenal of jet-black, shoulder-length falls—this one girlishly adorned with white bows— the indomitable forty-eight-year-old Susann had accessorized for the ship's maiden voyage with one of her fabulous displays of too- muchness: caterpillar-thick false lashes, white eye shadow, lips and nails painted the color of overripe Dekopon oranges, and an eye- strobing, paisley-patterned white Pucci dress. Susann, a master of self-promotion and pioneer of branding, comported herself in a manner befitting her status as one of the world's most newly famous and recognizable personages. Squiring her was her spouse of nearly three decades, fifty-eight-year-old Irving Mansfield (né Mandelbaum). For the occasion the gimlet-eyed former publicist, TV writer, and producer had decked himself out in white evening formal wear. This made a nice change from his array of expensive linen shirts unbuttoned (at least) one button too many, exposing his 24-karat-gold, jewel-encrusted ankh medallion, the ancient Egyptian *crux ansata* symbolizing the life force, resting atop a nest of chest hair. One indulgence he refused to forgo: he'd crisped his skin to a brown somewhere between sienna and russet.

Susann swanned her way into the ship's 147-seat ballroom, pausing to air-kiss the film's young stars Patty Duke, Sharon Tate, and Barbara Parkins (her special favorite) and to chat with director Mark Robson and wife, Sara, and various 20th Century Fox executives. Susann was, as always, polished, outgoing, quippy, magnetic, and lethal if crossed. Attention and deference had to be—and *was*—paid to her. This was, after all, a night of nights for the author who had rocked the publishing world with a cultural phenomenon pecked out with two fingers on a blue Royal typewriter over eighteen months of eight-hour-daily writing sessions in her leather-walled, Pucci-draped 200 Central Park South aerie. Susann had created a juicy, lurid, compulsively readable roman à clef about three ambitious young women scaling the Broadway and Hollywood heights only to turn to liquor and pills when their dreams, successes, and romances turn out to be devastating letdowns. *Valley of the Dolls* more than delivered the goods to millions of celebrities, working women, and housewives, the unwashed masses who could live vicariously through characters who seemed an awful lot like Marilyn Monroe, Judy Garland, Ethel Merman, and more.

As the *Princess Italia* set sail, twenty-one months had passed since the publication of *Valley of the Dolls*, and Susann's book still rode high on the *New York Times* bestseller list. Mocked gleefully by the press and the literary intelligentsia as sudsy, poorly written swill, the book would eventually go on to be cited in the *Guinness Book of Records* as what was then the single bestselling novel of all time, moving thirty million copies. That's bigger than *Gone with the Wind* and topped only by the Bible, the Quran, and, decades later, *Harry Potter and the Sorcerer's Stone.* The book's runaway success was a sweet victory for the relentlessly driven, hardworking Susann, who had been struggling unsuccessfully since the 1940s as a model, TV personality, stage actress, and playwright. It was a more personal vindication for Susann who, in 1962, underwent a mastectomy to try to stop the spread of a malignancy.

And on this November night, along with members of the British, French, German, Italian, and Swiss press; the moviemakers; and the cast members, Susann was about to view what was predicted to be one of the year's most unmissable movies. Susann told the press that not only had she not yet seen the film, but she also hadn't even been shown the shooting script. But she took heart from the relentless drumbeat emanating from the 20th Century Fox publicity department and from the studio's decision to launch *Valley of the Dolls* with splashy Old Hollywood publicity hoopla—a first-ever twenty-thousand-mile, one-month roundelay of catered shipboard parties and screenings. Some on both sides of the camera believed that their personal and professional fortunes were about to hit the sky.

Then the houselights dimmed, and the projector whirred.

Fade in on a portentous white-on-black title card—held for almost fifteen seconds—reading: "The producers wish to state that any similarity between any persons, living or dead, and the characters portrayed in the film you are about to see is purely coincidental and not intended." Knowing murmurs ripple through the crowd. The famous 20th Century Fox fanfare sounds out, the logo fades, and over a credit sequence featuring Alberto Giacometti–influenced abstract figures and tumbling pills, Barbara Parkins begins to intone in her alluring purr, "You've got to climb Mount Everest to reach the

Valley of the Dolls . . ." and when she's done narrating, then Dionne Warwick begins warbling Dory Previn and André Previn's wistful, haunting title tune. So far, so good.

But then something goes terribly wrong. The sound begins to boom and echo weirdly around the hall. The action and sound go wildly out of synch, speeding up and making the cast members sound like Alvin and the Chipmunks and move like Keystone Kops. Quiet titters build into raucous laughter that ricochets around the auditorium. What is happening? It turns out that 20th had lavished a fortune on food and finery but had provided only one 35-millimeter projector and a makeshift film screen a journalist later described as "no larger than one a film buff might use for showing a home movie." To avoid the inevitable lengthy delays that would have been neces- sary if the projectionist had to change one of the film's twelve reels every eleven minutes, all 123 minutes of *Valley of the Dolls* had been loaded onto a single unwieldy reel of film.

Up go the house lights. While the Italian projectionist labors fran- tically to fix the snafus, veteran film-editor-turned-movie-director Mark Robson rises and begins to speak in a style a reporter de- scribed as "soothing, patient as if he were explaining his latest sci- entific experiment to all the boys and girls out there in TV land. Golly, Mr. Wizard." Robson, a man given to bow ties and inscruta- ble expressions, delivers glib apologies and attempts to stall by inviting questions from the audience. Few take the bait. Finally, the beleaguered projectionist restarts the show from the beginning, but everything sounds even worse—and funnier—than before. The laughs and guffaws grow so loud, the dialogue becomes inau- dible. All that time and money the studio spent on vocal coaches for the leading ladies, and they wind up sounding like Minnie Mouse on helium. A reporter in attendance commented, "Remem- ber that scene in *Singin' in the Rain* where they're having a sneak preview of a silent movie with sound and dialogue added, *The Duelling Cavalier*, and everything that could possibly go wrong *did*? This *Valley of the Dolls* premiere was like that—an unmitigated disaster." The projectionist eventually resolved the mechanical issues. But the rancid dialogue and over-the-top performances got the audience laughing louder than ever.

Barbara Parkins recalled that she and Sharon Tate saw an "appalled, angry, hysterical" Jacqueline Susann leap up in the middle of the screening and say, "They've ruined my book!" Later the writer cornered director Mark Robson to tell him, "You've made a piece of shit!" Refusing to honor her commitment to stay aboard the *Princess Italia* to meet the press and critics in different ports, Susann somehow got herself and her husband off the ship and had them both whisked to the Canary Islands and back to New York where, according to songwriter and radio-and-TV reporter Ruth Batchelor, a friend and colleague of Susann's, "she stayed zonked out on pills for two weeks."

Susann wasn't alone in expecting that the movie had every reason to be stylish, sexy, provocative, powerful, attention getting, even *important*. What went so wrong? The backstory of the making—and unmaking—of *Valley of the Dolls* reveals how that disastrous screening was only the latest in an epic series of mishaps, betrayals, broken promises, blood feuds, and acts of vengeance involving virtually everyone involved. It all began with . . .

CHAPTER ONE

Jackie

Valley of the Dolls is the novel Jacqueline Susann was born to write. In a way she had been rehearsing for it since her birth on August 20, 1918, in Philadelphia. She was the sole child of a prim and fastidious schoolteacher, Rose (Jans), and Robert Susan, a dashing, successful portrait painter and womanizer who charged high-society types $5,000 (roughly $63,000 today) to flatter them shamelessly on canvas. Rose, a woman of some force and agency, took it upon herself to append another "n" to her daughter's Dutch and Sephardic Jewish surname. Determined to ensure that that new name would be correctly pronounced "SuZANN" rather than "Susan," Rose inadvertently provided her daughter with a stage name. A posed photo of Susann and her father from the summer of 1926 shows the young girl in a long-sleeved linen shift—unsmiling, hair bobbed, bangs brushing her grave, dark eyes. Her right hand rests on her breast. Her left lies intimately draped over her father's shoulder. They're on the front stairs leading to the grand porch of their columned home, and the dark-haired, faintly Hollywood-inspired Susann, dressed in plus fours, saddle shoes, and argyle socks, stares off with a faraway air of restlessness. Jackie used to confide to her friends about her dad's essential unreachability. Decades later she told journalists that as early as age eight, her father lamented not having a male heir. When he said, "There will be no one to carry on the name Susan," little Jackie assured him, "I'll carry it on. I'm going to be an actress." The way Susann told it, her father grinned and said, "Well, if you're going to be an actress, be a good actress. Be a people-watcher."

Adoring her seductive, elusive father as she did, she took his advice to heart, and, years later, he would go on to become her model for a number of the attractive, unfaithful, and essentially unattainable male antiheroes in her novels. As one of his many acts of defiance against his wife, he fed his little girl's show business fantasies. He squired her to all the newest movies and plays. He fostered her dreams of stardom and delighted that she plastered her bedroom walls with photos of (mostly female) theatrical idols of the day. He crowed proudly when she auditioned for local plays and radio shows. On April 16, 1936, in a beauty contest for which her father was a judge, she was crowned at age seventeen "Philadelphia's most beautiful girl." Buoyed by Robert Susan's constant and florid boosterism, she would agree with that assessment. As part of the beauty contest prize, she was sent to New York for a Warner Bros. screen test. They passed. Undeterred and now more than ever determined to make a name for herself, she tore off to New York to stay, over Rose's howls of protest. Jackie, as she now preferred being known, took up residence at Kenmore Hall, a compact 145 East Twenty-third Street hotel, where, as she was well aware, the residents once numbered Nathanael West, Erskine Caldwell, and Dashiell Hammett, who finished *The Maltese Falcon* there. (Decades later, in *Valley of the Dolls*, patrician heroine Anne Welles would room at the Martha Washington Hotel at 29 East Twenty-ninth Street between Madison Avenue and Park Avenue South.) Jackie's fellow residents included many show people on the way up or down. Among them was a diminutive, tough-tender, scrappy young vaudeville performer named

Ethel Agnes O'Neill—nicknamed Effie—with whom she'd become friends. Effie would go on to be an inspiration for *Valley of the Dolls* heroine Neely, a forename Susann poached from Betty Smith's 1943 novel, *A Tree Grows in Brooklyn*. Susann would meld elements of Effie with thinly disguised aspects of the life of the blazingly talented, gallant but self-destructive Judy Garland, the film, stage, and recording powerhouse. Nothing was lost on Susann, who, heeding her dad's advice, studied people constantly and who possessed a remarkable memory for dialogue.

Jackie launched a full-on assault at stardom. After dozens of unsuccessful auditions, she managed to snag a tiny role in a big show—the original 1936 Broadway production of *The Women*. Her father had called in a favor to get her cast, but Jackie got sacked during rehearsals. Still, she refused to completely let go of the chance to appear in Clare Boothe Luce's seminal all-female comedy, which famously featured crackling, bitchy dialogue and two knock-down, drag-out catfights. Even after her dismissal, she took the opportunity to study the play by watching every performance from the wings. While hoping to be rehired, she also developed what Irving Mansfield, her publicity flack/producer/promoter-to-be, would later describe as a "fierce crush" on the show's leading lady, Margalo Gillmore. Gillmore viewed Susann's intense Eve Harrington–worthy devotion to her as "a bit much." In the end, Jackie did get hired to replace Beryl Wallace (the showgirl tootsy of theater producer–showman Earl Carroll) as the lingerie model billed as "First Model." She began performances on June 2, 1937. Meanwhile, Jackie grew close to actress Beatrice Cole, an elegant and refined blond beauty billed in *The Women* as "Second Model." Susann and Cole (both would become prototypes for the cool, classy Anne Welles character in *Valley of the Dolls*) modeled and demonstrated such products as Lux Toilet Soap. Jackie doggedly auditioned for showier roles, but it took meeting press agent Irving Mansfield at a showbiz-friendly Walgreen's to heat things up. Jackie, who frequently referred to herself as "a tearing beauty" and "lovely me," had mercenary intentions in her attraction to the physically unprepossessing Mansfield, the publicist for such top radio programs as *The Rudy Vallee Show*. Letty Cottin Pogrebin, founding editor of *Ms.* magazine, who first encountered Mansfield when she was assigned to publicize the novel *Valley of the Dolls*, likened Irving to "a Jewish uncle, a throwback to an earlier generation who'd turned himself into a character out of Damon Runyon and *Guys and Dolls*, all slicked-down hair, flashy suits, fast-talking—and, as the perfect press agent, always selling you something. He was a can-do person, which I liked." Although Mansfield was not Susann's type—aside from older actresses, she found Jewish comedians irresistible—he was nevertheless a shrewd, unusually well-connected NYU grad who in 1946 became a major producer with CBS, where he developed high-profile programming, including *Arthur Godfrey's Talent Scouts* and *The Jane Froman Show*. He possessed the clout and contacts to do for Jackie what the press-agent character Mel could do for Neely in *Valley of the Dolls*: get her flattering mentions and photos in all the widely read gossip columns, push and prod her to the next level. In Jackie's mind, all that stood between herself and stardom was a publicity blitz. Says Pogrebin, "Her self-confidence and self-possession were breathtaking and unshakable. She wasn't going to *be* somebody, she already *was* somebody."

Jackie and Irving set up residence in a swank Essex House apartment, but when Mansfield was otherwise engaged, Susann leaped headfirst into a fling with the very married, much older Eddie Cantor, as big a deal as anyone could be in vaudeville, the Ziegfeld Follies, radio, films, and stage. For Susann such side affairs with father substitutes tended to be transient and mercenary. The Cantor liaison produced the kind of dividend she most valued: a walk-on in the star's newest Broadway vehicle, *Banjo Eyes*, which opened in December of 1941. In March of 1942, Jackie repeated the pattern. Irving had been drafted into the army, and Jackie was in Chicago playing in the all-female cast of *Cry 'Havoc'* appearing in town at the time was Joe E. Lewis, the cocky, mobbed-up comedian often called "the father of stand-up." Lewis had been a pop singer in Chicago nightclubs and gin joints during Prohibition. Famous for his ribald patter between songs and for his boozing it up onstage, Lewis enraged the owners of his North Side home club the Green Mill when he announced he was relocating to the rival Rendezvous Club Café. A week after Lewis's successful opening, Al Capone's enforcers invaded the entertainer's hotel room, fractured his skull, slit his throat, and sliced off part of his tongue. Lewis recovered, reinvented himself, and enjoyed a major comedy career. Frank Sinatra called him one of the four or five greatest artists in American pop history and played him in the movie biography *The Joker Is Wild*.

As unlikely as it may seem, Susann fell hard for Lewis. She took up residence at the Royalton and left Mansfield, telling a friend that she refused to live with a man who now only made an army recruit's salary. After Mansfield's army discharge, he and Jackie recoupled circa 1946, but Susann never stopped caring for Joe Lewis. When she acquired her adored black poodle in the '50s, she named the dog Josephine in tribute. A catchphrase of Lewis's nightclub act was "You only live once—but if you work it right, once is enough." On his deathbed in 1971, Lewis told Susann he was mistaken: "Once is not enough." Jackie made that the title of her third novel, published in 1973.

But if Susann was sufficiently satisfied with ex-G.I. Mansfield's booming career to relocate with him to the Hotel Navarro on Central Park South, she was much less so with her casting in New York stage revivals of *Blossom Time* and *Let's Face It*. Something a bit better came up in 1945 with *A Lady Says Yes*, a short-lived Broadway musical featuring bubbly, buxom, statuesque 20th Century Fox contract blonde Carole Landis, one of a number of stunners signed by priapic studio boss Darryl F. Zanuck with an agreement of guaranteed sexual access. Vibrant, good-hearted, well-read Landis, the victim of an almost Dickensian childhood of abandonment and sexual abuse, was similarly exploited by Hollywood, where she was nicknamed, variously, the Chest, the Blonde Bomber, and the "Ping" Girl.

While appearing together in *A Lady Says Yes*, Susann and Landis—both of whom had been sexually involved with vaudevillian, actor, and singer George Jessel—grew exceedingly close. (Jessel famously renamed Frances Gumm as Judy Garland; twenty-two years after *A Lady Says Yes*, he would also appear as himself in an awards ceremony scene in *Valley of the Dolls*.) Landis gifted Susann with earrings and a fur coat; Jackie described to several of her closest female friends how "sensual it had been when she and Carole had stroked and kissed each other's breasts." After audiences said no to *A Lady Says Yes*, the two stayed in touch during Landis's two-year marriage to a Broadway producer and, after their divorce, through an intense, tortured affair with caddish actor Rex Harrison. But in 1948, at age twenty-nine, the much-married Landis ended her life with a Seconal overdose, reportedly due to her despondency over Harrison's refusal to divorce wife Lilli Palmer and marry her. Susann kept the tragic Landis foremost in her mind when she created the character of the gorgeous, modestly talented showgirl Jennifer North in *Valley of the Dolls*.

Susann and Mansfield suffered a life-changing tragedy with the birth of their son, Guy Hildy Mansfield (his middle name a tribute to cabaret singer Hildegarde, another of Susann's crushes), on December 6, 1946. The handsome baby displayed behavioral issues from the outset and, at age three, was diagnosed with what doctors would today call severe autism—about which little was known at the time. Guy's doctors prescribed a series of shock treatments that did nothing to lessen the little boy's agonies and only intensified those of his parents. The Mansfields were shattered when told that Guy would require institutionalization for the rest of his life. Several close friends, such as actress Joan Castle, asserted that Jackie's devastation precipitated and accelerated her voracious appetite for prescription drugs. Guy would so haunt Susann that she tried to exorcise some of her grief in the *Valley of the Dolls* character of childlike singer Tony Polar, institutionalized as a young man because of a degenerative hereditary disease. Susann wrote the novel in a home office converted from what had been Guy's nursery. She came to call the room her "torture chamber."

Through the late '40s into the '50s, Susann poured herself into several pursuits. One was her complex and troublesome fixation on Ethel Merman. Becoming chummy with the siren-voiced fifty-one-year-old musical comedy legend quickly turned into Susann behaving, according to singer Hildegarde's manager Anna Sosenko, "absolutely loony, like a 12-year-old . . . she had really fallen for her." The open-secret relationship between Susann and Merman raised eyebrows among denizens of the Great White Way, as had rumors of Susann's earlier relationship with fashion designer Coco Chanel. Manhattan partygoers attest to having witnessed Merman and Susann making out late one night on a couch—horizontally and at some length. Susann proudly boasted to intimates how she had performed a sensual bump and grind private striptease to help Merman prepare for her career-defining "Rose's Turn," the now legendary 11 o'clock number in the hit 1959 Jule Styne–Stephen Sondheim musical *Gypsy.*

Though both women were volatile and quick to anger, their relationship seemed to be going along swimmingly until a loud, nasty argument broke out between them at a New York restaurant. Things got so heated that Irving hurled a drink at Merman, not only publicly humiliating bona fide show business royalty but also outraging his wife. According to multiple sources, Susann was so shaken by the incident that she turned up that night at Merman's apartment door, loudly weeping and repeatedly wailing, "I love you!" Susann grew so unhinged that Merman called security to have her ejected and, from that time forward, froze her out of her life. Susann, shaken and desolate, threatened suicide convincingly enough that Irving persuaded her to check into a psychiatric hospital, where she suffered a nervous collapse. Years later she exacted revenge by using Merman as an inspiration for foul-mouthed, combative, sexually frustrated, slipping-down-Broadway gargoyle Helen Lawson in *Valley of the Dolls*.

On her release from what Helen Lawson would indelicately call "the nuthouse," Jackie redoubled her mission to immortalize her father by becoming a famous actress. Or a famous *something*. She grew weary of being "cast as what I looked like—a glamorous divorcee who gets stabbed or strangled." After the Merman fiasco, Susann was determined to get herself back in the public eye, whatever it took. She became the on-air spokesmodel, writer, and producer of TV ads for the Schiffli Lace and Embroidery Association, and for five years, she got constant exposure as "the Schiffli Girl" on such programs as *The Mike Wallace Interview* and *The Ben Hecht Show*. She'd sometimes appear in the ads with her beloved poodle, Josephine. It was not enough, though. Susann held an unshakable belief that she could write. She and cowriter, Bea Cole, had, after all, achieved a bit of success back in the mid-1940s with a tickle-and-tease sex farce titled *The Temporary Mrs. Smith*; directed by the droll actress Jessie Royce Landis, the play opened on Broadway in December of 1946 with the new title *Lovely Me*. Risqué enough to pack the theater early in its run, the show was so trounced by critics that ticket sales slowed and the producers rang down the curtain after thirty-seven performances. *Daily News* critic Douglas Watt's review enraged Susann to the point that she walloped him in full view of other famous, gossipy patrons at Sardi's.

Undaunted by the failure of *Lovely Me*, Susann and Cole decided to collaborate on a down-and-dirty tell-all novel, *Underneath the Pancake*, about the challenges of being female in show business. Although they abandoned their effort in the early stages, Susann thought they were on to something. In the years following, she toyed with the possibility of blending some of the ideas and characters she and Cole had concocted with a new brainstorm: a novel to be called *The Pink Dolls*, an exposé of drug and alcohol addiction among the rich and famous of New York and Hollywood. Meanwhile, Susann wrote lively letters to her friends around the world detailing her latest adventures—and tales of the exploits of her poodle, whose painted portrait eventually adorned the flank of Susann's Eldorado. It took theatrical impresario Billy Rose and his wife, Joyce Mathews, who were living in a villa in the South of France, to suggest that she make Josephine the central character of a book.

So, at age forty-five, Susann cleared the decks and, nine months later, emerged with a manuscript called *Every Night, Josephine!* Irving shopped it to all the top agents without getting a nibble. But when the manuscript reached the desk of Annie Laurie Williams, the Manhattan literary agent who, partnered with her husband, Maurice Crain, amassed a client list that included recent Nobel Prize winner John Steinbeck and newly anointed Pulitzer winner Harper Lee, Williams thought the book charming and commercially viable. Susann signed with the agent, who was described as possessing "a face and figure like Mae West and a mind like a steel trap." Williams promptly submitted *Every Night, Josephine!* to Doubleday; their editors sat on it for months.

Irving sent the restless Jackie and her mother on a diversionary trip around the world. In Japan, Susann stocked up on over-the-counter Seconal, the insomnia fighter that ranked high among her many "dolls" of choice. While there, she sent Irving a letter in which she crowed enthusiastically about her early idea for another book: "I think I have a great title—*Valley of the Dolls*—all based on our little red dolls in the medicine chest." But in that same letter, she nonchalantly mentioned a small lump she had discovered on her breast and asked Irving to make a precautionary appointment with her physician. Back in New York, her doctor delivered a sobering diagnosis: infiltrating ductile carcinoma. Mansfield wrote later about how his wife, when up against the wall, would make deals with God. "I've got to leave something worthwhile on this earth before I go," she wrote in her diary on the first of January 1963. Susann promised God that if He gave her ten more years of life, she would become the world's top-selling writer. Celebrity columnist Cindy Adams said of Susann, "This woman had to be known, to be seen, to be heard. She would not be a nonentity."

Doubleday's editors eventually informed Susann that, although they found *Every Night, Josephine!* to be winning and publishable, they'd already contracted with brilliant comic Beatrice Lillie for a book about *her* pet, and so could not publish Susann's tome. The crushing disappointment, coupled with her medical diagnosis, sent Susann into therapy and deeper into popping pills, some of them prescribed by her therapist. But either way, she always had easy access to a stash of the day's most popular "dolls," including Seconal, Benzedrine, and Valium.

In February 1963, thanks to Irving, Jackie's manuscript landed on the desk of their newspaperman friend Earl Wilson, known for his juicy, popular, six-day-a-week "It Happened Last Night" gossip column. Wilson quickly sent the manuscript by messenger to publishing maverick Bernard Geis, a former Prentice Hall editor who, in 1959, launched Bernard Geis Associates, working out of a wee East Fifty-sixth Street office. A smart, literate, waggish firebrand, Geis—known as "Berney"—loved attention as much as he enjoyed smacking New York's conservative literary establishment on its upturned nose. Financially backed by celebrity clients, including Art Linkletter, Groucho Marx, Ralph (*This Is Your Life*) Edwards, and TV game show producers Mark Goodson and Bill Todman, Geis's agency published what were known by literary critics and the industry at the time as "non books." Nevertheless, those "non books" produced a run of *New York Times* bestsellers by Marx, Linkletter, Max Schulman, Abigail "Dear Abby" Van Buren, President Harry Truman, and Helen Gurley Brown with her boundary-shattering *Sex and the Single Girl.*

Geis was particularly attracted to self-publicizing clients, and his fortunes and influence expanded so quickly that he annexed another floor of his building, connecting the offices by a fireman's pole.

The pole sliders soon numbered not only agile clients but also the associates Geis began to add to the organization, described by one observer as "the epitome of the Swinging Sixties." The dozen or so employees included the sophisticated, highly literate Don Preston (who famously recommended rejecting the manuscript of Susann's *Valley of the Dolls*), Letty Cottin Pogrebin (future founding editor of *Ms.*), and savvy senior editor Jackie Farber. Geis and his wife, Darlene, a children's book author and book editor for Harry N. Abrams, both liked *Every Night, Josephine!* Geis agreed to add it to the Bernard Geis Associates list. "I always say I was 'born' that day," Susann once wrote. To celebrate Jackie's triumph, Irving spent almost as much on her new Van Cleef poodle brooch as Geis paid for the book rights. Pogrebin, who served as Geis's publicity director from 1960 to 1970, recalls, as "a buttoned-down 21-year-old girl from Queens," her first meeting with Susann in her office: "Jackie was larger than life, glamour personified. She was exotic, bursting with self-confidence and she moved through the world with such self-importance that it was magnetic, *riveting*. Her ego was such that it was like cultural anthropology watching her. There she was all dolled-up, commanding the room in heels, full make-up, hair done and in Pucci at 9 a.m. Well, no sooner had I met her than she hiked her Pucci skirt all the way up to adjust her pantyhose. She didn't have on any panties, so there was her rear end, her pubic hair, everything. I'd say that was a pretty memorable first meeting but that was Jackie."

Susann and Irving turned out to be a full-service, no-trick-too-cheap publicity machine. The pair's relentless self-promotion, combined with Geis's Hollywood-style publicity tactics, proved to be as unusual in the publishing world as it was unbeatable. Anything was fair game, including planting fake items in gossip columns, gimmicky personal appearances, and brassy publicity stunts. Said Pogrebin, Geis "made authors into celebrities and celebrities into authors. Jackie and Irving would do anything to sell the book and, in those long-gone days of publishing, I had $100,000 budgets per book. It was high-flying stuff, the sixties, you could do anything and Kennedy was president. It was a whole new world, where you could break all the rules. With Jackie's publicity, nothing was too bizarre. Berney jazzed up and shook up the publishing world and Jackie was the perfect client. I couldn't do with Helen Gurley Brown or Rona Jaffe what Jackie would do." CBS TV network executive James Aubrey called Susann "the most charming, outgoing, gregarious person—not at all what one would picture a writer to be." When in November 1963 bookstores began stocking Susann's entertaining paean to her poodle, Jackie decked out Josephine and herself in matching leopard-skin hats and coats as they ran a marathon of TV interviews, personal appearances, and book signings. When Geis refused to shell out $6,000 for a full-page *New York Times* ad for the book, Irving himself sprang for it. But when the November 22 murder of President John F. Kennedy stopped the world, it also stopped plans for Susann's big promotional tour of Los Angeles, the city that encapsulated both her long-denied dream of Hollywood stardom and her *Made it, Pa—top of the world!* aspirations. On November 22, Susann entered the Geis offices to keep appointments with her publicists. When she found everyone glued to the TV to watch the unfolding national tragedy, she wailed, "Why the fuck does this have to happen to me? What's going to happen to my bookings?" Pogrebin said, "She just bitched and bitched. She was like Trump—the quintessential solipsist—everything revolved around her. She couldn't get that, with the president having just been shot, nobody was going to book an interview with a lady writing about her French poodle."

Still, Irving pressed on, making certain that he and Jackie got to Los Angeles and San Francisco. But when they hit the West Coast and none of the targeted bookstores had copies in stock, Jackie phoned Geis in the middle of the night and read him the riot act. He shipped out books by air freight. Irving and Jackie masterfully worked their major league contacts and followed the publicity blueprint laid out for them by a major power couple, *Sex and the Single Girl* writer Helen Gurley Brown and David Brown, the head of the 20th Century Fox story department. After the two women had met in Manhattan months before and purportedly by chance, the Mansfields cultivated a strategic alliance and friendship with the Browns, one that would soon have major implications for Susann's access to Hollywood.

In part because of Helen's advice, Susann mapped out a book promotion campaign on the level of a military campaign. Brown called Susann "a superior promoter. She's really the best." Susann learned how important it was to make it a practice of buying and autographing copies of her book and gifting them to bookstore owners and managers. She compiled detailed notes on every reporter, media host, and bookstore employee she encountered ("Nice, but nothing," she wrote about one; "Eats with his fingers," she observed of another) and routinely sent birthday and holiday gifts. But no one had to advise her what to do if she scoped out a bookseller with a large gay clientele and/or sales staff. For personal appearances at these venues, she'd go full diva, swathed in her showiest skintight Day-Glo Pucci creations, fake ponytails, falls, and lashes, with Josephine tucked in her arm. Irving, meanwhile, engineered stunts like pressuring the Geis office into arranging for an actress on a popular TV soap opera to perform a big scene while holding a copy of *Every Night, Josephine!*

In the end, the publicity push and the book's considerable charms helped *Every Night, Josephine!* sell thirty-five thousand copies; its sales eventually reached one million. Not only was Susann officially on the map, but Geis also paid her a $3,000 advance for whatever she concocted for an encore. The publisher didn't know— and Susann didn't reveal until later—that she had already strategized her next move. The very day she had first met with agent Annie Laurie Williams, she rushed home and wrote Chapter One of *Valley of the Dolls*, based on notes she had made years before for

Underneath the Pancake and *The Pink Dolls*. Those notes were a treasure trove of inside show business gossip, sexual confidences, covering up of extramarital dalliances, and pharmaceutical dos and don'ts exchanged with her self-titled Hockey Club, a half dozen intensely close, loyal women friends with whom she met regularly. (The group was notorious enough for Jules Feiffer to write about them in his 1963 novel, *Harry, the Rat with Women.*)

CHAPTER TWO

Jackie Climbs Mount Everest

For the next eighteen months, religiously from 10:00 a.m. to 5:00 p.m., Jacqueline Susann devoted herself to writing *Valley of the Dolls*—five drafts of it. After hours, she'd hit the gym. She also made a study of her literary models (or, as she thought of them, her rivals): Grace Metalious, Rona Jaffe, and Harold Robbins. *Especially* Robbins, who was the wildly successful self-promoting and bestselling author of sexy, sprawling romans à clef, including *The Carpetbaggers* (with characters patterned on Howard Hughes, Jean Harlow, Louis B. Mayer, and Harry Cohn).

Setting herself the task of cracking the code of Robbins's winning formula, Susann bought multiple copies of *Where Love Has Gone*, published in 1962. Robbins swore up and down there was no connection, but few readers could possibly miss the obvious resemblance to the real-life 1958 tragedy of young Cheryl Crane's stabbing to death her movie-star mother Lana Turner's mobbed-up lover Johnny Stompanato. Susann sliced up the novel's pages and organized these snippets chronologically for each major character. She then assigned each character a different color index card in order to chart his or her arc within the narrative. Later, she'd distill those down to chalkboard shorthand. Her conclusion? The public had a voracious appetite for novels about characters struggling with the same life issue, often in the same setting. In *Valley* the common link between the characters would be uppers and downers. She heard Robbins loud and clear when he blustered, "I'm the world's best writer—there's nothing more to say." The press may have scoffed but they printed whatever self-aggrandizing nonsense Robbins spewed. Susann also took note that Hollywood paid handsomely for the movie rights to pretty much everything Robbins wrote. So, hopes high, she pecked out her own narrative on a portable typewriter given to her as a wedding present by comedian, radio and TV writer, and columnist Goodman Ace. On her first attempt she used cheap white paper (for a draft in which she'd simply let it all hang out); then yellow paper for the second draft (reserved for work on characters); then pink (story motivation); and blue (heavy editing); and last, fine white paper for the final draft. Her forays into playwriting had taught her all that.

She never found the process natural or easy, but she settled into a kind of groove, likening writing the book to using a Ouija board, because "characters would spring up. I had to write it. I had to have my say." By January 1965, she was in the throes of an early *Valley of the Dolls* draft when agent Annie Laurie Williams informed Bernard Geis: "Don't laugh, but Jacqueline Susann's writing a novel." Months later Susann sent to Williams and Maurice Crain what she considered a finished manuscript—598 pages that sparked negative response from the entire Geis editorial staff. Geis editor Jackie Farber thought *Valley* "a bad, bad book" that was "hardly written in English." Pogrebin called it "a salable book by a terrible writer and, if you knew the dramatis personae she was writing about, a *roman à clef*, ha-ha, wink-wink." Fellow editor Don Preston characterized Susann as "a painfully dull, inept, clumsy, undisciplined, rambling and thoroughly amateurish writer" who "hauls out every terrible show biz cliché in all the books." Preston judged the tome as "cheap soap opera" that failed even on the level of other "popular potboilers" by Jackie's touchstones Robbins, Metalious, and Jaffe. Preston predicted it would be "roasted by critics, not for being salacious but for being badly done, dull." But Geis's savvy writer-editor wife, Darlene, compared reading the book to the delicious pleasure of eavesdropping on a phone conversation between women discussing their husbands' bedroom prowess—or lack thereof. Nora Ephron would later call her first exposure to Jackie's book "like reading a very long, absolutely delicious gossip column." Who'd pass up publishing something like that, let alone a book that also tackled—in its own lumbering but subversive way—female bonding and the old question *What do women want?*, along with a subsidiary exploration, *What will men do to keep them from getting it?*

Swayed by his wife's enthusiasm, Geis decided to publish it and assigned Don Preston to wrestle with Susann's weighty, unwieldy manuscript. Preston spent six intense weeks cutting roughly one third of the book's most purple prose, performing major reconstruction and rewriting—some of it requiring in-person sessions with a mostly cooperative Susann. Still, there were hitches. Preston wanted Jackie to use the word "nipples." She said she preferred "boobs." Preston tried persuading her to inject some emotional intimacy and tenderness to the sex scenes. She refused, apparently incapable of grasping anything beyond, in her words, "humping" and "fucking." On the other hand, Preston claimed that Susann showed sensitivity and delicacy in writing sex scenes between women. Unquestionably one of Preston's smartest upgrades was to insist that she bring together the novel's two most vivid and enjoyable hellions—the Judy Garland-ish Neely O'Hara and the Ethel Merman–esque Helen Lawson. It was his idea to pay off their longstanding feud in a trash-talking, wig-pulling, and flushing-it-down-the-toilet showdown in a posh ladies' powder room. Preston's addition is deliciously resonant for fans of legendary theater and movie bitchery. It slyly alludes to stage and screen actress Coral

Browne, who followed vitriolic gossip columnist Radie Harris into the ladies' room of a swank restaurant, slipped into the stall next to hers, reached under the partition, snatched the newswoman's detached wooden leg, and made off with it in a taxi, leaving Harris mortified and stranded. At the same time, Preston alludes to the two famous confrontations/catfights in *The Women*, a baffling oversight by the crafty Susann, especially considering her participation in the 1936 Broadway cast of Clare Boothe Luce's scathingly witty play.

Susann massaged the manuscript as Geis and Preston required. Well, sometimes, anyway. Pogrebin recalls the writer "storming into the office, rising to her full height, and refusing to make certain changes of Don's with which she didn't agree. She wasn't budging on some of it, but she argued with passion and dignity." Once she had tendered her third rewrite, she announced that she was calling it quits. If Geis wanted more, let Preston do it. (Later, she relented and penned two more drafts.) But although no one liked her melancholy, unhappy ending between characters Anne Welles and Lyon Burke (spoiler: she's over him), she refused to slap a happy face on it. Sure, she wanted to make money. But more than anything she wanted to make an entrance at the storied 21 Club and set fellow diners of that restaurant and former speakeasy buzzing about "Jacqueline Susann, the author," the way they never buzzed about Jacqueline Susann, the actress. Geis approved of Preston's many changes, especially those involving more pages devoted to his favorite, Helen Lawson. No arguments from Susann, who told everyone how much she loved the character who, as she boasted, "could emasculate men with her strength." Said Susann, "I understood her loneliness. A woman, to be a star, has to fight for her rights. When she gets on stage with a man, he's no longer a man, she's no longer woman. She says, 'Is my best side to the audience?,' 'Are my lyrics better than his?' I think that a woman like Helen Lawson is sad and beautiful and wonderful. Her loneliness that she has is very real. She doesn't realize that she brought her loneliness on herself. She doesn't realize that no man could relate to her as a woman anymore because the power of a Helen Lawson is frightening to a man."

But despite Susann's obvious empathy for Lawson, she also freely admitted the obvious to the publisher: she had based the character on Ethel Merman, with whom she had a score to settle. Geis witnessed firsthand evidence of the women's animosity while dining one evening at Sardi's with the Mansfields. From across the room, he and the Mansfields spotted "the Merm," customarily a brunette, with her shock of hair newly dyed a singularly brassy shade of red. Susann had purposely written Helen Lawson as a redhead in a halfhearted attempt to throw readers (and lawyers) off the scent. Shooting daggers at the hennaed Merman, Susann growled, "That bitch. She just did it to confuse my readers." That night, Susann rushed home to alter the manuscript, turning Lawson's hair a deep dark black. The following morning Geis received this note: "Irving says I'm silly to even worry . . . but you did seem surprised at the red hair on the REAL Helen last night . . . so this is at least a 'saver.' Unless that bitch goes and deliberately dyes her hair back black and lets it grow. Love, Balzac Mansfield." Another evening, Pogrebin and her husband dined at Sardi's with the Mansfields. She recalls, "Jackie and Irving knew everybody in town and, as each person came in, she and Irving would whisper frantically, 'Can you believe that thing she's wearing?' and 'Oh, my god, look at the bad table they got.' Suddenly, in comes Ethel Merman and Jackie said, *Do not look at her! Don't say anything! Make no sign that we notice her!* It was such a colossally pained reaction that, my husband and I knew, something had happened that warped Jackie's feelings about Ethel Merman and maybe herself. We didn't *dare* look at Ethel Merman."

With the manuscript ready to go, it was clear that, with a mighty assist from Geis and his editors, Susann had cannily jazzed up, trashed up, and given a '60s spin on an old-fashioned genre—the up-by-the-bootstraps career girl sagas that dated back to Fannie

Hurst's '20s and '30s novels *Imitation of Life* and *Back Street* as well as Edna Ferber's and George S. Kaufman's Broadway and Hollywood success *Stage Door*, and even, in a sense, Margaret Mitchell's *Gone with the Wind.* Susann consciously aped Harold Robbins but just as consciously absorbed the influence and power of Grace Metalious in her sensationalistic 1956 condemnation of small-town hypocrisy, *Peyton Place*, and Rona Jaffe with her timeless 1958 sex-and-the-city groundbreaker, *The Best of Everything.* Into the mix Susann had stirred stinging memories of her rejection as an actress as well as those of the heroines of countless backstage-to-back-alley movie musicals, with a dash of details from Christopher Morley's eyebrow-raising 1939 novel, *Kitty Foyle.* She'd also helped herself to incidents and moods from showbiz autobiographies such as Lillian Roth's harrowing saga of addiction, sin, and redemption, *I'll Cry Tomorrow.* In all, *Valley* was an unapologetic guilty pleasure—part autobiography, part roman à clef, part book-length gossip column. She had, quite simply, in the words of Simon & Schuster editor in chief at the time, Michael Korda, "reinvented the woman's novel."

The publisher brought the book to market with a compelling cover design featuring a bold black-and-gray title treatment on a field of white dotted with red Seconal sleeping pills, yellow Clomipramine antidepressants, and multicolored amphetamine pills. With a relatively modest first printing of twenty thousand copies, *Valley of the Dolls* hit bookstores on February 10, 1966, at $5.95 retail. Months before, Geis had begun orchestrating the earliest and biggest possible paperback rights sale. He first offered the novel to Dell Publishing's top editor, Leona Nevler, who had helped turn *Peyton Place* into a paperback sensation. Although Nevler responded to the book's narrative drive and roman à clef marketability—Geis proudly touted how Susann had nailed Merman "down to a T"— she considered it glaringly amateurish and gave it a hard pass. So *Valley of the Dolls* went to auction. Newspaper columnist Earl Wilson observed, "Some people are amazed that there are book readers who go in for this kind of book. They wonder, 'Why do they do it?' Are they gossip column readers, primarily, who are finding an enlarged gossip column?" It didn't matter. When Bantam Books tendered what Geis considered a soft bid, he gambled by bluffing, warning them they had deep-pocketed competition. Bantam raised their bid to upward of $200,000. Geis grabbed the offer and then funneled a whopping $50,000 of that advance into an aggressive publicity campaign.

Geis's invaluable publicist Letty Cottin Pogrebin engineered that campaign to maximize what she called "all-out glamour, shimmer, glitter, the works," what singer-actress-vocal-coach-vocal-arranger Kay Thompson called "the old Hollywood-bizazz." (Thompson said "bizzaz," not "pizzaz," but when the legend becomes fact, print the legend.) To complement the cover design, Pogrebin devised the witty gimmick of mailing potential reviewers eye-catching teasers in the form of prescription pad pages reading: "Take 3 yellow 'dolls' before bedtime for a broken love affair, take 2 red dolls and a shot of scotch for a shattered career, take *Valley of the Dolls* in heavy doses for the truth about the glamour set on the pill kick." As a chaser, those same reviewers later received a colorful sugar-filled pill taped to an advertisement reading: "This is an imitation 'doll.' But *Valley of the Dolls* is no imitation! Watch for the sensational truth about the glamour set on a pill kick." Said Pogrebin, "Jackie and Irving took credit for that and almost everything I did, but who cared? A lot of the ideas were mine but the way they promoted it? The hard work was theirs." Michael Korda thought the book and its movie-style promotional push "seemed to many of the old guard of publishing like the beginning of the end, Hollywood vulgarity at the door of the temple of culture." Which was exactly Geis's and Pogrebin's point.

The Geis office followed up those efforts with 1,500 advance galleys to critics and other influencers such as newspaper columnists, celebrities, and highly connected Manhattan and Hollywood yentas. The recipients included Senator Robert F. Kennedy (who influenced a character in the novel, which is maybe why his office politely responded but declined) and author Norman Mailer (whose spokesperson impolitely blew it off). Mostly, though, the gambit worked. Long before its publication date, the book got written about in the right show business columns and gossiped about by the *right* people. Irving Mansfield showed the book early to James Aubrey, the wildly successful former ABC and CBS network executive who was nicknamed, not for nothing, the Smiling Cobra, and whose formula for TV programming success was described as "broads, bosoms, and fun." Said Aubrey in 1967, "I was never as convinced about anything in my life as I was that this would be not only a successful novel but a highly successful novel. And I was probably much more convinced of it than Jackie was because, naturally, she had doubts and reservations, as did Irving. But I hope that some of my enthusiasm for it helped them in their resolution to make the kind of a deal for it that they did eventually." That deal included, according to Oscar Dystel, the president of Bantam Books, requiring his company to "[commit] a very large sum of [acquisition, publicity, and promotional] money long before the hardcover book was published." Goaded by Aubrey's bullish response to the novel, Irving Mansfield pushed Susann's agents to go in for a big financial kill. "When [Aubrey] said this to me, my ambition knew no bounds," said Mansfield. "I became a real killer . . . because in a sense what [Aubrey] said to me was something I believed but was afraid to express. I went out after it in a big way. Nothing could hold me back."

Susann was in her glory. So, for that matter, was Mansfield, who ended all of his TV producing commitments to concentrate solely on his wife's career with a single goal—to turn her into a star at long last. Susann was more than ready for it. Having kept a meticulous diary of the book distributors she had encountered while flogging *Every Night, Josephine!*, she wrote personal letters to each, dropping the names of their mates, children, and other relatives. In every letter she asked for help in promoting *Valley of the Dolls*. No wonder some called her "a politician" in single-minded pursuit of power and success. The Mansfields also hired personal publicists in Los Angeles and Miami, while Jackie—naturally vivacious, funny, and bigger than life—embarked on a coast-to-coast publicity on-slaught, even posing for the many ridiculous promotional photo opportunities engineered by Irving. Over the course of ten days, eleven cities, and thirty interviews a week, all of them fueled by doses of the amphetamine pills she was taking on the sly, she was unfailingly quotable and generous in giving her time to the press. As she reasoned, "A new book is just like any new product, like a new detergent. You have to acquaint people with it. They have to know it's there. You only get to be number one when the public knows about you."

More than once, though, even Susann had to curb Irving's "No publicity is bad publicity," P. T. Barnum–like hucksterism. In At-lanta, Georgia, for instance, the Mansfields made a pilgrimage to Peachtree Street, where, in 1949, a car fatally struck *Gone with the Wind* author Margaret Mitchell. Irving wanted Jackie to pose for photographers in the middle of the street with a car bumping her gently. Jackie thought it was beyond the pale and refused. There's no telling whether Mansfield understood why. But this he did un-derstand: the public perception of his wife had changed overnight. *Every Night, Josephine!* brought fan letters from everyone, from everyday dog fanciers to Elizabeth Taylor, the Duchess of Windsor, and Buckingham Palace. *Valley of the Dolls* brought notoriety. "A whole different attitude surrounded our entrance into a room," Mansfield said. *"There she goes. Boy, she must be quite a swinger. How does he stand for all of these things?* . . . [Then], all of a sudden we got offers to join marriage swap clubs."

Meanwhile, the reviewers, the male-dominated literati, ganged up on her and raked her over the coals. *Publishers Weekly* called the novel "big, brilliant and sensational" though "poorly written." *Time* magazine's critic called it the "Dirty Book of the Month" and "a highly effective sedative, a living doll." You could practically hear Eliot Fremont-Smith sniffing when he dismissed it in his *New York Times* review as "Hedy Lamarr's kind of book." When *The Best of Everything* author Rona Jaffe was asked whether she thought Susann had written a dirty book, she said, "Oh, I don't think it's dirty. What is a dirty book, you know? I mean, today nothing's dirty. Everybody is so sophisticated."

One exception—though one not hard to understand—came from author and reporter Cleveland Amory in *Cosmopolitan*, the brainchild of the Mansfields' friends and advisers Helen Gurley Brown and David Brown. Amory later said, "Jacqueline honestly never wrote this book to sell. It's a story that she knows well—the seamier side of show business. The chips fall where they may. It isn't everybody's literary cup of tea. But it's a genuine cup of tea." Helen Gurley Brown herself told her husband after reading it that she found it "maddeningly sexy" and wished she'd written it herself. She said a year after the book's publication, "Obviously, other people are the most interesting thing in the world to other people. Women want to know what other men and women are doing in bed or in the kitchen or socially or in the swimming pool or wherever they do what they're doing because they want to know *Is that how Fred and I do it?* Or a*re they having a better social life than we are? Are they taking more pills?*, just as women are interested in people." Cleveland Amory wrote, "The story has been told before but Miss Susann makes you *care*—not only about the dolls themselves but also about the other, medicinal, 'dolls'—pep pills, sleeping pills, etc."

Meanwhile, fellow writers Truman Capote, Norman Mailer, and Gore Vidal publicly mocked her. After Jackie ridiculed Capote's fey mannerisms on *The Tonight Show*, Capote appeared on the same show weeks later and said she looked like "a truck driver in drag." (The Mansfields consulted super attorney Louis Nizer, who advised against their proceeding with a libel case.) Later, Irving told friends privately that Capote envied Susann's expertise in working the media. Publicly he took a swipe at Capote, saying, "[Jackie] could do what—let's say a man like Truman Capote—did not know how to do. Of course, Capote could have done it and I don't know why he didn't. After all, he does have a glowing voice like [operatic soprano] Lily Pons and a sense of humor like Bennett Cerf."

Because Susann's novel was so outlandishly popular, the literary lions set out to prove its worthlessness—and the public's bad taste. Class-obsessed TV hosts like David Frost and guests like film critic John Simon treated her with utter disdain. When Simon called the novel nothing but "a piece of trash on which you can get famous, rich, known quick, and make money," Jackie asked if his name was Goebbels, Göring, or Simon, "because you sound like a storm trooper." In the face of these attacks, she soldiered on like a Mack truck defiantly painted in Pucci's flashiest patterns and hues. Said Letty Cottin Pogrebin, "She maintained a double identity. As a wealthy Philadelphian, she could really lay down the attitude, conveying the sense that she was stepping down from the mountain into the muck of show business. With her critics, her stance was 'I am class but I am having fun. You are taking me seriously, which makes you a jerk.' She was like a glamorous phenomenon like the high-voiced singer Tiny Tim—a silly phenomenon, with a quotient of freakiness you could make fun of. But what she did, she really did well. You always got the sense that she was in on it, that she knew exactly what she was doing. Whether or not they knew it, she had everyone by the *cojones*." Feminist icon, *New York* magazine columnist, and *Ms.* magazine cofounder Gloria Steinem's scalding, snobby review truly got under Susann's rhinoceros hide, though. The novelist famously took exception to Steinem's mention of *Every Night, Josephine!* as having been the only book on display for months at the Sixth Avenue Delicatessen, where the menu also featured the "Every Night, Josephine" sandwich. Pointing out that *Valley of the Dolls* was also on display at 21 and Sardi's, Susann said, "Obviously, Miss Steinem spends most of her time in the Sixth Avenue Delicatessen. I'm not angry. All I can say is I hope that if she writes a book, it sells half as many copies as *Josephine* has sold sandwiches." Steinem notwithstanding, Susann told British journalist Fergus Cashin in his *Daily Sketch*, "Women understand. They understand the dread of thirty, forty, fifty. I have just told the truth. There is no deliberate sensationalism. As an actress I have lived through the things I write about. I have seen them happen. Look at the stars of the '40s and '50s. The men are still there mugging with the new crop of girls but where are the women? Most of them cashed in happiness for success and are now lonely and alone in Beverly Hills mansions with sagging facelifts." Although she publicly defended her female readers, in private her sense of sisterhood was less powerful: "I write for women who read me on goddamn subways. They want to press their noses against the windows of other people's houses and get a look at parties they'll never be invited to, the dresses they'll never get to wear, the lives they'll never live."

Susann invented her life, becoming an opening night fixture at the big new Broadway shows, smoking up a storm, chowing down medium rare steaks, downing gimlets with dolls as chasers. Everyone wanted to know about Susann's knowledge of show business, a business that, to her credit, she never stopped writing about or discussing as particularly devastating to women. She told one journalist, "[Show business] brings you up so high and there's no place to go. And no matter how high you get, there's a time you have to retire. This is harder on the women stars, who face this problem almost all of their careers. No one cares if a man has a line on his face. It helped Bogart and Spencer Tracy. The men can go on as stars but the women are left to play in horror pictures." Asked if she herself took pills, she would often fire back, laughing, "Of course. Doesn't every normal, healthy person in show business?" She was joking but not lying. Her intake of pills and alcohol was high. But on a more serious note, she added, "So many people out here are hooked on pills, you wouldn't believe it. Just take a look at the number of people who have died from accidental overdoses—Dorothy Kilgallen, Marilyn Monroe, Alan Ladd, and so many more."

Decades before our current spectacle of TMZ and celebrity-centric reality shows, when misbehaving, falling-down, hardcase celebrities can no longer hide—and some don't even bother to—*Valley of the Dolls*, a product of the now-quaint "blind item" era of thinly veiled celebrity gossip, generated tons of press about bruised celebrity egos and newly spawned feuds, real and imagined. Novelist Rona Jaffe said, "People were saying, 'Well, do you think it's really so-and-so?' Everybody likes to read the sordid truth about so-and-so if she or he is a big star or something." Susann stoked the publicity fires (and dodged potential lawsuits) by playing footsie with the press about her character inspirations. "People have two businesses," said Susann. "Their own and show business. People start saying 'I think this character is this person,' and so forth, and there's a big guessing game. But look, twenty women sued Gustave Flaubert saying they were 'Emma Bovary' in *Madame Bovary*."

But as the Mansfields' friend Rosemary Wilson, wife of columnist Earl Wilson, once read aloud in a TV documentary Jackie's inscription on her copy of the book: "It's not sweet, pure or clean. But let's face it, you'll find some of our best friends between these covers. Love, Jackie." Walter Winchell reported in his column that since the publication of the book and Susann's depiction of Helen Lawson, Ethel Merman and Susann were absolute "don't invites" to the same party. Susann quipped about Merman, "We weren't talking before I wrote it. Now we're just not talking, only louder." Other stars, including Sophie Tucker and Mary Martin, also suspected that they were being slandered. The latter Broadway legend reportedly ordered a number of copies of the book sent to her sprawling farm in the jungles of Brazil but was also spotted at the famous Manhattan lunch spot and candy emporium Schrafft's eagle-eyeing the novel all by her lonesome. When *Los Angeles Times* reporter Richard "Dick" Houdek asked Susann which of the dolls in *Dolls* she was most like, she quipped, "If I were any of those girls, I would be in one of those glass jars at Harvard."

Soon Susann and her book were gaining so much fame and attention that the scalding reviews began to matter less and less. David Brown said of Susann, "As far as she was concerned, her 'reviews' came from bookstores." In fact, *Valley of the Dolls* had a slow sales start, which led Mansfield to swing into action. Determined to move product in a big way, he dispatched his and Jackie's friends to buy out every available copy at the 125 national bookstores consulted by the *New York Times* in compiling its bestseller list. If the store had sold out, Mansfield's cronies would order more copies and make certain the book was prominently displayed in stores. Not until March, a month after publication, did the novel hit the bestseller list; "Mostly because Irving bought up so many copies, turning it into a 'bestseller' before it actually became a bestseller," says Letty Cottin Pogrebin. By May *Valley of the Dolls* hit the number one position on all the bestseller charts, holding on to that spot for twenty-eight of its then-unprecedented sixty-five weeks on the list. But few knew at the time that, in promoting the book, Jackie and Irving had in their corner a powerful, rich, and self-interested ally. The movie rights had been bought by 20th Century Fox, the bosses of which were committed to making the book a mammoth, talked-about phenomenon.

CHAPTER THREE

Hollywood Goes for
Booze and Dope

Consider the irony. Susann's all-consuming, lifelong slouch toward Hollywood acceptance finally pays off. But not because of her celebrity connections. It's because of a relatively anonymous *Publishers Weekly* reviewer. George Wieser, that modestly paid book reviewer, had a couple of things going his way. First, he enjoyed early access to as-yet-unpublished literary material. Second, he had a nose for spotting highly commercial Hollywood-baiting properties. That's how he kept food on the table, by moonlighting for aspiring film producer Robert Evans, who paid him $175 weekly or, in today's market, $1,300 for his access and acumen. Back then, Evans was known mostly as a former actor discovered in 1956 by Norma Shearer, the retired movie queen of the '30s and '40s whose career flourished under the aegis of her husband, Irving Thalberg, MGM's head of production, its "boy wonder," who died in 1936 at age thirty-seven. In an incident that sounds like what a Jackie Susann–scripted *Sunset Boulevard* might have been like, the Widow Thalberg reportedly first eyed slim, handsome, sun-kissed Evans near the Beverly Hills Hotel swimming pool. Despite the fact that the thirty-one-year-old Evans had no acting experience, Shearer successfully promoted him to play the role of Irving Thalberg in the 1957 movie biography, *Man of a Thousand Faces*, starring James Cagney as actor Lon Chaney. As show business wise guys quipped about Evans's discovery, "He dove into a swimming pool and came out a star." That same year, Darryl F. Zanuck, 20th Century Fox's mighty, brilliantly astute, much-feared boss, spotted Evans dining at El Morocco, signed him to a contract, and assigned him to play a dashing young bullfighter in a movie version of *The Sun Also Rises*. Despite howls of protests from the novel's author, Ernest Hemingway, and the film production's stars, Tyrone Power and Ava Gardner, Zanuck refused to fire Evans. The kid, as Zanuck called him, stayed in the picture.

But after Evans got his shot in six movies, even Zanuck might have agreed with his calling himself "a half-assed actor." Using Zanuck as one of his role models, Evans, buoyed by cash from his and his brother Charles's successful Evan Picone women's clothing line, launched what he called the "nonexistent" Robert Evans Production Company. It was headquartered in his Manhattan town house. In the late summer of 1965, many months before its publication, Wieser slipped Evans a galley of *Valley of Dolls*, calling it "hot pulp" and recommending that Evans not only take it off the market preemptively but also lock up the virtually unknown Susann's next three novels.

Evans devoured the book in a single sitting and immediately recognized it for the sizzling, wonderfully soapy stuff it was. After all, his last acting role had been in that *Valley* forerunner, 20th's 1959 movie version of *The Best of Everything*, novelist Rona Jaffe's equally hot and pulpy, pre-women's liberation precursor in which five career gals waste their time on (mostly) philandering, useless boyfriends. Evans said that he "naively" brought the galleys of Susann's book to David Brown, 20th Century Fox's Manhattan-based vice president of story operations. (Could Evans have been so new in the movie business that he was unaware of the friendship between the Browns and the Mansfields?) Evans considered Brown not only an influential Hollywood powerbroker but also a personal fan who, during Evans's acting days, had proposed he costar with Montgomery Clift and Brigitte Bardot in a 1961 movie project to be based on Vivian Connell's censorship-plagued 1942 erotic novel *The Chinese Room*. That is until 20th Century Fox's distribution bosses labeled the project "too hot to handle" and plans were scrapped.

In any case Evans, who famously said, "There are three sides to every story: your side, my side, and the truth," recalled dropping the *Valley of the Dolls* galleys on the desk in Brown's office and announcing, "David, I think I have Fox's next big picture. I can get a lock on the author, too." Brown reportedly thanked him, assured him of an answer within the week, and read the book shortly after. He fired off several pages of his impressions to Darryl F. and Richard D. Zanuck, calling it "a good bad book that sometimes gets a certain notoriety and circulation" but admitting that he was "hypnotized by the corny, coarse, crass story it tells."

Brown put *Valley of the Dolls* squarely in the category of Harold Robbins's *The Carpetbaggers*, "with elements of *I'll Cry Tomorrow*, *A Star Is Born*, and even *The Snake Pit*," and ordered the book to be distributed widely among the movie producers affiliated with Fox, including Ernest Lehman (*The Sound of Music*), Robert Aldrich (*Hush . . . Hush, Sweet Charlotte*), and Harry Kurnitz (*Goodbye Charlie*). Brown advised the Zanucks: "It is the kind of story which may be easily snapped up by a Ross Hunter or a Joe Levine. . . . I believe the book will be read avidly by women—particularly girls—even though the critics will murder it. . . . With luck, as a movie, it might get into *The Sandpiper* or *Butterfield 8* category."

Darryl F. Zanuck encouraged Brown to huddle with Richard Zanuck about acquiring the screen rights. On September 16, Brown sent the younger Zanuck Susann's agent's acquisition quote of $200,000 plus 2.5 percent of the gross but advised, "We feel it can be had for a great deal less." Because Zanuck Sr. thought *Valley of the Dolls* a good idea, it is almost axiomatic that Zanuck Jr. would pump the brakes. On September 23, 1965, Brown cabled the elder Zanuck: "Dick is frankly not impressed by this book as film material even if it does become a big bestseller."

Before Richard Zanuck made his final decision, though, he consulted the 20th producers who had read the novel. Although most would not touch it, David Weisbart (*Goodbye Charlie*) showed considerable interest. Respected and personally well regarded, the dashing fifty-one-year-old Weisbart had launched his career in the '40s as a film editor at Warner Bros., eventually cutting such high-profile pictures as *Mildred Pierce* and *A Streetcar Named Desire*. Moving into producing for Warner Bros. in 1952, Weisbart wrangled many of that studio's starriest players for his projects, including Gary Cooper, Barbara Stanwyck, and Humphrey Bogart. Increasingly over the years he specialized in showcasing new young talent—James Dean in *Rebel Without a Cause*, Elvis Presley in *Love Me Tender*, Pat Boone in *April Love*, and, in *The Pleasure Seekers*, Ann-Margret (whom he would soon champion for *Valley of the Dolls*). In Weisbart's intrastudio memo to the bosses, he suggested that the book "could, with careful handling, be turned into a very good contemporary film. It is a kind of *Darling* with three girls instead of one . . . the characters are interesting and it should attract top performers."

Zanuck Jr. remained on the fence about *Valley of the Dolls*, but he trusted Weisbart, who laid out compelling reasons to make the movie during a long meeting with the studio boss and David Brown. Although no one could possibly mistake *Valley* for great literature, it had the makings of a highly entertaining movie—even one that spoke some home truths as it conjured a world of vivid characters and spun a grabby plot. "So," Weisbart concluded, "I think the result can justify the plunge." Later, Weisbart explained to a Hollywood columnist, "I'm not exactly a crusader, but when an opportunity comes along to say something significant in motion pictures, I like to take it." He went on to say that he considered

Susann's book "a very moral story. There is a great deal to be learned from it . . . about the corruption of people under pressure. . . . Some are geared for success; others tumble into it and can't cope with it. These are the tragedies. It's a story that has a lot to say about our sense of values."

Decades later Robert Evans commented on losing *Valley of the Dolls* to Weisbart and Brown: "For five Gs, I could have had an option on the film rights to what was to become not only a bestselling novel, but a smash film to boot. Once, a mistake. Twice, a failure. It never happened again." But as many good Hollywood stories as there are, there are just as many different versions to every one of them, including the one about how *Valley of the Dolls* got sold to the movies. Jacqueline Susann's literary agent Annie Laurie Williams had previously sold film rights to Margaret Mitchell's *Gone with the Wind*, Lloyd C. Douglas's *Magnificent Obsession* and *The Robe*, John Steinbeck's *The Grapes of Wrath* and *Of Mice and Men*, and Harper Lee's *To Kill a Mockingbird*. Having cultivated a close working relationship with 20th Century Fox since 1955, Williams claimed that it was she who sent the *Valley* manuscript directly to David Weisbart, who read it overnight and the next morning brought it to the attention of Richard D. Zanuck.

In any case, Richard Zanuck continued to drag his feet during the negotiations, but Zanuck Sr. and Brown pushed him to finalize a deal—so long as he did it at the right price. David Brown recalled in his memoirs the most common cause for hesitation: "We said, 'But the author has done only one book before—a nonfiction book. How do we know anything will happen to this book?' We didn't. We just had an instinct." Armed with that instinct, and money to back it, Fox began negotiations for the film rights in the first week of July 1966. In grand old Hollywood cutthroat tradition, Evans got kicked to the curb.

Literary agents Annie Laurie Williams and Maurice Crain and Fox struck a preemptive prepublication arrangement that paid the Mansfields' company, Sujac Productions, $85,000 (the equivalent of about $693,000 today) for the worldwide motion picture and allied rights. The contract also included an elevator clause if Susann's book became a big seller, guaranteeing the author seventy-five cents on each hard copy sold in excess of 20,000 with the ceiling topping out at $200,000 (minus the initial $85,000 payment). Thanks to Williams's agentry, Susann—who waived both the option to pen the screenplay and to assert any creative control over the movie— eventually went on to become richer by another $200,000 (today the equivalent of $1.5 million). Hardly chump change. But, by comparison, consider *Peyton Place*. Just weeks after its September 24, 1956, publication, Fox producer Jerry Wald paid first-time author Grace Metalious $250,000 (about $2.3 million today) for the movie rights alone; Metalious's profit participation eventually brought her over $400,000 (about $3.7 million today).

For years, the Mansfields would rail against Williams's not advising them to hold out for a postpublication movie sale. Who could foresee that *Valley of the Dolls* would climb to the top of the bestseller charts—and stay and stay and stay there? Irving Mansfield went to his grave grousing that if only Williams had advised them to wait until the novel hit the bookstores, she could have extracted from Fox a minimum of $450,000 ($3.5 million today) plus a healthy percentage of the movie's profits. The Mansfields' decision to take Fox's preemptive deal laid the groundwork for a grudge match with the studio that would eventually play out in a bitter lawsuit.

As for Robert Evans, soon after being dealt out of *Valley of the Dolls*, he never again brought a knife to a gunfight. Evans (thanks again to George Wieser) took a $5,000 option on a big-city crime and corruption thriller, *The Detective*, another red-hot property by a first-time novelist. About one month after the *Valley* incident, Evans again marched straight to David Brown's offices, dropped ex–private investigator Roderick Thorp's gritty novel on his desk, and said, "I didn't do too badly with *Valley of the Dolls*, did I, David? Insiders say this is the sleeper of the year." When Brown again promised he'd get back to him in a week, Evans volleyed, "Thanks, David. Oh, and by the way, I own this one," and made a stylish exit. (Years later Wieser got Evans to lend money to his friend Mario Puzo to pay off his bookies; a bit later, Puzo, still broke, came to Evans with a thirty-five-page treatment titled *Mafia,* for which Evans paid $12,500 before it got retitled *The Godfather.) The Detective* rocketed to the top of the bestseller chart and sparked a heated Hollywood bidding war. Most of the interested suitors tried buying out Evans, including David Brown, who, on behalf of 20th Century Fox, offered $500,000 and a meaningless vanity producing credit to buy him off. But Evans instead insisted on a three-movie 20th development deal, a suite of secretary-staffed offices in the Executive Building, and full-page ads in the *Hollywood Reporter* and *Variety* featuring a photo of Evans with Richard D. Zanuck—if not with both Richard *and* Darryl Zanuck—signing his production deal. As Evans wrote in his 1994 memoir, "Ego? You bet! Revenge? Even more so."

The Zanucks wanted *The Detective* movie rights badly enough to meet Evans's demands. But the ink had barely dried on his contract when he flummoxed the studio executives by pitching a deal: the 20th studio could keep *The Detective* (and several other Evans projects) in exchange for letting him out of his contract. Zanuck took the deal. It turned out that Evans had been handed the much richer offer that led to his becoming head of production of the then-shaky Paramount Pictures. Assuming the risky executive position, he turned around the company's fortunes and became a major competitor and producer. Evans never forgot the machinations of Brown, who, along with other industry powerbrokers, could only watch in envy as Evans outmaneuvered Fox on prize properties, including *Rosemary's Baby, Love Story, The Odd Couple,* and *Marathon Man,* all of which became major financial successes. Eight years after Brown snatched *Valley of the Dolls* from under him, how could Evans not derive satisfaction from outmaneuvering Brown and the Zanucks on grabbing the movie rights to *Once Is Not Enough* by none other than Jacqueline Susann?

Evans had been working with director Mark Robson on readying

The Detective for the screen. He intended to hang on to the property, even when hard-to-handle Frank Sinatra moved to the head of the pack of stars eager to play the leading role. Robson and Frank Sinatra had a history, having made 20th's hit World War II train hijack POW escape thriller, *Von Ryan's Express*, released in 1965. Throughout filming, the two had locked horns. Though Sinatra could be a weapons grade bully and agent of disruption, Robson himself was no pushover. He had first made his bones in the 1940s editing Orson Welles's and Val Lewton's movies at RKO before punching his way up to directing such socially conscious melodramas of the late 1940s and early 1950s as *Champion* and *Home of the Brave*. Under a multifilm 20th Century Fox commitment, he had more recently drifted to slick, soapy, *tastefully* sexy bestsellers like *Peyton Place* and *From the Terrace*. Robson signaled his determination to direct *The Detective*, even agreeing to sideline his then-ongoing negotiations with Akira Kurosawa to allow Robson to direct Anthony Quinn in an Americanized version of *The Hidden Fortress*, one of the Japanese director's masterworks. It was one of the many projects favored by Darryl F. Zanuck but not by his son Richard; they did this combative, competitive dance of death throughout their joint and separate reigns at the studio. Meanwhile, in the background, Sinatra began lobbying 20th to shove Robson off *The Detective* in favor of pliable, reliable old-timer Gordon Douglas, with whom Sinatra had made the gangster musical *Robin and the 7 Hoods*. To help keep Sinatra and Robson happy—and *separated*—in stepped Zanuck Jr. and David Weisbart to persuade Robson to consider directing the film version of another, more sexy, female-centered novel that was flying off bookstore shelves at an unprecedented clip. Robson was in.

CHAPTER FOUR

We Two Kings

Valley of the Dolls might have landed at any major Hollywood studio, but something felt right—almost predestined—about 20th acquiring the property. Studio chief Darryl Francis Zanuck, who ran the studio and defined its brand from 1935 to 1956, was powerful, larger than life, charismatic—a big game hunter, horseman, and sportsman—exactly the sort of figure that could have come out of a Jacqueline Susann novel. He alone decided which pictures to make, which screenwriters and directors to assign to them, which actors to put under contract, and how to light, costume, and promote them. It was he who watched the dailies of every project under production and who fine-tuned every aspect of them, "fixing" them through rewriting, reediting, or reshooting when he felt they were falling short of the 20th standard. The films he chose to make, and micromanage, courted controversy, defined his studio and, sometimes, their eras—*Alexander's Ragtime Band*, *The Mark of Zorro*, *The Grapes of Wrath*, *How Green Was My Valley*, *Laura*, *A Tree Grows in Brooklyn*, *The Razor's Edge*, *Pinky*, *All About Eve*, and *The Longest Day*. In the early 1950s, to help lure audiences away from television, Zanuck channeled $10 million (about $94 million today) into an ultimately futile battle to make widescreen Cinemascope *the* antidote to the small screen. He also began a humiliating, expensive, equally futile effort to make a movie star out of his modestly talented bisexual Polish mistress, Bella Darvi—her screen surname, astonishingly, a combination of "Dar" for Darryl and "Vi" for Virginia, Zanuck's equally smitten, long-suffering wife. Due in part to Zanuck's World War II battle experiences, to world weariness, and to his marital and extramarital malaise, he stepped away from the day-to-day running of the studio in 1956 to explore independent production opportunities in Europe under a lucrative 20th deal. But he returned to running the studio in 1962 in a desperate attempt to save it from the financial debacle of the elephantine *Cleopatra* and the aborted Marilyn Monroe movie comedy *Something's Got to Give*. Shortly afterward, he installed his twenty-eight-year-old son, Richard Darryl Zanuck, as head of production. Their rivalry, one-upmanship, and feuds, undergirded by deep love and affection, are the stuff of legend. In the final public act of one of Hollywood's most oedipally charged father-son relationships, Zanuck humiliated and discredited his son by railing against his "incompetence" during a 1970 meeting of the board of directors and blindsided him by firing him on the spot.

By the time of *Valley of the Dolls*, the senior Zanuck spent much of the year in France and may have appeared to advise, from afar, on his son's projects. But that might make it seem as though he didn't have much interest or sway over that project or his son's other projects. Internal studio memos, cables, and records of phone calls reveal a much different story. Unlike his son, Darryl F. Zanuck immediately grasped the movie potential of *Valley of the Dolls* and wanted 20th to jump on it. After all, the novel's big-screen potential fit into the elder Zanuck's moviemaking tenets on many counts. Being an exposé of America's pill-taking habits, it would follow in his succession of "problem" pictures that included *Gentlemen's Agreement* (anti-Semitism), *The Snake Pit* (the horrors of psychiatric hospitals), *Pinky* (race relations), and *The Man in the Gray Flannel*

Suit (post–World War II conformity and suburban discontent). Susann's novel also meshed perfectly with Zanuck's abiding fascination with—and recycling of—"the three-girls" movie genre, which 20th had been doing since the '30s with *Sally, Irene and Mary*; *Walking Down Broadway*; *Moon Over Miami*; *Three Coins in the Fountain*; *How to Marry a Millionaire*; *The Best of Everything*; *The Pleasure Seekers*; et al. The narratives rarely varied. Three beautiful girls go to (fill in the name of the major city) to seek career success, romance, maybe marriage but get badly knocked around while trying.

The studio ethos at 20th served as an all-too-real example of the show business excesses—and treatment of women—Jacqueline Susann exposed in *Valley of the Dolls*. Alongside the pugnacious, arrogant senior Zanuck's ferocious negotiation skills, screenwriting and editing acumen, and nose for good material, there was his reputation as an insatiable cocksman and predatory sexual opportunist. The legends about Zanuck abound: His daily 4:00 p.m. "private time," during which his office doors got locked and no one was allowed to disturb him as he was sexually pleasured by one of the studio's handpicked female contract stars and starlets. The back corridor and the subterranean passages from which these actresses could slip discreetly after their obligatory assignations. How any actress who balked would wind up blackballed and maligned (Carole Landis) or dropped (Joan Collins, among others). The speculation about how intimately Zanuck may or may not have been entangled with members of 20th's stable of stars including Betty Grable (to whom he exposed himself), Linda Darnell, Gene Tierney, Jayne Mansfield, and Marilyn Monroe (whom he claimed to detest). The stash of expensive perfumes, negligees, and jewelry he kept in cabinets behind his massive desk and dispensed to women who particularly pleased him. The solid gold life-size replica of his phallus prominently displayed to women in an effort to intimidate, amuse, and arouse. "Impressive, huh?" Zanuck reputedly boasted to Joan Crawford while showing off the golden idol, who shot back, "I've seen bigger things crawl out of cabbages." "Anyone at the studio knew of the afternoon trysts. . . . He was not serious about any of the women. To him they were merely pleasurable breaks in the day—like polo, lunch, and practical jokes," wrote Marlys J. Harris in *The Zanucks of Hollywood: The Dark Legacy of a Hollywood Dynasty*.

Had Zanuck not existed it would have taken a Jacqueline Susann to invent him. Observed an actor who appeared in several 20th films of the '50s and '60s, "Darryl Zanuck was everything anybody ever said he was. I heard the stories about him through Marilyn Monroe. He was just an awful, horrible lech who cornered or chased every starlet around his office, as I heard all the time from so many actresses. He expected they would comply—and apparently, a number of them did, to further their careers. Back then, certain producers, directors, and studio bosses considered sexual access to be their divine right. I know it all sounds like a Hollywood cliché but as we know from the history and from people like Harvey Weinstein and Les Moonves, it happens all the time." Lovely brunette actress Lara Lindsay, while under a seven-year 20th contract in the mid-sixties, recalls, "Some of us from the studio were invited to the Beverly Hills Hotel. I was very naïve and I wasn't warned about Darryl Zanuck, who was a sly old man, manipulative. Anyway, I was in the swimming pool and all of a sudden, Zanuck came up and grabbed me and I got away from him. I was divorced and had a child and had another person to answer to but let's just say that Zanuck and others at that time would never have survived in the era of Me Too. Hollywood was a breeding ground for sexuality. I have *so* many stories but I'm one who believes if you have something to say, say it at the time or be quiet."

Jeff Maxwell, best known for playing Private Igor Straminksy on the 20th TV series *M*A*S*H*, began work as a teenager on the 20th lot in 1967 printing screenplays and delivering interoffice memos for top-tier studio personnel who occupied offices in the three-story Zanuck-run Executive Building; he and movie-director-to-be

John Landis also delivered studio mail, and Maxwell graduated to working in the Casting Department before pursuing his acting career. Recalled Maxwell, "More than any of the other studios, 20th was a big deal. All the history, all that real estate and production was booming. Darryl Zanuck was in the news all the time. He was spending less and less time at the studio and more time in Europe but I saw him in the incredible commissary, really the heartbeat of the studio, and he was dynamic, charismatic. His executive offices were on the first floor just across from the printing and mail office. Being crazy about the history of the studio, I looked into every nook and cranny on the whole lot. I got very friendly with all the secretaries and knew that in the basement was a big swimming pool built for Zanuck or one of the other moguls. I'd ask the secretaries about the pool and they'd roll their eyes and say nothing or else say something like, 'Oh, you know what they're doing down there. . . .' When I'd go down there, it looked creepy, all white tiles like something out of a horror movie. Around the lot, it was common knowledge that the pool was where the moguls, executives, and actresses frolicked sexually. I also remember a young actress under contract to the studio at the time—kind of trashy, very gregarious, sexual, flirtatious, out there, always in short, short skirts, an *event*. She'd often come to the Executive Building and just always seemed to vanish somewhere but I finally stayed around to watch and saw her go to what I thought was a nondescript closet door. She unlocked it with a key and went in. Thirty seconds later, a very big executive walked out of his office, went in that same door, and closed it. I finally found out that it led to a private patio for Zanuck, or was used by some other executives, and hidden from prying eyes. But this actress and that executive went there to enjoy each other—*often*. I also found out about the two-story building Zanuck had near the back of the lot for his own use. By the time I worked there, the building housed low-level producers and assistant producers. On the second floor was what looked like a soundproof booth with headphones and a big switchboard and equipment that would have been the most advanced of its day. That's how I learned that Zanuck had a phone room dedicated to allowing him to listen to any phone conversation in any executive's office on the lot."

As the early days of preproduction began on *Valley of the Dolls*, 20th had recovered from the nearly ruinous *Cleopatra*, the highest-grossing film of 1963 yet a loss leader because of its original budget having ballooned from $1 million to $7 million due to many factors, including production overruns. The studio's soundstages bustled with film and TV production, flush with the phenomenal world-wide box-office success of *The Sound of Music*. Meanwhile, TV shows filmed at the studio included *Daniel Boone*, *Voyage to the Bottom of the Sea*, *Lost in Space*, *12 O'Clock High*, *Batman*, *The Felony Squad*, and *Judd for the Defense*, and its ratings-busting nighttime soap and national obsession, *Peyton Place*. But the long-standing tensions between Zanuck *père et fils* were beginning to boil over. Zanuck Sr. was highly dubious about many of the projects his son was greenlighting—*A High Wind in Jamaica*, *Rapture*, *Wild on the Beach*, *Morituri*, anyone? Even sure-fire productions like *The Blue Max*, *The Sand Pebbles*, and *Fantastic Voyage* lost millions. Meanwhile, the senior Zanuck was obsessed with finding a project to top his own 1962 blockbuster, the Word War II epic *The Longest Day*. If the elder Zanuck envisioned an elegant, polished, stylishly sexy version of *Valley of the Dolls*, the junior Zanuck wanted a hip, young, *now Valley of the Dolls*. Neither of them won that battle. The young Zanuck fumed as his father lavished some of the studio's gigantic *Sound of Music* windfall on expensive, "all-star" period road show duds, including *Those Magnificent Men in Their Flying Machines*, the Friedrich Dürrenmatt–based revenge tragicomedy *The Visit* with Ingrid Bergman and Anthony Quinn, and the French-American World War II coproduction *Up from the Beach*. The star of the latter, Cliff Robertson, dubbed the movie "Up From the Bitch," a reference to Irina Demick, Zanuck's most recent mistress, whom he foisted on the moviegoing public in all of those aforementioned movies. Even then, though, Demick was on her way out and the sixty-three-year-old Zanuck would soon replace her with nineteen-year-old Genevieve Gilles. She called him a Picasso of sex; he handpicked for her the leading female role in *Hello-Goodbye*, a comedy romance directed by Jean Negulesco. Audiences and critics didn't take to Gilles any more than they had to Zanuck's previous paramours: Bella Darvi in *The Egyptian* or her successor, the gifted French chanteuse Juliette Gréco, in *The Sun Also Rises*, *The Naked Earth*, *The Roots of Heaven*, and *Crack in the Mirror*, let alone Demick. His highly public dalliances and creative missteps became an embarrassment to the stockholders, and they wanted him out of power as expeditiously as possible.

As Zanuck Sr. repeatedly told his son, had *Valley of the Dolls* been a product of the Hollywood studio system at its apex, in less than a week he would have assigned it to a contract director, one or more of the studio's stable of thirty-plus top screenwriters, an available cameraman, production and costume designer, a composer, and a cast selected from 20th's contract talent roster. It isn't hard to imagine a forties-era *Valley of the Dolls*. On tap at the studio were any number of great beauties and "types," some of them quite talented. And if those weren't quite right, Zanuck might have arranged to borrow talent from other studios. There was Gene Tierney, Linda Darnell, or Jeanne Crain to play the reserved New Englander Anne Welles. Betty Grable, Rita Hayworth, or Lana Turner might have played the luckless showgirl Jennifer North. The young Bette Davis, Susan Hayward, or Ida Lupino would have fit as brilliantly talented, tormented Neely O'Hara. Tyrone Power/Gregory Peck/Cornel Wilde could have slipped easily into the role of suave, slippery Lyon Burke, alongside Dana Andrews as press agent Mel, Vincent Price as Charles Revson–inspired cosmetics empire maven Kevin Gillmore, and Clifton Webb as fashion designer Ted Casablanca. For good measure, Zanuck could have thrown in Gertrude Lawrence as fading Broadway virago Helen Lawson, Frank Sinatra/Dean Martin/Vic Damone as Tony Polar, and Geraldine Fitzgerald as Miriam, sister of the sexy, childlike crooner. Or had Zanuck made the movie later in his career, he could have helped himself to the talents of, respectively, Hope Lange, Diane Varsi, or Shirley Jones as Anne, Marilyn Monroe, Joan Collins, or Debra Paget as Jennifer, Joanne Woodward as Neely, Richard Burton or Stephen Boyd as Lyon, Roddy McDowall as Ted Casablanca, Claudette Colbert or Mary Martin as Helen, Elvis Presley as Tony with Angela Lansbury as Miriam. But in 1966, the days of the studio system and exclusive contracts were on life support. With the long shadow of Darryl F. Zanuck looming over *Valley of the Dolls*, it would take Richard D. Zanuck, producer David Weisbart, and director Mark Robson long, torturous months and many reversals before the casting—let alone the entire production—finally pulled together. And, from his Paris headquarters, Zanuck Sr. thought that was laughable—when he didn't find it infuriating.

CHAPTER FIVE

You've Got to Climb Mount Everest

Although not entirely willingly, Richard Zanuck vaulted *Valley of the Dolls* to the top of the short list titled "highest-priority projects." Said *Sweet Smell of Success* screenwriter Ernest Lehman, whose blue-chip work for 20th had already included *The King and I*, *From the Terrace* (directed by Mark Robson), and *The Sound of Music*, "Naturally, Dick wanted to get that book on-screen before the novel petered out and fell off the bestseller list, which lots of us thought was bound to happen sooner rather than later. Of course, the book didn't peter out, but how was Dick or anyone else to know that?" When it had looked as though Mark Robson's work on *The Detective* was going to make him unavailable for *Valley*, David Weisbart presented for the Zanucks' approval an eclectic target list of possible directors and then met, formally and informally, with a number of the candidates. The studio executives hoped to counteract as much of Jacqueline Susann's sudsiness and melodrama as possible. Weisbart's list of candidates—constantly added to by Richard and Darryl Zanuck—ran the gamut. Among the picks were Martin Ritt (most recently, *The Spy Who Came In from the Cold*), Robert Wise (*The Sound of Music*), Philip Dunne

(*10 North Frederick*), George Cukor (*My Fair Lady*), Robert Aldrich (*Hush . . . Hush, Sweet Charlotte*), Jean Negulesco (*The Pleasure Seekers*), Joseph Losey (*Modesty Blaise*), Richard Fleischer (*Fantastic Voyage*), and John Huston (better represented by *The Maltese Falcon* and *Reflections in a Golden Eye* than by his then-current project, *The Bible: In the Beginning . . .*). Also on the studio's "possible" list was an intriguing, if unlikely, choice: Joseph L. Mankiewicz. Signed by Darryl F. Zanuck to a long-term deal in 1944, writer-director Mankiewicz had made eleven highly qualifying calling cards under studio contract—*A Letter to Three Wives* and *All About Eve* being the ones that most positioned him as a possible director for *Dolls*. But he'd also most recently made the ultimate disqualifier, *Cleopatra*, the one that nearly sank 20th and pretty much sank Mankiewicz with it. Missing from the list, though, might have been the best choice of all—Douglas Sirk, that undisputed king of ultra-glossy, subversive, ironic, culturally critical melodramas, including *All That Heaven Allows*, *Written on the Wind*, and *Imitation of Life*. But after the smashing box-office success of the latter, Sirk, weary of making pictures for producer Ross Hunter, had decamped to Europe to plan a film about the troubled life of painter Maurice Utrillo. When that project collapsed, he became ill and, despite Hunter's offer of several projects, Sirk retired from filmmaking.

Weisbart pushed hardest for Don Siegel. Tough, unpretentious, and rough and ready, Siegel had already worked amiably with Weisbart on the Elvis Presley vehicle *Flaming Star*, released in 1960. Siegel had subsequently shown impressive range and skill in making A-level movies on B-movie budgets, including *Invasion of the Body Snatchers* and *The Killers*, but, in 1966, he was working mostly in episodic TV, years away from getting the opportunities that helped him become *the* Don Siegel, who helped make a movie icon out of Clint Eastwood on five movies, including *Dirty Harry*. Weisbart's correspondence with the Zanucks championed Siegel as "fast, tough and fully capable of dodging those soap opera traps" while still making a movie that would appeal to the novel's female and male fans. Correspondence from Siegel to Weisbart—including Cleveland Amory's positive *Cosmopolitan* review of Susann's novel—suggests that the director was sufficiently intrigued by the challenge to want to be kept in mind when the hiring decision got made.

In the end, though, once Weisbart and Zanuck learned that Mark Robson was suddenly off *The Detective* and extremely eager to work, that director moved into first position. Robson's biggest selling point was his having made a classy enough 20th film out of *Peyton Place* that it went on to receive nine Oscar nominations, including Best Picture and Best Director, and earned its rank as Hollywood's second biggest moneymaker of 1957. When Robson and the studio struck their *Valley* deal, the director was guaranteed a salary of $82,500 (the equivalent of $647,273 in 2020), plus a percentage of the box-office take, a take that reportedly went on to reward Robson in excess of $300,000 (or $2.4 million in 2020). In the 1940s, the Montreal-born Robson (né Rabinovitch) had shown his mettle and versatility on bitter, tough-minded low-budget crime and horror melodramas, working in tandem with directors Nicholas Ray, Robert Wise, and others. He worked his way up to shrewdly and beautifully editing (usually uncredited) well-known RKO pictures directed by Orson Welles (including both *Citizen Kane* and *The Magnificent Ambersons*) and Jacques Tourneur (*Cat People, I Walked with a Zombie, The Leopard Man*). He put himself on the map by directing such movies as the 1949 boxing drama *Champion*, starring Kirk Douglas, and in the same year, the pioneering racially charged World War II movie *Home of the Brave*. But once Samuel Goldwyn tapped him for bigger budgets and higher-profile projects, he tended to drift away from the grittier stuff and veered awkwardly toward soapy women's movies with Susan Hayward.

By 1966, Hollywood viewed Robson, fifty-three, as one of its more reliable, workmanlike, and regularly employed directors, who occasionally batted one out of the park, like 1954's critical and box-office hit *The Bridges at Toko-Ri*, starring William Holden and Grace Kelly. Solid and unflashy, he and his wife, Sara (married for thirty-three years at the time), and their three daughters lived in leafy, manicured, upper-class Brentwood in a home that began as a stately Georgian but which the Robsons expensively remodeled five times inside and out until they eliminated the vintage details to "accommodate changing time," as they put it. They also expanded the house to make room for Robson's prized art collection of twenty-plus years, some of it gathered in Thailand, India, and during various global film location trips. No wonder Robson once explained his nonstop work schedule but sometimes questionable choice of material by saying, "I have a large family to feed and it's only occasionally that I find a story that interests me." One of Robson's daughters, Martha Bardach, the former Los Angeles bureau photo editor for *Time* magazine, described her father as not always the easiest man to get to know. "When it came to choosing movie projects after the '40s and '50s, he struggled. He wanted to remain relevant and become part of the changing tide of Hollywood, but he had difficulties making that transition."

In mid-August of 1966, Robson called himself, in a letter to his London agent Norma Paulsen, "mixed up and frustrated," professionally speaking. He was still holding on to the possibility that he and Robert Evans might yet get together on his most coveted project, *The Detective*, but admitted "[Evans] has just moved into Paramount and he's kind of mixed up." Meanwhile, Robson was dickering with several other projects ranging from the World War II–set projects *Patton*, *The Devil's Brigade*, and a prison camp escape thriller *The Long Pursuit* to an original Arnold Schulman–penned romantic comedy along the lines of *Roman Holiday*, and a drama about the social and political awakening of a working class woman meant to star Audrey Hepburn. But not one of them was ready for production. Wrote Robson, "Here at 20th, David Weisbart wants me to do *Valley of the Dolls* which has been the number one book in this country for a long time.

The Detective can't go until the Spring of 1967, and with all of the projects up in the air I'm like a juggler. Unless I get something to go pretty soon I'll be 'blocked out' until *The Detective* goes. This would be disasterous [*sic*], of course . . . such a waste of time, though I'm hoping one of my own three projects can go first." Looking to avert disaster, Robson hopped aboard the runaway train that was *Valley of the Dolls*, perhaps thinking it his best chance to be new, modern, relevant—and immediately employable. Robson took to defending Susann's source material as "honest," "forthright," and "full of wonderful characters, compelling characters who have veracity and are memorable"—especially when colleagues and the press called it "unconvincing claptrap," "trashy," and "filthy." He said, "Public attitudes have changed. People aren't as shockable as they were when *Peyton Place* appeared. It's old-fashioned now. But although we're planning *Valley of the Dolls* to be as truthful as possible, we're not trying to offend anyone. Besides, it's a theme I've dealt with many times before. It's the drive for success, as in *Champion*, and the blaming of society for failure."

On the 20th lot, Robson occupied a modest suite of offices on the third floor of the Executive Building, appointed with a receptionist posted in an outer foyer and, in the inner sanctum, an anteroom for Robson's personal secretary, Cecile Kramer, with dark wood-paneled walls lined with French landscape prints, a big polished desk (almost unfailingly neat), and a few overstuffed, hand-me-down club chairs upholstered in dark green and red leather. He also worked out of larger, more personal headquarters of his Red Lion Productions, first located in Hollywood at 1438 North Gower Street and later relocated to 259 South Beverly Drive, Los Angeles, less than ten miles west of 20th. Actor and dancer Christopher Riordan, who had by then appeared uncredited in *Viva Las Vegas*, *My Fair Lady*, and Mark Robson's *Von Ryan's Express*, would soon be considered by the director for the roles of both singer Tony Polar and fashion designer Ted Casablanca. He recalls 20th as "a funny place. Some of the top directors, producers and writers had these little cubby holes for offices—bare, utilitarian. I'd see them and think, *How can anyone be inspired working in a room like this?* Some of the offices were grand, quite nice, very well done. By some interior decorator, of course. I mean, you certainly couldn't imagine that Darryl Zanuck's office would have been decorated by Zanuck. I mean, just imagine what he would have had displayed!" (Taxidermy, big game hunting trophies, war memorabilia, animal hides; think Hemingway meets Patton.)

Beneath Robson's gung-ho public attitude toward his new movie project, however, he carried a private well of resentment and mistrust that led to a battle—one of many that flared up and wrought havoc during the making of the film. Robson's festering discontent could be traced to the previous summer, when on location in Italy he found himself in the weeds trying to deal with the outrageous abuses of Frank Sinatra while filming *Von Ryan's Express.* The 20th production, coproduced by Robson and first timer Saul David, was fraught and contentious—so much so that, returning to Hollywood from a location visit, Stan Hough, 20th vice president in charge of production operations, reported in a memo to Darryl and Richard Zanuck that he had never before seen a company so frightened of a star, to the point "where, actually, some of the crew wet their pants when he arrives on the scene." The pugnacious, macho Sinatra had been imposed on Robson by Zanuck and producer David. Although Robson praised Sinatra for always being on time and "eager to work," the actor constantly undermined the director's authority, belligerently refusing to do more than one take and ignoring any suggestion he thought could better Sinatra's performance and the movie. Fed up, Robson angrily wired his agent, Phil Gersh, calling Sinatra "impossible" and "an obstructionist for whom favors must constantly be done" and whom one must "fight for everything." Sinatra further infuriated Robson by demanding—and getting—from 20th a $25,000 "slush fund" (Robson's term) so that he could take off several days' work for a yachting trip with his "henchmen" (again, Robson's term), costars Brad Dexter and Dick Bakalyan, whom Sinatra called "indispensable." The mandate stung Robson professionally and personally. Richard Zanuck had contractually guaranteed Robson a bonus if he brought in the movie on time and on budget. But Sinatra's $25,000 perk would be charged against that bonus fund and wipe it out. The studio brass also turned a blind eye to the antics of Trevor Howard, another troublesome actor whom Zanuck and David had imposed on Robson. The director cabled the studio and his agent that the much-admired Howard often reported to the set "slobbering his lines . . . shoeless and wearing a Panama straw hat to complement his German military uniform." Howard infuriated Robson during filming of a big action sequence, when he stopped delivering his lines, turned to costars Edward Mulhare and Michael Goodliffe, with whom he'd worked for weeks, and asked, "Who the hell are you?" then shoved them aside and hobbled toward the titular train's boxcars like, Robson complained, "Quasimodo, the hunchback of Notre Dame." During filming of a brief, crucial reaction shot of Howard, he toppled headfirst into the mud and began to wallow around in it muttering incoherently; while shooting another action scene, the sound of mortar fire sent Howard diving to the ground where he crawled around erratically. (Despite Howard's much-publicized heroism while serving as an officer in World War II, the British Army discharged him for what was termed a "psychopathic personality.") Robson insisted that the studio assign Howard a round-the-clock male nurse to help him get his scenes wrapped and get him off the movie.

Despite Robson's "greatest admiration and affection" for Howard, he complained to Gersh that any footage he'd shot of the actor was unusable. Sinatra and Howard's shenanigans were "offensive, unprofessional and stupid"—a manifestation of "Fox's masochistic streak" when it came to the handling of out-of-control actors, a streak that "may have finally caught up with them." He laid blame squarely at the feet of Zanuck Jr., who had "stepped into a job beyond his experience, and as the son of [Darryl F. Zanuck], a titan in our industry, he is out to prove that he is a rough, tough studio head who can stand on his own and who can handle anyone regardless of his reputation or stature." He asked Gersh to remind Zanuck personally "that this kind of behavior on the part of 20th died in the early 40s. They are no longer running a factory—nor can they press buttons and order people to jump." When Zanuck and Saul David called Robson "uncooperative," the director warned Gersh that he would refuse to even set up a camera shot if Trevor Howard "showed up once again in a condition which will prove detrimental to the film. . . . I previously warned [Zanuck] over and over again about the loaded casting. . . . It is the fault of Dick Zanuck and 20th and it is not up to me to solve their problems." The "screaming and yelling" by his two main actors had Robson considering walking off the movie unless Zanuck invoked force majeure over Howard's alcoholism. Unsatisfied by the inaction of Zanuck, David, and his agent, Robson leapfrogged over them all and personally called Darryl F. Zanuck in his Paris office. The senior Zanuck gave Robson a more than sympathetic hearing and, soon after, raged at his son not only for pressuring Robson to cast two troublesome actors the director hadn't wanted in the first place but also for letting a volatile situation get so out of hand. The Zanucks' ongoing firestorm raging again, Gersh cabled Robson a warning from Richard Zanuck that Robson's phone call "would disrupt the entire [studio] chain of command." But once Zanuck Sr. intervened, it was obvious that Sinatra and Howard had been persuaded to at least curb their excesses long enough to complete production. Richard Zanuck sent Robson an apologetic cable ending with: "Let's not be upset any longer as our working relationship and personal relationship is too important for this."

Despite the Sturm und Drang, *Von Ryan's Express* went on to become the tenth biggest moneymaker of 1965 and earned Sinatra (deservedly) some of the best reviews of his movie career. Zanuck hoped to smooth things over by paying Robson his $25,000 bonus and by passing over other directors to assign him *Valley of the Dolls*, viewed by both Darryl and Richard Zanuck as a plum assignment, almost a reward for Robson. After all, unlike *Von Ryan's Express*, Robson might have viewed *Valley* as a cakewalk. No filming on grueling locations, no major action sequences, a shorter shooting schedule, plenty of interiors shot right on the studio lot, and not being forced to cast masters of disruption like Sinatra and Howard. Soon, though, Robson would be reliving his worst nightmares on *Valley of the Dolls*, this time with multiple difficult stars. *If you want to make the Hollywood gods laugh, tell them your plans.*

CHAPTER SIX

Going Back to Harlan—Ready, Screenwriter One

As moviemakers, studio bosses, and blood kin, Darryl F. Zanuck and Richard D. Zanuck had their differences. On at least one *Valley of the Dolls*–related matter, though, the dueling Zanucks concurred: it had been a wise decision not to press Jacqueline Susann into having the first shot at writing the screenplay. Fortunately, Simon & Schuster had paid Susann a whopping advance for the rights to her next novel, *The Love Machine*, so rather than return to the valley she instead chose to return to her "torture chamber" to complete the book—especially with the added incentive of knowing that although 20th had a first-look option, several other studios and producers promised a bidding war for the movie rights, a war that would go on to send the asking price soaring to a then-record $1.5 million. For public consumption, though, Susann focused on comparing *Valley of the Dolls* to a beloved child and said that to slice a narrative spanning twenty years to fit the limitations of a two-hour movie would have forced her to perform "self-emotional surgery." So, by contract, she ceded creative control over any aspect of the movie version, including matters of casting. Jackie said, "The book was mine. No one had told me how to write it, what to say. The picture was Fox's. They certainly were not paying me a huge sum of money so they could destroy my book. Thank God, thank David Weisbart, thank Mark Robson that I can say, 'I have nothing to do with it, it's all up to them.'" The following year, she would choke on those words.

The Zanucks consulted regularly on production decisions and hiring, starting with the question of the right screenwriter to tackle a slick, racy, but censor-resistant movie adaptation. Weisbart and the Zanucks initially perused the studio's short list of some of the best, most Oscar-nominated, highest-paid screenwriters of the era—all men. Among them were Philip Dunne (toiling most recently on adapting Irving Stone's novel *The Agony and the Ecstasy* for 20th), Ivan Moffat (*A Place in the Sun* and *Giant*, a favorite of Mark Robson's), John Michael Hayes (who had adapted *Butterfield 8*, *The Carpetbaggers*, and *Peyton Place* for director Robson), Rod Serling (*Seven Days in May*), and Ernest Lehman (*North by Northwest*, *West Side Story*, *Who's Afraid of Virginia Woolf?*). Some were unavailable, some indecisive, some thought Susann's novel too smutty and lowdown to bother with. Said Lehman, "I'd been doing movies on and off at 20th since *The King and I*, *From the Terrace*, and a picture Hitchcock and I nearly did. I went back there to do *The Sound of Music* and *Hello, Dolly!* but I also experienced the place after the *Cleopatra* days when things got so dire, Darryl Zanuck pretty much shut down the entire lot to try and save the studio. The place got so deserted, you didn't want to leave your office too late because you'd go to your car and see packs of coyotes prowling around and staring you right in the eye. After *The Sound of Music* put Fox back in business, *Valley of the Dolls* was one of those things Dick Zanuck saw as potentially very profitable. I had no interest in doing *Peyton Place*, which Mark Robson directed, but I adapted *From the Terrace*, and Mark Robson directed that one. But that was John O'Hara's novel. When *Valley of the Dolls* came along? No, that one I avoided like the plague. I wouldn't have known how to do it but, anyway, to me, that one was death on toast." Weisbart and Zanuck Jr. 's choice threw many in Hollywood for a loop—including several of the aforementioned screenwriters—and spun the project in an entirely different direction.

On February 23, 1966, *Daily Variety* and the *Hollywood Reporter* ran the announcement that Weisbart had signed as screenwriter for *Valley of the Dolls* Harlan Ellison—the thirty-one-year-old former drifter, *Rogue* magazine editor, and blazingly talented, legendarily combative speculative fiction writer nicknamed Mad Dog. The studio paid Ellison $11,000 (about $88,000 today) for a treatment, the first lap of the old egg-and-spoon race known as a "step deal"; the contract included options and escalator clauses for additional drafts, a full screenplay, and rewrites. Ellison was very new to movies. Having moved in 1955 from his birth city, Cleveland, Ohio, to New York to pursue a writing career, within two years Ellison had under his belt more than a hundred short stories published, as well as stories for EC Comics (Entertaining Comics) and other venues. He migrated to Hollywood in 1962 and won gigs writing episodes of TV's *Route 66*, *Burke's Law*, *The Outer Limits*, and *The Alfred Hitchcock Hour*. Weisbart hired Ellison for his talent, edginess, and youth, and on the buzz off his yet-unseen adaptation of director-pulp-writer-screenwriter Richard Sale's irresistible, knowing 1964 novel *The Oscar*, in which fictional Academy Award nominee Frankie Fane lies, cheats, steals, abuses women, and uses every dirty trick in the book to discredit the four other stars against whom he's competing. Fane is the sort of Machiavellian monster with whom Jacqueline Susann's *Valley* divas Helen Lawson and Neely O'Hara might have compared life goals and stratagems. As Ellison told writer Nat Segaloff, "I had already been signed to do *Valley of the Dolls* and was doing it at the time it came out"—"it" being *The Oscar*. Said Ellison, "They would not let me look at the dailies. I never saw one frame of that film until the night I saw it. And as I saw it, I literally sank lower and lower and lower in my seat. I had the distinct thought, 'This is the end of my film career.' It was so bad." As Ellison points out, he had also signed his *Valley* deal before the Zanucks, Weisbart, and Robson were allowed to see the film version of *The Oscar* released to Manhattan theaters on March 4, 1966. In the end, the script for that flagrantly awful, pseudopoetic, hugely enjoyable mess was "credited" to Ellison, Russell Rouse, and Clarence Greene.

Nevertheless, Ellison put his nose to the grindstone while working out of an office in the Swiss chalet–style Writers' Building at 20th. Longtime Ellison associate Segaloff observed, "*Valley of the Dolls* was career pragmatism. It's always easier to get a job if you already have one, and the wise Hollywood writer lands that new assignment before the last one is released, especially if it carries the odor of a flop." Ellison, right on time, turned in his 124-page treatment for *Valley of the Dolls*, dated May 6, 1966. The writer's descriptive powers are in fifth gear from the first paragraph. He envisions a credit sequence beginning on a pair of female hands grabbing for a pill bottle, then a pair of eyes brimming with anguish, and then—pow!—searing kaleidoscopic colors and fish-eye aerial views distort as Manhattan skyscrapers melt and collapse upon themselves. Aside from Ellison's many suggestions for trippy visuals throughout, his dramatics are surprisingly square and reasonably faithful to Susann's novel. Ellison's psychedelic visuals sparked an impressive portfolio of bold, artful production illustrations for a movie envisioned to exist alongside such then-edgy films of the era as *Blow-Up* and *Darling*. So what did Ellison do that is good, bad, and different from the movie as we know it?

1. He raises the curtain in 1953 with Neely ("fire in her eyes, lightning in her feet") and her supporting singer-dancers the Gaucheros (one an "obvious homosexual," the other Neely's brother-in-law) in rehearsal for *Hit the Sky*, the newest stage musical starring Broadway's queen of mean, Helen Lawson. Ellison's Neely has "electricity . . . a dissension, a physical presence," and she's ambitious, kind to the guys in her act, blazingly charismatic, and—a quality somewhat lacking in the final movie—*sympathetic*. The role cries for a reigning young supernova or, better yet, one about to happen.

2. The script details ten full-on musical numbers and is replete with knowingly campy Busby Berkeley–style visuals and staples of Showbiz Movie Montage—spinning theater marquees, shots of cheering audiences, maps depicting a Broadway show's out-of-town theater engagements. Alternating with these are druggy, Day-Glo-tinged sequences—each of the three young heroines gets at least one—as well as montages with distinctly Richard Avedon–influenced fashion imagery.

3. Neely, Anne, and Jennifer become roommates, and their lives, career trajectories, and bad romances are inextricably linked. Their relationship is salty, warm, sisterly, protofeminist, and a throwback to such earlier 20th movies as *How to Marry a Millionaire* and *The Best of Everything*.

4. Flashbacks dramatize young Anne's mother and her aunt Amy warning her about how no "real lady" enjoys sex; in another, young Anne fights off date rape on a New England beach.

5. Powerful theatrical agent Henry Bellamy describes his client Jennifer North to Anne as "if possible, even more beautiful than you. She is very possibly too beautiful to be alive and I have never met anyone who was such a perfect victim." To further hammer home Jennifer's sex-bomb appeal, Ellison, surely pulling the legs of 20th executives—whether or not they knew it—conjures, Frank Tashlin–style, Manhattan streets teeming with slack-jawed businessmen who ogle her, drop their briefcases, collide with one another, literally stopping traffic.

6. Ellison '60s-izes Lyon Burke, Susann's cardboard lady-killer, would-be novelist, and all-around drag, as a long-haired, bearded, "barely restrained wild thing" who is introduced nearly hurling his current lover (she's "born for the bedroom") to the rocks during an argument on a windswept Northern California seacoast cliff. "You're a bum trip, buddy!" yells the young beauty, to which Lyon retorts, "The bummiest, baby."

7. Lyon reluctantly returns to work for his former employer Henry Bellamy and thanks Anne for finding him a great apartment by wining and dining her at a restaurant featuring a circular ring in which a blonde with a riding crop rides a white pony. For a chaser, Lyon regales her with tales of his former wild days and his novel-in-progress. For some inexplicable reason, Anne falls for him.

8. The triumphant opening night of *Time* magazine cover boy singer Tony Polar brings together at one ringside table Helen Lawson ("the Ethel Merman-ish star of the Broadway stage . . . with a voice like a shotgun"), her straight/gay entourage, and Anne fuming with jealousy because Lyon brings client Jennifer as his date. Erotic sparks fly between Tony and Jennifer.

9. Neely gets canned from the new Helen Lawson musical *Hit the Sky*, but one of her performing partners, who is bedding Lawson, stays on. Helen courts Anne's friendship despite Neely's warning that Helen is "a monster . . . a killer . . . the Queen Mother of all piranha fish."

10. As the Tony-Jennifer liaison heats up, Neely takes up with nebbish press agent Mel—"a gentle sort of little guy with owl glasses, a mild, sweet manner." In a deliberate nod to Irving Mansfield's constant comment about Jacqueline Susann, Neely observes of Mel, "Isn't he great?" Soon, Neely shocks prim and proper Anne by sharing news about her sex life with Mel: "I lost my cherry!" Helen invites herself to dinner with Anne and wheedles *Hit the Sky* producer Gil Case into scoring her some sleeping pills.

11. Meanwhile, when Helen fires from *Hit the Sky* another scene-stealing young up-and-comer, Anne helps get Neely the job. In a lavish production number called "Dreams Are a Dime a Dozen," Neely scores as an evangelical Salvation Army worker. (The number is Ellison's deliberate takeoff on Ethel Merman's show-stopping "Blow, Gabriel, Blow" from Cole Porter's 1934 *Anything Goes*.) A drunken Helen Lawson refuses Neely's congratulations on opening night, snarling, "Get the hell away from me, ya little snip, before I rap you in the mouth. . . . If you wanna say anything, it's prolly, 'So long, Lawson, I'm stealin' your show.'" Neely tries to placate her, but Helen lunges for her, held back only by the show's producer, who refuses Helen's demand to fire Neely. Later, Ellison dramatizes Neely's first turn for the ugly when Lyon overhears her telling an appalled Anne, "Helen Lawson doesn't fight with losers. She was afraid of me, Anne. Really scared. I'm a threat to her. And I'm gonna show that old bag. I'm gonna come out of this bigger 'n her."

12. Lyon and Anne's tiresome *Will they or won't they?* routine ends with a simple, inevitable *They will*, consummated in a New Haven hotel room. Rather than dwelling on their passion, Ellison cuts instead to a bout of "naked lust" as Jennifer fights off Tony's attempted rape, complete with his "grappling, muted sounds" and a touch of "Grand Guignol." A wheedling phone call from Jennifer's manipulative mother ("You're treating me like dirt after I spent the best years of my life raising you!") interrupts the attack until Tony roars, "Come on, baby—*I'm on fire!*"

13. Ellison ends a *Hit the Sky* montage—done with spinning theater marquees and audiences cheering quick musical excerpts featuring Neely, Helen, and Jennifer—with a grotesque Janus-faced close-up of Helen, one side slathered in stage makeup, the other side horrifically wizened. Helen begs Anne—who had promised to go back to New York with Lyon now that they are lovers—to instead stay with her so that she won't "go bugsy" and wind up with "some bum in the hotel bar just so I won't have to be alone."

14. Tony's sister, Miriam, in Tony's "palatial apartment," calls Jennifer "a money-grubbing gold digger . . . a whore." Tony gets from Jennifer an "It's her or me" ultimatum and, as delineated by Ellison, the camera goes tight onto his "childlike face" as his gaze shifts from his sister to his lover.

15. Ellison depicts Jennifer's high-fashion photo shoot "à la Richard Avedon" and "Julie Christie in *Darling*." Between wardrobe changes, Jennifer confesses to Anne her terror that the camera has begun revealing her true age and that she's hooked on Seconal. In Tony's apartment, she studies her reflection—"anxious, frantic." When she tries to get Tony to elope, he rapes her.

16. Lyon storms out of a book editor's office when the editor praises his book but tells him that it needs more sex and a more sympathetic main character. Lyon takes out his anger on Anne, damning her "constant mothering and prying" as "the worst thing a woman can do to a man having trouble with his art." Lyon hurls his manuscript into the fireplace and walks out on Anne, who heads straight for a bottle of dolls.

17. Jennifer, bored senseless while Tony makes movies, commiserates with Mel, who complains that costume designer Ted Casablanca now rules Neely's life, putting her on crash diets with pills and worsening Mel and Neely's already strained communication. Neely—now hip, flashy, cynical, and addicted to Nembutal and Seconal—returns home, pops amphetamines, and secretly confides that she and Casablanca have spent the afternoon "humping" in his studio: "And may I tell you, lady, he is anything but a fag." She and "The Head" (the studio boss) have arranged for Mel to be caught with a girl to ensure the public's sympathy when Neely divorces him. When Jennifer announces her plans to make Tony impregnate her, Neely provides the name of Hollywood's go-to abortionist.

18. Jennifer accepts Anne's invitation to stay with her and cosmetics magnate Kevin Gillmore (living in sin!) in their posh New York digs, but when Jennifer devolves into an unemployed pill-head, Kevin demands Anne kick her out. In one of Ellison's many loopy "poetic" touches, Jennifer watches the flight of a solitary bird and, apparently inspired, starts packing. Miriam materializes at the front door of Anne and Kevin's apartment, finally spilling the beans about Tony's degenerative condition. (MIRIAM: "Do you want your child to be a lunatic? Retarded? Convulsions, pathetic, gone to rot in some insane asylum?")

19. Months later, while dining out with Anne and Kevin, Jennifer, divorced and post-abortion, gets spotted by Claude Chardot (a "Roger Vadim–style French film director"), who tells her that he's in New York preparing a psychological thriller, "possibly a *Repulsion*," an eerily prescient reference to Roman Polanski, considering that Sharon Tate, who went on to play Jennifer, married Polanski. The sexual sparks between Jennifer and Chardot prompt Kevin to comment: "Too bad we never had fireworks like that, Anne." She replies, "Ours may not be as bright, Kevin dear, but it will probably last much longer."

20. Anne berates Jennifer for accepting Chardot's offer for her to star in his film, wailing, "But in the nude, Jenny! Naked! My God! . . . Oh, Jen! Sex pictures!" "*Art* pictures," Jennifer protests. Later, Anne receives a copy of Lyon's newly published novel, dedicated to her. She reads it, weeps, and gulps down some dolls.

21. When Neely, stoned, wakes up to find Ted and a nudie cutie cavorting in their swimming pool, she lowers the boom: "The little boys, I don't mind too much. Dr. Kensington said it was good therapy for you every once in a while, because you were insecure. What about *her*? Is *that* 'little boy' therapy?" Ellison wittily punctuates the scene by describing Neely's tirade as so loud, the lights of every adjacent Beverly Hills mansions switch on.

22. Once Ted walks out on Neely, Ellison indulges in many, many pages depicting a long, super trippy montage of "psychoanalytic probing deep inside Neely's life, her thoughts," as she loses her grip. It's all described in "matte overlays, spiral crosses, flip frames, freeze frames, solarization, jump-cuts" and fragments of film showing lots of doll taking, an "Assistant Director's face in extreme close-up yelling, 'Where the hell is Neely? This is the 15th time she's been late!' and glimpses of her winning *six* Oscar nominations. She winds up in an expensive sanitarium where, when visited by Anne, now a super-chic top fashion model, she reveals that her singing voice is shot, possibly for good.

23. Kevin gives Anne an ultimatum: him or Lyon. No contest. She and Lyon canoodle and kiss in his hotel suite as the camera spins around them again and again, *Vertigo* style. Returning to Kevin, Anne finds him dead of heart failure and finds herself a rich widow.

24. Chardot's brutal manipulation of Jennifer's age-related insecurities sends her rushing to an exclusive clinic straight out of "Fritz Lang—all swirling knives, lights reflecting off her skin, and the shiny brightness of metal." After recuperating from her face- and body-lift, she is swarmed by the paparazzi at Kennedy Airport, her visage revealing a "tightness but peculiar freshness," her forced smile betraying "an edge of horror, a tinge of fear."

25. Ellison plays a scene of Anne and Jennifer visiting Neely in the institution from the viewpoint of an unidentified "inmate" who moves through the crowd, his gaze "shimmering, a bit out-of-focus and tilted weirdly, distorted." When a miraculously healthier Neely finishes performing "Dreams Are a Dime a Dozen," a man—the aforementioned "P.O.V."—steps up and says, "You always had it, Neely—we both did." Neely is horrified to recognize him as "the shattered remains of what was once Tony Polar" as he wanders zombie-like and unseeing right past Jennifer, whose gaze shows an "edge of madness and desperation." Better believe, for Jennifer, the road leads straight to dolls.

26. As Lyon and Anne discuss their future as a couple, Lyon confesses, "You're losing me, and I've never found myself." Anne uses her inheritance money to secretly buy Lyon the Bellamy Agency. All the characters converge to celebrate Anne and Lyon's wedding. Neely, hoping to get "The Head" to notice her revitalized talent, sings a sad ballad; the studio mogul is too busy accepting Chardot's offer to sell him Jennifer's contract, which includes "complete services"—beginning that night. The head is obviously Ellison's riff on a Darryl F. Zanuck or Louis B. Mayer and one can only imagine Zanuck Sr.'s and Jr.'s reactions to reading *that* little bit of business.

27. Jennifer learns that Chardot sees her only as "a saleable commodity," "a dancing bear," and swallows a fatal dose of sleeping pills.

28. Weeks after the funeral, Helen Lawson strolls into a nightclub, and she and Neely duke it out in the ladies' room, "two real professionals tearing at the soft underbellies of each other" until Neely yanks off Helen's wig, revealing shards of hair ruined by "a bad dye job."

29. Neely exploits a gossip columnist's questions about Jennifer's death into a shameless exercise to promote her next career move. When the crowd cheers Neely's impromptu performance in a supper club, she announces to Lyon that she's ready to reestablish her career—"every goddamn mile of it."

30. Neely's career renaissance gets encapsulated in snippets from a nightclub performance, a triumphant Hollywood Bowl concert, and a TV special. Later, Anne gets suspicious when Lyon packs for Hollywood to "hand-hold" Neely as she starts filming her new movie. Late one night on a soundstage, a naked Neely tries to seduce Lyon and, when that doesn't work, she reveals that Anne bought the agency for him. Lyon, humiliated and furious, indulges Neely in a bout of revenge sex.

31. At a restaurant, when Henry Bellamy confirms to Anne that Lyon and Neely are having an affair, Anne stubs out her cigarette in her slice of cake. (Similar to moments in *Rebecca* and *To Catch a Thief*, directed by Alfred Hitchcock.)

32. During Anne and Lyon's first wedding anniversary party, Ellison describes Neely threatening to sabotage herself and him. Anne overhears it all, goes to her bedroom, and lies down in the dark. Moments later she overhears Lyon and his new starlet girlfriend arguing. Lyon warns her: "Any woman who puts her career before her man is exchanging the griddle for the fire." Once they leave, Anne chugs some dolls—"She loves Lyon less so it hurts less now"—and stares through her bedroom window at "the promised land . . . glittering gold and diamonds."

And final curtain, with everyone in the morality play ending up dead, miserable, or resigned to her fate, pretty much as Susann wrote it and certainly the way Ellison intended his adaptation.

• • •

The Zanucks, Weisbart, and Robson had hired an iconoclastic youngblood in the hope that he might slash through Susann's purple excesses and give *Valley* a contemporary urgency and energy. They also hoped that Ellison might bring dimensionality to the male characters. Robson, especially, wanted to attract a younger audience. They miscalculated. But, according to the filmmakers, for all the promise in the treatment, it didn't seem like the way forward for the kind of movie they wanted to make. Read today, Ellison's work is funny, hip, visual, very much of its period—and something of a revelation. At the time, though, false rumors ricocheted around Hollywood that his script was filthy. Immoral. Savage. Not just druggy but, well, drugged-out. And that's why few were surprised when word spread that the moviemakers were on the hunt for another screenwriter to take things from there.

For years, it has been reported that Ellison left the project and refused credit on the final film out of anger at any attempt to give the movie a Hollywoodized happy ending. Maybe so, but he revealed to more than one friend and journalist, including author, podcaster, and film critic Alonso Duralde, another reason why he became persona non grata on *Valley*. The story goes that during a 20th publicity party thrown to celebrate the launch of the movie project, Ellison got seated near Jacqueline Susann and Irving Mansfield. The three were having a gossipy good time slinging show business (and other varieties of) mud. But the atmosphere apparently turned frosty when Ellison began regaling Mansfield with tales of an attractive young woman he knew, a bona fide math genius who, in her spare time, moonlighted as a well-paid gentleman's escort. It turned out that Jackie knew that Irving was a frequent client. That, supposedly, was one of the things that *really* led to Ellison's being tossed from *Valley of the Dolls*. "I never got a major film assignment after that," Ellison told Nat Segaloff, who said, "My reading on all this is not that Harlan necessarily did a bad job, but that the book's continuing sales scared the producers and the studio into wanting to cover themselves by bringing in more experienced writers. Harlan would have made *Valley of the Dolls* the camp exercise it turned out to be, only he would have done it on purpose. Although he had no experience with drugs (he famously eschewed any kind of intoxicant), he knew a lot about star mentality and the pressure on people in Hollywood to be part of the scene. He had a writer's eye and ear and the skill to create a film that was at once dramatically involving and just emotionally removed enough to laugh at the absurdity of Susann's self-serious work. With so much money at stake, you have to take it seriously. My sense is that Harlan didn't."

By late summer of 1966 the novel was already in its twelfth printing, with 354,000 hardcover copies in print. It had spent twenty straight weeks topping the *New York Times* bestseller list and twenty-one at the top of *Time* magazine's list. Zanuck, feeling his father's growing insistence on making a hit movie out of *Valley* right away, leaned on Robson and Weisbart to hire another screenwriter so that they could get *Valley* before the cameras by fall or, at the very latest, early winter. They had tried "young and hip." Now they wanted solid, dependable, and female.

CHAPTER SEVEN

A Helen Not Named Lawson and a Friend of Dorothy's— Screenwriters Two and Three

After David Weisbart and Richard Zanuck considered, rejected, and got rejected by a number of potential screenwriters, witty, literate Helen Deutsch became their choice to course-correct *Valley of the Dolls* after what Darryl F. Zanuck termed "the Ellison experiment." Deutsch, sixty-one, never learned to type; she spoke her screenplays into a Dictaphone machine. She was a respected Hollywood pro who saw herself easing into the final stretch of a notable run. She'd launched her post–Barnard College career in the 1930s by managing and reading prospective material for the influential Provincetown Players, whose history of innovative affiliated artists included Eugene O'Neill, Edna St. Vincent Millay, Louise Bryant, Theodore Dreiser, and Wallace Stevens. She later became a theater critic and theater commentator for the *New York Herald Tribune* and the *New York Times* and, later still, the press representative for the original Broadway productions of

Robert Sherwood's *The Petrified Forest* starring Leslie Howard and Humphrey Bogart; Maxwell Anderson's *Winterset*, for which she masterminded the publicity campaign to promote young Burgess Meredith's stardom; and Laurence Housman's *Victoria Regina*, starring Helen Hayes. In 1935 at the Algonquin Hotel, Deutsch, Brooks Atkinson, Walter Winchell, Robert Benchley, and others launched the New York Drama Critics' Circle. In her leisure she published more than twenty stories in the *Saturday Evening Post*, *Ladies' Home Journal*, and *McCall's*.

MGM took note of her literary talent and influence and test drove her scriptwriting skills in adapting Anna Seghers's novel for the 1944 Spencer Tracy anti-Nazi drama *The Seventh Cross*, one of director Fred Zinnemann's earliest feature film efforts. Capping that success with an even bigger one, Deutsch nicely adapted Enid Bagnold's 1935 girl-and-her-horse novel *National Velvet*, cementing what was to be a thirteen-year relationship with Metro-Goldwyn-Mayer. Known for story construction and memorable dialogue, she earned top dollar anonymously doctoring not only many of her home studio's movies of the '40s and '50s but also some of Warner Bros.' challenging scripts, particularly the never-filmed adaptation of *Ethan Frome*, a pet project of Bette Davis's; she burnished her reputation by scripting a mixed bag of films including *King Solomon's Mines*, *The Glass Slipper*, *The Unsinkable Molly Brown*, and *Lili*, for which she was Oscar nominated and for which she lyricized what she called the "dreadful" hit song "Hi Lili, Hi Lo."

She was an anomaly among screenwriters. She surprised MGM's directors, cinematographers, and editors by shadowing them, observing, "How can one write successful screenplays without knowing some mechanics of the film business?" She spoke seven languages; regularly read works in Middle Latin, Middle French, Middle English, French, and German; and was invariably at the ready with a snappy quip or comeback. Columnists routinely reported on her stylish Malibu beach house, her flair for haute couture, and how she refused to work full days on Tuesdays so that she could keep a standing appointment with her Beverly Hills hairdresser. Then there were her frequent outings at swank nightclubs—squired one evening by dashing Argentinian actor Carlos Thompson (Lana Turner's *Flame and the Flesh* costar), the next by "Hollywood's Most Eligible Bachelor," the mighty Hollywood lawyer Greg Bautzer, who famously bedded some of his clients, many of them Hollywood's most desirable women. Deutsch's 1946 marriage to Rhodes scholar and UCLA economics professor Spencer Drummond Pollard came as a "surprise" to her colleagues; the marriage was annulled in less than a year.

She didn't suffer fools. Controversial, scholarly, overly serious MGM studio head Dore Schary called her "not a totally calm woman." When a studio executive urged Deutsch to tailor Daniel Defoe's 1719 epistolary shipwreck novel *Robinson Crusoe* for swashbuckling actor Stewart Granger, making sure it contained recurring dream sequences filled with gorgeous dames, Deutsch admitted, "I threw the guy out of my office." On her studio office wall hung two framed mottoes. One, apparently a nod to Mary Wollstonecraft, read "The mind, too, must lie fallow a while," meant to warn off any executive who might wander in and criticize her taking one of her regular daily catnaps; the other motto, pure Deutsch, read "When in doubt, cut to the chase."

She was smart, talented, self-determined, glamorous, and assertive, just the kind of dame Jacqueline Susann might have immortalized in the pages of *Valley of the Dolls*—if the author hadn't found her so threatening. Privately Susann referred to Deutsch as "a snob." Snob or not, perhaps Deutsch's strongest calling card for replacing Harlan Ellison as screenwriter was her adaptation of Broadway singer-actress Lillian Roth's tough, hard-luck 1954 autobiography, *I'll Cry Tomorrow*. The drama with musical numbers charts Roth's battles with an overbearing mother, her harrowing fall from stardom into alcoholism, and her battle to recover her life and stage a comeback. Deutsch's script ignited ferocious jostling for the lead role among Grace Kelly, Jane Wyman, Janet Leigh, Jean Simmons, Piper

Laurie, and Jane Russell. Twinkly MGM sweetheart June Allyson was set to take the lead, but when director Daniel Mann (*Come Back, Little Sheba*) replaced original director Charles Walters (*Torch Song*), Mann jettisoned the wholesome Allyson for the fiery Susan Hayward, who did her own singing, earned an Oscar nomination, and took home the Best Actress award at Cannes in 1956.

In the summer of 1966, David Weisbart signed Deutsch for *Valley*, and the writer and Mark Robson would routinely meet and discuss the script for hours before she'd return to Malibu to write at night. When veteran *Los Angeles Times* reporter and critic Philip K. Scheuer asked for Jacqueline Susann's reactions to Deutsch's hiring, the novelist said, "Helen told me, 'I want to follow your story completely.' I spent a year and a half struggling with the book's dialogue and another half year promoting the book. I didn't want to sweat over the screenplay; I'd rather use the time for writing my next book. So, she's completely on her own. The rest is up to her."

Deutsch submitted her first-draft screenplay in mid-October of 1966 and filed slight revisions on November 3. Weighing in at 184 pages, enough for a three-hour-*plus* movie, Deutsch's approach differs radically from Harlan Ellison's. Her scope is wider, her tone more serious, and she front-loads her version with themes, the major one being an often-repeated "*Vincit qui patitur*," that is: "The one who endures, wins." Lyon Burke philosophizes to Anne: "You win if you can take it, if you can last. For success in show business, a major requirement is the ability to survive. . . . There's no business quite like show business because the people deal not in commodities or services but in their own souls, in their own lives, in their own bodies."

Although it was generally agreed that the script needed work, the moviemakers felt confident enough to include Deutsch in a September 1 press luncheon and roundtable discussion where they chummed the waters for the media sharks. *Compared to Jacqueline Susann's novel, how frank would the movie's language and adult situations be? Would it be a damning indictment of show business?*

Did the moviemakers expect run-ins with the censors? David Weisbart assured the reporters that the moviemakers were aiming to
reach a "wide general audience"; Robson called the material "very
valuable for a broad cross-section of people to see. I'd like for
younger people to see it. It shows the pitfalls of certain ambitions."
Trying to have it both ways, Robson declared to the reporters that
Deutsch's dialogue would be "in good taste" but that "Helen [Law-
son] will use the language called for where it is part of the fiber of
the character." The moviemakers stated that the intention of Zanuck Jr. and Sr. was to create a "tasteful" *Valley of the Dolls*, imply-
ing that it would be a movie with just enough topicality, sex, and
scandal to become a sensation. Robson added, "I don't see nudity
or violence as being anything particularly bad. It may have value as
a catharsis. What I don't like is censorship in any form. I think it's
up to the public to judge. If they don't like it, they won't go." Deutsch
admitted, "I'm struggling to keep it within the bounds of good taste.
There will be no bad language simply for sensationalism, but if it's
for characterization, yes. So far, there is no need for four-letter
words, and they will not be used unless absolutely necessary in the
language, but they may be put to use for certain scenes and certain
behavior of the characters. The last thing I want to do is to take
advantage of the lessening of censorship and end up with something dirty."

Deutsch's mentions of "the lessening of censorship" and "something dirty" had more than a little to do with Edward Albee's Pulitzer
Prize winner *Who's Afraid of Virginia Woolf?* Warner Bros.' controversial film version of the play had been released to theaters just
months before on June 22. Jack Warner, the seventy-four-year-old
studio boss, had famously viewed the most expensive black-and-
white movie made to date and told fellow executives, "My god,
we've got a $7.5 million dirty movie on our hands." Screenwriter-
producer Ernest Lehman and director Mike Nichols had fought to
retain for movie audiences as much as possible of Albee's frank dialogue, which had shocked Broadway audiences. When the National

Catholic Office for Motion Pictures rated *Virginia Woolf* "morally objectionable in part for all," Jack Warner made an end run by self-labeling the movie "For Adults Only" and requiring theater owners to sign contracts stipulating that no minors would be admitted unless accompanied by an adult. Starring Elizabeth Taylor and Richard Burton, the film became a box-office hit, earned thirteen Academy Award nominations, and became such a watershed event that even Jack Valenti, the longtime president of the Motion Picture Association of America, called it "the Fort Sumter of film censorship."

But what about the characters who are seen as fictionalized versions of Judy Garland, Ethel Merman, and more? Weisbart took pains to emphasize that the movie's characters would "be fictitious and not reflect any phase of show business. Some of the people will be nice; others not so nice. Some have warts, others don't." He was, of course, gaming the press. On the one hand, 20th wanted the public to believe that the price of a movie ticket would guarantee audiences a ringside seat from which to gawk, fantasize, and tsk-tsk at the private sex lives and drug taking among the Hollywood and Broadway set. On the other hand, the studio's phalanx of lawyers seriously considered the possibility of being slammed with lawsuits over its playing a winking game of "Guess who?" There was precedent. In 1932, a jury awarded Princess Irina Alexandrovna of Russia $127,373 (roughly $2.3 million today) in damages and a $250,000 ($4.6 million) out-of-court settlement in her suit against MGM over *Rasputin and the Empress* for its suggestion that the Russian mystic Rasputin had raped "Princess Natasha," widely understood as the movie's version of the princess herself. To dodge further legal challenges, MGM pulled the movie out of distribution for decades. (Fun fact: highly respected cinematographer William H. Daniels, who shot *Rasputin and the Empress*, would soon be hired to film *Valley of the Dolls*.)

Closer to home, in 1939 Ziegfeld funny girl Fanny Brice saw 20th's musical drama *Rose of Washington Square*, starring Alice

Faye, Tyrone Power, and Al Jolson, and promptly sued each of them, along with Darryl F. Zanuck, for a total of $100,000 ($1.8 million today), charging defamation of character and unauthorized use of her life story. The movie was so obviously a thinly disguised version of Brice's life and her marriage to professional gambler and con artist Nicky Arnstein that the studio had little choice but to settle out of court for between $30,000 and $40,000 (about $630,000 today). To settle an additional lawsuit filed by Arnstein, 20th paid him $25,000. Few who have read about the Brice-Arnstein relationship dynamic or even seen the Barbra Streisand biopic *Funny Girl* would be surprised to learn that the wealthy Brice footed all of Arnstein's legal costs, even though they had been divorced for twelve years.

Imbroglios like the ones surrounding *Rasputin and the Empress* and *Rose of Washington Square* helped usher in decades of Hollywood studios' attempts to protect themselves against similar suits by slapping boilerplate disclaimers onto their films. By the mid-'60s, many studio lawyers had decided that the "Any resemblance to actual persons, living or dead, or actual events is purely incidental" notice offered no real legal protection. Only MGM and Columbia Pictures continued to use the disclaimer; Paramount Pictures, Universal Pictures, Walt Disney Studios, and 20th had dropped it altogether. But 20th had already decided to revive the notice in a major way for *Valley of the Dolls*, largely—but not only—for publicity purposes.

Meanwhile, the *Valley of the Dolls* filmmakers made an effort to reassure the thin-skinned citizens of a company town that the movie would not indict the film business as had, say, *Sunset Boulevard*, *The Big Knife*, or *In a Lonely Place*; Deutsch asserted that the movie would not be "of the Hollywood exposé type." Said Weisbart, "This is not a picture about Hollywood. There's only one studio scene in the film. It's about show business, yes, but mainly about . . . four girls under extreme pressure and how they react to it." When one journalist asked whether big movie star names would be attracted to such a controversial property, Weisbart replied, "At least thirty people have given evidence of interest to work in *Valley of the Dolls*. This is very reassuring." Behind the attempt to maintain a bullish, upbeat front, however, both Zanuck and David Weisbart fretted about whether they'd be able to continue to attract top-shelf talent on both sides of the camera if the production was perceived as anti–show business, risqué, and tacky.

Reading Helen Deutsch's richly detailed screenplay drafts today, one notices the first major difference (and improvement) when she begins the movie with Anne, Neely, and Jennifer each voicing a section of a slightly longer introductory narration that begins with Anne's, "You've got to climb Mount Everest to reach the Valley of the Dolls. . . ." It continues with Jennifer saying, "You stand there, waiting for the rush of exhilaration—but it doesn't come. You're alone—and the feeling of loneliness is overwhelming," and ends with Neely saying, "You've made it—and the world says you're a hero—but you're too far away to hear the applause—and there's no place left to climb. There's no place left to go but down—down into the Valley of the Dolls." When it comes to the character descriptions, one wonders whether Deutsch got the memo about downplaying the roman à clef elements. She describes Anne Welles as "exquisitely beautiful but does not play it up. Prototype: Grace Kelly"; Neely O'Hara is "a young singer turned a vicious, egocentric addict. Prototype: Judy Garland"; and Jennifer North is "an international sex symbol victimized by everyone. Prototype: Marilyn Monroe." But although the screenplay hews closer in style and spirit to Susann's novel than did Harlan Ellison's version, Deutsch did make some significant nips and tucks.

1. Jennifer has a musical number in Helen Lawson's new Broadway-bound show, during which two burlesque-style slapstick comedians strip down her "voluptuous body" to only glittering panties and bra. The producer and director argue over whether Jennifer is even bright enough to pull off a reaction to being stripped.

2. Helen Lawson's role is bigger and better developed. In one scene, press agent Mel Anderson tells Helen backstage during rehearsals that she's been booked on Johnny Carson's show. Helen bellows, "You set up Helen Lawson to drag herself around to plug the show?! Not me, bub."

3. When Lyon congratulates Helen but berates her for firing Neely for being too good, Helen says, "[The new show] will sell to pictures and I'll sit back and watch a film star play my part." Anne listens to Lyon refer to New York as "one big slum full of unhappy, driving people, all seeking and not finding, only half-alive, rude, irritable." When Lyon calls Helen Lawson "a barracuda—she makes her own loneliness," Anne observes, "Perhaps. But that doesn't make it any more endurable to an aging woman."

4. Deutsch has a ball dramatizing Jennifer's money-grubbing leech of a mother, "a fattish woman of about fifty with a whining voice . . . sitting in a big upholstered chair . . . holding food in one hand and the phone in the other." A handwritten note in one script draft indicates that Shelley Winters was a casting target.

5. A scene, written to be a knockout, begins with Lyon entrusting Ted Casablanca with transforming Neely from a sow's ear into a silk purse. Lyon warns the designer, "She looks like nothing. No taste. No style. But she's got something, Ted, and you're the man to bring it out and give her a style all her own. . . . You have exactly four and a half hours to turn Clara Agnes O'Neill into Neely O'Hara." Ted, his staff, Anne, and Jennifer perform the makeover, with Deutsch throwing a nod or two toward early-'60s Barbra Streisand and Liza Minnelli. Finally, Ted lets Neely view herself in the mirror for the first time—just as we do—when Mel gets to voice one of the funniest, sure-fire clichés in the entire script, "Now go out there and sing it—the way *that girl* would sing it!"—a riff on Warner Baxter telling Ruby Keeler in *42nd Street*, "You're going out a youngster, but you've got to come back a star!"

6. Lyon Burke invites Anne to move with him as he takes over the talent agency's West Coast offices. She tells him, "You want to have me and yet be free to play the field. Until some day you run into a girl who won't be as easy as I've been, and then you'll marry her." He snaps back, "Our world has grown old-fashioned about marriage. To me it's a fiction perpetuated by economics, divorce laws, and Victorian ethics. So I shall not lie to you about what I'm offering." Anne wants to be "Mrs. Somebody and not be constantly embarrassed because the rest of the world *hasn't* yet outgrown old-fashioned marriage." Later, Anne disappoints her boss by asking to be transferred west to be with Lyon, admitting: "I lie awake thinking of him with other women. I know what he is. I know what I'm getting into. But I can't help it. I've met lots of other men, but I'm in love with Lyon. And I've discovered that a little of what you really want is better than large quantities of what you don't."

7. Meanwhile, a celebrity panelist on the TV show *What's My Line?* hails Neely as "the most exciting new actress in years, the shiniest new star in Hollywood!" Deutsch paints an ironic montage of Hollywood's "shiniest new star" getting robbed blind by her business manager, knocking back booze and dope while her movie coworkers enable her, and another (delicious) moment in which a stoned Neely encourages a hack Hollywood columnist to fabricate an entire interview. Neely explains her drug addiction to Mel, "I need them more by day than at night. They make me seem relaxed, like Perry Como. They make me more attractive; otherwise sometimes I feel like I'm going to scream for no reason at all. [My psychiatrist] asks me why I think I want to scream. How the hell do I know?"

8. Deutsch—in a direct "message" to the censors—describes Jennifer's debut in a French "art" film as something that will be shot strictly from "above the waist": "In general, what we are seeing on the film screen is much like certain art films which have been released during the past few years. A tinge of travesty would be excellent and perhaps be achieved by cutting meaninglessly from cigarette to leg to ear, lingering on a big toe, showing a hand resting on a thigh with two fingers beginning to tap with boredom, etc."

9. While visiting Neely at the psychiatric hospital, Lyon and Anne deliver the news that Broadway producer David Merrick (known as the Abominable Showman) wants her for a new Broadway musical. "I've tried to get you a picture," says Lyon. "But you promised too often to be a good girl and you let them down each time. They won't take a chance on you in films—not until you've proved what you can prove on Broadway—that you're capable of showing up night after night for a performance and in good condition." Neely announces her new credo: "I'm going to take what I want. Grab what I need. . . . [I'm a] big star. Way up on top of the mountain, hmm? You climb the mountain . . . and the air gets thinner . . . and harder to breathe . . . and you get to the top. And what do you find on the other side? The valley of the dolls, down, down, down. . . ." Neely declares her intention to pursue everything and everyone she wants—starting with Lyon. Anne laughs; Lyon calls himself "Lucky-Lyon-in-the-middle." But Anne's smile fades when she notes Neely's hardened expression.

10. Jennifer's sleazy French director Claude Chardot tells Miriam that he is canceling her new film because the camera is exposing her age. To prove it, he opens Jennifer's jacket and manhandles her breasts, saying, "She's sagging! She's over the hill!" This image gets repeated in montage as the screenwriter visually dramatizes Jennifer's descent into loss of control. At home, Miriam proffers Jennifer some dolls and advises her that she must forget Tony for her own survival, and as she comforts her, she runs her hands over her body "in a manner that is far from sisterly." When Jennifer pushes Miriam violently away, Miriam throws her out of the house. Jennifer phones her mother, begging her to let her come back home; her mother tells her to send her money immediately. The screenwriter describes—in quick flashes—Jennifer reliving her degradation by Chardot, seeing Tony being dragged away by hospital attendants, Miriam coming on to her, images from Jennifer's nudie film, and Jennifer being stripped by the vaudeville comedians. Downing more pills, Jennifer sits before a dressing table mirror, slathers herself in cold cream—"a horrifying attack by Jennifer upon her own sexuality"—then staggers to the bed, collapses, and dies.

11. Anne tells Lyon that she's had enough of show business and of his catting around. She declares, in what sounds suspiciously like a screenwriter's self-confession, "I'm no longer enchanted with the art of films. It may be an art, but I no longer see that—I see promotion and wheeling-dealing. . . . This has been coming on for a long time. I guess my entire upbringing makes this way of life wrong for me." Deutsch pulls off a clumsy, funny paraphrase and update of Scarlett O'Hara's dialogue from the famous *Gone with the Wind* scene in which she asks Rhett Butler, "Rhett, if you go, where shall I go? What shall I do?" In Deutsch's version, Anne answers Lyon's, "What will you do? Where will you go?" with "I don't know. But right now I'm on my way to the valley of the dolls, and I'd rather not let that happen to me." When Anne returns to Lawrenceville, Deutsch depicts her finding pleasure in strolling the beach, going on a picnic alone, and acknowledging the wolf whistle of a man painting a fence. She is "full of vitality, happy." But this being a soap opera, once she sits down at the shore and watches the sky and sea, her smile fades and tears fall.

12. In New York, Neely—"startlingly beautiful, dressed in a gorgeous, offbeat cocktail gown"—crashes the after-party celebrating Helen Lawson's new show. From there, the now infamous scene between Helen and Neely plays—with minor dialogue variations—pretty much the way it does in the film version as we know it. The biggest difference is that, when Neely flips Helen's wig: "She is *bald* with a few gray wisps of hair here and there on her pate."

13. Neely makes a disaster of her opening night, appearing onstage stoned, missing her entrances and musical cues, her voice cracking, and yelling drunkenly, "Cut! Now leshtart again." The screenwriter suggests cutting to a reaction shot of producer David Merrick in the audience. Later in her dressing room, Neely pops pills and refuses an offer from her dresser to see her home: "I said go 'way. I don't need you. . . . I don't need anybody." Ushered out of a bar by a kindly, familiar bartender, she collapses in an alley next to the theater. And with Neely screaming the names of Lyon, Mel, Anne, Jennifer, Ted, Clara Agnes O'Neill, and *God*, Deutsch drops a musty, cliché-ridden curtain on *Valley of the Dolls*.

For all of Deutsch's elaborations and cutting, she kept her word to Susann about sticking to the contours of the novel. But she also labors too hard to turn gloriously pulpy melodrama into something top-heavy with Truths and Major Statements—so much so that boredom, alongside melodramatic camp, leaps off the page. And as it turned out, she and director Mark Robson were not simpatico. Although Robson gave Deutsch generally positive and respectful feedback, he wanted things pacier and punchier. He directed her to attempt several versions of the three-character narration that opens the movie, insisting on more emphasis on "the pills" and the theme of the "the sacrifice people make for careers in show business." He also pinpointed several scenes he wanted her to make sexier; depicting Neely's attempt to seduce Lyon in Las Vegas, he advised the screenwriter to have Neely invite Lyon to her hotel room, where she awaits stark naked. But the director and writer were a classic case of irresistible force meeting immovable object. Robson complained, "Frankly, I would sit with Helen for seven or eight hours and we'd talk about one scene. The next day, we'd go through the same thing, and nothing would come of our conferences." No matter how hard Robson pushed Deutsch, the screenwriter refused to make major changes with which she did not agree.

On November 3 and 6, Deutsch delivered Robson's requested revisions. Although the Zanucks, Weisbart, and Robson remained unsatisfied, the producer began using the script as a work-in-progress blueprint from which to come up with a proposed budget based on a tentative shooting schedule, location requirements, set and costume costs, and other technical aspects. Just before the dawn of the new year, Deutsch sent Weisbart a letter expressing concern about the "*Vincit qui patitur*" theme she had introduced into her screenplay. The letter was occasioned by the publication of a nonfiction book by Dr. Sam Sheppard titled *Endure and Conquer*, in which the doctor defended himself in the infamous case in which he was accused and convicted of brutally murdering his wife. The tone of Deutsch's letter betrays a certain defensiveness when she asserts how the theme had been on her mind "for many, many years" and was even the motto of her girlhood summer camp. She urges Weisbart not to eliminate it from the film; otherwise it would lose "body and stature."

Between the lines one can sense that Deutsch had realized that her screenplay had not hit the bull's eye. Although Jacqueline Susann frequently told the press that she never read any of the screenplay drafts, Deutsch told friends and associates that Susann had indeed read her script, not liked it, and couldn't wait to get her hands on it. "She meddled and meddled with that screenplay," Deutsch complained. In the end, Deutsch disavowed the script and petitioned, as Harlan Ellison would later do, the Writers Guild of America to scrub her name from the credits. (The request was denied.) Calling her *Valley* stint a "sour note" on which to cap her career, she retired to a high-rise at 185 Park Avenue. Whenever Hollywood later came calling, she'd invariably respond: "Occupation: a recluse in New York." *Valley of the Dolls* would be her final movie credit.

Richard D. Zanuck grew increasingly impatient with what he called the project's "non-progress." Robson said, "We had to get on with it, so I brought Dorothy in"—alluding to another former MGM contract writer, Dorothy Kingsley. Best known for her work on scripts for *Girl Crazy*, *Kiss Me Kate*, and *Seven Brides for Seven Brothers*, Kingsley, fifty-seven, was another whip-smart, highly independent sophisticate. When David Weisbart sent her a copy of the novel, Kingsley, a self-described "sweetness and light" type known for writing "clean" movies, read it in two hours flat. Her first reaction? "Oh, come *on*." But, said Kingsley, "I read it over again trying to figure out how I could do it—and I found my answer." Cynics might speculate that 20th's lucrative salary offer might have helped Kingsley see the light, but she was serious when she said, "I only accept assignments that are challenging or interesting—and *Valley of the Dolls* fell into that category." She certainly didn't need the money, being married to seafood tycoon William Durney and co-owner of, among other properties, a thousand-acre Carmel, California, ranch (with four hundred acres in vineyards), an impressive Beverly Hills spread, a Monterey bungalow, and a high-rise apartment in Century Towers on the former back lot of 20th Century Fox. To celebrate the *Valley of the Dolls* assignment in early January of 1967, Kingsley treated herself to a black-and-white mink she found in Copenhagen.

Robson became as fond of Kingsley as he had been disenchanted with Deutsch. The director advised her to "retain the excitement of the novel but cut out the offensive parts. Clean it up but keep it strong." He instructed her to incorporate more of the novel's key scenes and as much of its original dialogue as possible. For the next three months, Kingsley—Robson jokingly nicknamed her "Dirty Dot"—worked in her office at 20th, rewriting the screenplay in *longhand*. "Sure," she said, "much of the book is sensational, but if you get under that layer, it has something to say that's important. Pills are having a strong sociological impact on today's society. People can't stand on their own two feet anymore. They take pills to go to sleep and pills to wake up. The real importance of this book is that it points up the terrible dependence on pills." Kingsley had come by her show business know-how honestly. Her mother, Alma Hanlon, appeared in twenty-three movies from 1915 to 1919, often playing vampy vixens. Her newsman father, Walter J. Kingsley, wrote for the *New York Telegraph* and the London *Daily Express* before becoming a colorful bon vivant press agent for Florenz Ziegfeld. After young Dorothy's parents divorced acrimoniously, in 1918 her mother married movie producer-director Louis Myll. Kingsley's parents drifted away from show business and relocated to tony Grosse Point, Michigan.

In the 1940s, Dorothy, a charmingly outspoken, nimble-witted, and attractive blonde, found herself a young, divorced mother of three in serious need of work. With an armload of material written on speculation for several of the radio era's biggest stars, including Jack Benny and Eddie Cantor, she hit Los Angeles to make the agency rounds. The tide turned when she met swank party doll Constance Bennett, whose brief days as Hollywood's highest paid actress were over. Pushing forty, Bennett cannily reinvented herself and restored her wealth by returning to the stage, creating a line of cosmetics and clothing, and partnering with ABC for her own radio show. Kingsley clicked with Bennett and began writing her jokes at $75 a week. After the cancellation of Bennett's show, Kingsley spent several years as gag writer for ventriloquist Edgar Bergen's hugely popular radio show. She began writing film scripts on the side, and MGM producer Arthur Freed offered her twice what she was being paid by the notoriously stingy Bergen. Kingsley doctored ailing screenplays for the earlier-mentioned *Girl Crazy* and for Esther Williams's aquatic musical *Bathing Beauty*, both big hits.

For the next fifteen years, Kingsley tailored screenplays for MGM contract stars Debbie Reynolds, Elizabeth Taylor, and Jane Powell;

she also made major contributions to the script for *Angels in the Outfield*, among many others. The quality of her writing is credited with helping achieve the near impossible—persuading Frank Sinatra to star in Columbia Pictures' film version of Rodgers and Hart's *Pal Joey*, despite the actor-singer's long-running feud with that studio's crude, much-despised boss, Harry Cohn. The 1957 assignment led four years later to Sinatra's agreeing to star in *Can-Can* based on seeing Kingsley's name on the cover of the script. Kingsley said, with typical candor, "I never think of myself as a real writer. I only wrote because I needed the money. I had no desire to 'express myself' or anything."

Weisbart approached Kingsley with a $100,000 offer: punch up and slim down *Valley of the Dolls*. By choice, she had not written a script since *Pepe*, an unsuccessful big-budget 1960 adventure vehicle meant to propel the American career of Mexican comic actor Cantinflas, who had made a splash in *Around the World in 80 Days*. With that, Kingsley unofficially retired and began spending more time with her husband, family, and grandchildren in the Pebble Beach area of Northern California. But with new offers suddenly materializing, she penciled in *Valley* to follow her commitment to adapt for Paramount the stage musical *Half a Sixpence*. In mid-December 1966, 20th publicity head James Denton fed columnists the news of Kingsley's "taking over the adaptation" from Helen Deutsch, who, as described by a gossip columnist at the time, had "completed her work and is now out."

With *Valley* announced as beginning production on February 1, 1967, the 20th brass staged a second press conference to help give the project a new jolt of publicity adrenaline. Kingsley, flanked at a table by Weisbart and Robson, admitted to reporters that the novel's frank language and situations would "pose problems." Nevertheless, she soldiered on and turned in her 130-page draft on January 6, 1967. In many ways, the screenplay was so old-school Hollywood melodrama that it might just as well have been dated January 6, 1947. Robson and Weisbart liked her work, and with the

Zanucks muscling them to get the movie under way, they retained Kingsley to make script revisions after the start of principal photography.

An old Hollywood adage goes, "There are at least three different movies. The script. What gets filmed. And what gets edited." Each *Valley of the Dolls* screenplay draft contains elements of Jacqueline Susann's novel and echoes of earlier films. Dorothy Kingsley's take departs strongly—though not necessarily in a superior way—from Helen Deutsch's drafts. Kingsley's is advanced and detailed, right down to the design of the opening credit sequence described as "three tiny Giacometti figures discernable in the distance, casting their tiny shadows before them. They lose their human resemblance and become red, yellow, and blue sleeping pills that soon disintegrate. Their colors run together and become the main title." Kingsley extends the opening narration to Anne's farewell to Lawrenceville, her mother, Aunt Amy, and her fiancé. As Willie pins her with his fraternity pin, we are intended to hear Anne's voice saying, "Aunt Amy was pleased. Willie's father owned the mill. But Mother asked me if I loved him. I told her no. When Willie kissed me, I didn't feel a thing. Maybe I was afraid. Mother said she was the same—until she met Dad—dear, darling Dad." It is worth singling out this small bit of character development because it helps suggest Kingsley's gift for deepening a character simply and succinctly. It was also meant to dovetail with the final scene: Lyon Burke, after deflowering, betraying, and abandoning Anne, returns at last to ask her to marry him. Her response: "Funny, for so many years I prayed for this moment—and now that it's come, I don't feel a thing." With that, she walks straight past Lyon, beckoning her dog to join her for a walk in the adjacent woods, where she flings out her arms triumphantly and whirls around. As Kingsley put it: "At last, she is free—free!" Although novelette-ish and mawkish, at least Kingsley's scripted version—in contrast to the same moments in the finished movie—tries to create a reasonably plausible emotional arc for Anne, let alone not expecting her to walk out of her own house and leave Lyon standing there like a lummox.

Kingsley's drafts are notable for tiny details that attempt a semblance of character complexity, humor, self-awareness, quirk. When Anne is being oriented to the Bellamy theatrical office by the boss's personal assistant, Miss Steinberg, Steinberg says of Bellamy, "He's a nice guy. Been married to the same wife thirty years and goes to Temple every Saturday. His real name's Birnbaum." Anne says, "Oh"—and Steinberg (described as looking "at her narrowly") says, "You're not anti-Semitic?" Anne replies, "Oh, no—I'm not anti-anything." When Bellamy sends Anne to the rehearsal space where Helen Lawson and Neely O'Hara are gearing up for the opening of a new Broadway show, Kingsley gets us in Neely's corner by letting her show some gratitude and humility. She tells her press agent boyfriend, Mel (whom Kingsley gives a *spine*), "Imagine *me*—rehearsing in a Broadway show—with my own song. Isn't that a *pistol*? Gee, if the kids in the old neighborhood could see me now—the ones who aren't in Sing, that is."

In a later scene, when Lyon tells Anne that he isn't looking for a wife—"Some men don't pull well in double harness"—Anne responds, "You know yourself. I don't know who I am, or what I want. I only know I have to find out." We then cut to Anne's hotel room at the Martha Washington, where she, "keyed-up and exhilarated" after being swept off her feet by Lyon, walks to the window in her undies, throws open the shade, hops into bed, and "wiggles beneath the blanket, tosses out her underwear, snuggles down—raw. She closes her eyes, sighs blissfully, the neon light flashing on her face." In the coded language of the era, the moment slyly suggests that Anne may be well on her way to finding out who she is *and* what she wants.

The script details a dizzying montage of Anne's rise to the top, culminating in her being one of the blindfolded celebrity guest panelists on TV's *What's My Line?* while Neely O'Hara, affecting a

British accent, is the Mystery Guest. According to studio records, the scene was shot but scissored well before the movie was released. Also filmed but cut were Kingsley's series of scenes of Anne and Kevin Gillmore arriving on the West Coast, traveling in a limousine and settling into their suite at the Minoru Yamasaki–designed Century Plaza Hotel. Opened on June 1, 1966, the hotel was built on the once vast 20th back lot, sold off in 1961 to help recoup the costs of *Cleopatra* and the aborted Marilyn Monroe comedy *Something's Got to Give*, among other costly misfires. In the suite, Anne unwraps a gift—Lyon's first novel, *The Beholden*, dedicated "To Anne, who made this book possible" and described by Gillmore as "not very good." After reading it, Anne declares Lyon's book "interesting. I don't quite understand the girl." Gillmore says, "Why don't you ask the author?" When she calls Kevin "a very understanding man," he says, "Not understanding, just caught in the bite of the line."

Kingsley's depiction of Neely finding Ted in their swimming pool with another woman was pretty much left intact and found its way into the finished movie. About a possible inspiration for the scene, editor and former A-list talent publicist Edward Margulies, said, "When it came to things like Hollywood lore and gossip, nothing was lost on Jackie Susann. I grew up in the film and TV business, and as a teenager, I heard from several people a juicy story involving Ida Lupino; her longtime husband, the handsome, macho Howard Duff; and another good-looking macho actor, Leif Erickson. The story went that Ida came home unexpectedly early from the studio one night and found Howard and Leif in a highly compromising position—either in the swimming pool or on a pool table. The rumors go that poor Ida was so badly traumatized that she suffered a case of accelerated hair loss the doctors couldn't stop. She wore wigs for the rest of her life. Who knows if any of it is true? But I'd be willing to bet that Jackie heard the same rumor a lot of us did and found a way to use it." Lyon later finds Neely in bed at home instead of on the set. He tells her she is being replaced: "You were out ten days with sleeping pills. You were also late on the set—walked off in the middle of the day—you boozed and ate through the picture." As, reportedly, did Judy Garland on several movies, including *Annie Get Your Gun* and *Summer Stock*. Neely ducks out of checking herself into a sanitarium, winds up in an all-night San Francisco flea pit where one of her movies plays to drunks and druggies, and awakens in a dive hotel with a derelict whom she barely remembers. Connoisseurs of vintage Hollywood gossip claim that this incident was based on the exploits of a fading '40s and '50s movie glamour girl known for turning up on the sets of her late-period melodramas needing major help from makeup artists to disguise her bruises after one of her boozy, out-of-town weekend trysts with macho, abusive blue-collar types.

Kingsley treats Jennifer's career in French soft-core "art films" differently than the other writers; she becomes a big international success and award winner who gets offered a studio contract in the United States. Yes, Susann's influences for Jennifer include Carole Landis and Marilyn Monroe, but some of Kingsley's elaborations slightly suggest Jane Fonda at a time when Hollywood mostly considered her a highly decorative but only modestly talented beauty. Fonda went to France and married director Roger Vadim, who had helped make stars out of Brigitte Bardot and Catherine Deneuve and who directed Fonda in the risqué *La Ronde*, *The Game Is Over*, and *Barbarella*. Those films may have burnished her image as a sexpot, but they also paved the way for Fonda, unlike the victimized Jennifer North, to reclaim herself and return to the United States a more confident, risk-taking actress who became an Oscar winner.

Reportedly filmed but later cut was a moment after Jennifer's suicide in which Anne lies to the press that Jennifer was "in good spirits," "excited about her new contract," and that her death was accidental. The script describes Anne breaking down when the sheet-covered stretcher carries Jennifer's body from a hotel to the ambulance. Burying her head on Lyon's shoulder, she whispers: "I couldn't tell them, Lyon. I just couldn't. I had to keep her secret—I had to let her die in peace." Similarly, after Helen Lawson has been de-wigged and humiliated, Kingsley has the character delivering to her agents what amounts to a long speech faintly reminiscent of one of Margo Channing's maudlin and full of self-pity *All About Eve* monologues.

HELEN: When you're young you think you'll always be young. Then one day you wake up and the names in the obituary column are your friends. . . . And you, Lyon? Oh, sure, everything's rosy now. You skip from one thing to another, one dame to another. But watch it, my friend. Get yourself a good girl . . . have kids or one of these days, you'll wake up alone, like me—and wonder what happened. I'm sick of hooting around town with guys that don't give a damn for me—picking up the tab—but what do I do from here on in? All I know is the stage. The only real part of my life is make-believe. . . . I tried to be a housewife once. Remember Frankie? That was way back, before your time. Wow. Twenty-three. We were married for two years . . . we even talked about having a baby—but that woulda meant blowing a whole season. Well, you pay a price for success . . . and part of the price is a messed-up private life.

As scripted, Kingsley's final scene differs slightly from the scene as we know it. On the davenport of her family home, Anne sits petting her dog as Lyon mansplains his failed love affair with Neely and why Anne should accept his marriage proposal. She answers: "Thank you, Lyon, but it won't work. It seems I don't need you anymore—I've gotten my old values back. I'm standing on firm ground again, and I like the feeling. I'm going back to work. I'm making a fresh start. So, no, Lyon, not now. Perhaps someday—I don't know. . . . (She gets to her feet, beckons the dog.) Funny, for so many years I prayed for this moment—and now that it's come, I don't feel a thing." And with that, Lyon watches ("his face drained, expressionless") as Anne briskly walks out the door with the dog "frisking at her heels," and in the woods, she "flings out her arms in exultation, whirls around. At last she is free—free! Camera moves in on her face, holds. It is alive, glowing."

Only occasionally alive and hardly glowing, Kingsley's script—with story elements and dialogue from Helen Deutsch's version and Harlan Ellison's treatment—got greenlit by 20th. Sales of Jacqueline Susann's novel were still booming, and public demand for a movie version was peaking, so there wasn't the time or money to keep hiring screenwriters, hoping that one of them could fix what may have been unfixable. Weisbart had originally budgeted the screenplay costs at $211,000 (about $1.6 million today), but 20th had already spent a total of $189,602. Robson thought Kingsley should receive sole credit. Kingsley agreed; Deutsch remained indifferent. But many months later, when production was completed and the screenplay credit went into arbitration, the Writers Guild ruled that Deutsch and Kingsley would share credit and in that order.

But first the censors needed to vet the script. Even though the iron grip of movie censorship had continued to loosen, one wrong word from eighty-two-year-old Geoffrey Shurlock, longtime director of the Production Code Administration of the Motion Picture Association of America (PCA), could spell serious trouble for the release of *Valley of the Dolls*. Even if the PCA okayed the screenplay, as they had in 1964 with Billy Wilder's *Kiss Me, Stupid*—about which Shurlock said, "If dogs want to return to their vomit, I'm not going to stop them"—Shurlock presumed that the Catholic Legion of Decency would weigh in negatively. While Dorothy Kingsley reworked some of the screenplay's last section, 20th sent the first ninety-nine pages to Shurlock's headquarters at 8480 Beverly Boulevard, Los Angeles. On February 16, 1967, 20th Century Fox Film Corporation's legal counsel received a letter stating that the censorship board deemed the script—*provisionally* at least—"basically acceptable under the Production Code." They did, however, raise the probability that it would be necessary to recommend that the film be released and advertised as "Suggested for Mature Audiences." The news brought sighs of relief from Robson, Weisbart, the

Zanucks, and studio vice president in charge of production operations Stanley Hough. Had the Production Code office thrown road-
blocks before *Valley of the Dolls* at this stage of the game, the movie
might have gone on to become a ratings cause célèbre of the kind
that could have gotten it banned from certain theater chains—or,
on the other hand, sparked just the right level of scandal and notoriety that would have translated into big box-office.

Pending receipt of the final script, though, Shurlock rumbled warnings about what he and his colleagues deemed dubious, if not outright unacceptable, language: "We direct your attention to these
items as follows: 'hell' Page 10; 'damn' and 'you bet your ass' Page
11; 'son-of-a-bitch' Page 12; 'boobies' and 'damn' Page 16; 'hell' Page
32 and Page 34; 'damn' Page 72; 'hell' Page 73; 'Geez' Page 74 and
Page 76; 'hell' Page 77; 'Damn' twice and 'whore' on Page 81; 'hell'
twice and 'bastard' Page 82; 'boobies' three times Page 85; and
'hell' Page 89." They also put the studio on notice that the lyrics to
the song Tony Polar sings during his nightclub act would need to be
reviewed once the song had been written and finalized for inclusion. Further, on Page 37, "There must be no exposure of Anne's
nudity in 'the semi-darkness of the bedroom.'" They also warned:
"As a matter of good taste, no notice should be made of the fact
that Neely has stripped off her brassiere" (Page 79); "There must be
no exposure of the nudity of the two people [Ted Casablanca and
his playmate] in the pool"; and "There must be nothing offensive in
the 'exaggerated torrid love scene' in the foreign film [featuring Sharon Tate's character]." The letter ends with the standard caveat:
"You realize, of course, that our final judgment will be based upon
the final picture."

On March 9, 1967, producer David Weisbart finalized the production details. Based on the requirements as detailed in the final
script, dated January 6, 1967 (with changed pages through February 22 and verbal reports on additional changes to come), 20th approved a budget of $4,440,200 (or, today: $35 million). Weisbart
earmarked the film for a fifty-eight-day shoot, with eleven of those

days spent in New York, one day in San Francisco, and forty-six on the 20th Century Fox lot in West Los Angeles. As for casting, screenwriter Dorothy Kingsley, even as early as the previous winter, had begun telling associates and the press, "At the moment our feeling is to go with unknowns in most of the parts. We don't need big names for the box-office. The book is our star." Even buoyed by the success of Jacqueline Susann's novel, the nearly $5 million budget was considered risky, especially when director Mark Robson startled many in Hollywood by announcing that Kingsley had been correct; he did hope to cast the movie largely with "new, lesser-known young performers." That hope launched one of Hollywood's longest and most cutthroat star searches in decades.

CHAPTER EIGHT

The Casting of the Dolls—
"Not Since Scarlett O'Hara . . ."

Considering how controversial and shocking Jacqueline Susann's novel was for its time, it was inevitable that movie casting speculations began running rampant the week *Valley of the Dolls* hit bookstores. Through the spring and summer of 1966, Zanuck, Weisbart, and Robson began circulating intra-20th memos floating casting ideas. Although each had his own favorites, most of the proposals were the province of 20th's West Coast casting chief, fifty-four-year-old Owen McLean, characterized by 20th's Extras Casting associate Jeff Maxwell as "a very big Kahuna but a dick" and by director Don Siegel as "a pompous ass." McLean had previously cast 20th's *Miracle on 34th Street*, *The Man in the Gray Flannel Suit*, *The Three Faces of Eve*, *The Diary of Anne Frank*, and *Cleopatra*. At McLean's right hand were the influential Jack Baur, recalled by Maxwell as a "very nice guy, with a booming, hearty kind of voice," and Joe Scully, whom Maxwell described as "a short, balding, very nice guy who really knew his job." Their West Coast associate was Terry Liebling, and Linda Schreiber headed up the East Coast office. Near the Los Angeles main casting office stood a separate casting office for extras and actors speaking fewer than five lines of dialogue, headed up by the upbeat, good-humored Carl Joy and assisted by Mark McLean, Owen McLean's son. Beginning at 4:00 a.m., candidates for smaller and extra roles would line up at a window and, says Jeff Maxwell, they "represented *all* kinds of humanity—super tall, super tiny, jugglers, clowns, some who'd been up all night long, doing whatever, some staggering and drunker than hell, and some, like, say, on a movie like *Valley of the Dolls* or one of Dean Martin's 'Matt Helm' movies, very sexy ones."

Of the latter, says Maxwell, who also helped cast TV's *Batman* and *Julia*, and such feature films as *M*A*S*H* and *Planet of the Apes*, "One of the casting kahunas had an office right next to the Extras Casting Office and it was equipped with an intercom that fed into ours. When I was just starting in this department, my boss said, 'Jeff, I'm going to interview an actress and I want you to listen on the intercom so you can learn how to do this.' So this girl goes in, I'm listening, and he asks, 'So what have you been doing, what you been in?' She tells him her recent credits, then he says, 'So tell me, are you a good actress?' There came this pause and she answered, 'No, but I fuck really good.' I'm in my office and my eyes are bugging. Did she just say that? She said, 'Well, where do you live?' When he mentioned a beach city like Santa Monica or Malibu, she said, 'Well, I'd sure like to see your house.' A few seconds later, the interview ends and through my office window, I see them zoom off on his motorcycle."

In the very earliest days of the *Valley* casting process, Zanuck and Weisbart envisioned landing the biggest stars possible for all the roles. But Robson kept lobbying for hiring—perhaps even discovering—newer faces. Even before Harlan Ellison began attacking the script, Zanuck's, Robson's, and Weisbart's phones jangled with calls from talent, agents, and managers. The director and producer winnowed out the craziest of the casting ideas and launched an exhaustive series of casual meetings, lunches, auditions, and screen tests of hundreds of candidates for top roles, largely based on the recommendations proffered by Joe Scully, who was responsible for casting TV productions shot on the 20th lot, including *Voyage to the Bottom of the Sea* and *Peyton Place*, and who had just recently been assigned to cast some of the studio's feature films, including *In Like Flint*, *The Flim-Flam Man*, and *Tony Rome*. During those earliest casting discussion days, 20th flew out Jacqueline Susann and installed her in a suite at the Hotel Bel-Air, that LA rarity, a place to be private rather than a place to showboat. Arriving onto the 20th lot, she disembarked her chauffeured limo parked in its own specially assigned space and stenciled (very temporarily) with her name, and then got treated to a royal guided tour of the bustling lot. Robson and Weisbart lunched with her in the private executive room of the legendary commissary. In a few months' time, the bill of fare would feature a *Valley of the Dolls* salad entrée, though everyone's favorite waitress, Doris—a crusty, gravel-voiced, salty bottle blonde who had been at the studio forever—mostly pushed the famously good cheeseburgers. The producer and director escorted her to Richard D. Zanuck's suite of offices, in the building known today as the Old Executive Building.

In this first of Susann's several visits to the lot, she could feel vindicated in the knowledge that Hollywood was finally treating her the way she had always dreamed—as a prized commodity whose opinions mattered. When the subject turned to casting, Jackie, in her classic gung-ho, swing-for-the-fences style, told the filmmakers pretty much what she had also been telling many national journalists who asked her to play what had become a favorite Hollywood pastime: "Let's cast *Valley of the Dolls*." For Anne, she envisioned a Grace Kelly, "but as she was 10 or so years—and 15 pounds—ago." To play Neely, Susann offered, "Tuesday Weld, but I'd *love* Barbra Streisand." She suggested for Jennifer "that new girl, Raquel Welch [who] looks the part." She also mentioned Tina Louise but was told that the statuesque redhead had aged out. Said

Susann, "Imagine, too old at thirty." Her alternate choice for Jennifer (the also thirty-year-old) Ursula Andress, apparently unaware that voiceover artist Nikki van der Zyl had dubbed all of the Swiss actress's dialogue in *Dr. No.* As Susann also did in press interviews, she fantasized about what ideal casting Lana Turner ("in her most luscious years") would have been for Jennifer. As for Helen Lawson, "I think Bette Davis, of course. And, you know, Judy Garland would be good, too." She thought Elvis could make a dandy, dumb, doomed Tony Polar. The executives listened patiently as Susann informed them that Davis, Shelley Winters, and Lee Remick had contacted her personally about getting hired for various roles; in fact, those same actresses, and dozens more, had already contacted *them* personally.

Meanwhile, newspaper columnists and actors—and their agents and publicists—worked overtime pushing (20th-endorsed) stories featuring the theme "Not Since Scarlett O'Hara," a hype calculated to somehow turn the *Valley* casting sweepstakes into a publicity stunt equal to producer David O. Selznick's spending two years searching for the coveted female lead in *Gone with the Wind.* If Scarlett was that Civil War epic's plum role, clearly the monstrous, all-devouring train wreck Neely O'Hara was *Valley*'s; for an older star, it had to be the monstrous show business legend Helen Lawson. *Chicago Tribune* columnist Herb Lyon reported on June 26: "Bette Davis and Barbra Streisand are on tap to play the overbearing star Helen Lawson and Neely O'Hara, respectively." Davis labored overtime to make the role hers, romping on the beach with "old friend" Jacqueline Susann for a series of staged photographs and telling reporters she believed playing Helen Lawson would give her career "a zesty push" akin to playing the forgotten silent film star Jane Hudson in *What Ever Happened to Baby Jane?* But *Valley* would go on to involve such a long gestation period that Davis ultimately got knocked out of the running. As for Streisand, she was pregnant at the time, and her manager, Martin Erlichman, and producer Ray

Stark, who had her under contract, weren't enthused about the project.

On July 3, Hollywood columnist Mike Connolly reported that David Weisbart was hot on the trail of casting Natalie Wood as Anne (she wanted to play Neely) and Lee Remick as Neely, with Carolyn Jones, who'd been doing TV for the past three years, close to signing a deal to play Miriam Polar. By late July and for months beyond, Remick was offered more than once the choice of playing either Neely or Anne but instead absented herself from the screen that entire year. In Dick Kleiner's "Show Beat" column for August 1, Weisbart reported that he was receiving easily twenty-five calls a week from household names like the aforementioned Natalie Wood (still lobbying to play Neely), as well as Bette Davis, Kim Novak, and more. He added that, of all the candidates in relentless pursuit of the role of Neely, the elusive Barbra Streisand was his prize catch. Aside from Streisand, among the earliest, most hotly debated candidates were Jane Fonda (who nixed it and the Jennifer role) and the more adventurous choice of Barbara Harris, whose tour de force Tony-nominated Broadway performance in *On a Clear Day You Can See Forever* and her Tony-winning stint in *The Apple Tree* prompted no less than stage legend Mary Martin to marvel, "I've not seen anything like her since Laurette Taylor." Even Streisand herself said, "I'm not a star. Barbara Harris is a star." But when Robson made a special trip to see Harris in *The Apple Tree*, casting notes record his having a "negative reaction" to her.

On September 13, thirty-four-year-old Debbie Reynolds made a surprising leap into the fray, telling the *Chicago Tribune*'s Herb Lyon that she wanted to muddy up her sunny, likable image by playing Neely: "I'm sure it would shake up a few people. I've been playing goody-goody roles for 18 years. It's time for a change." (Reynolds's most recent starring role had been in *The Singing Nun*.) Newspaper columnists also ran stories about Shirley MacLaine's interest in playing Neely. Then what to make of a spate of newspaper columnists reporting that the Neely character had so angered Judy Garland supporters like MacLaine and June Allyson that friends had warned Jacqueline Susann to avoid running into them at all costs?

By September 18, though, it looked as though the casting derby was over. The *Hollywood Reporter* announced that 20th had Candice Bergen on the hook for Anne, Ann-Margret for Neely, and Raquel Welch for Jennifer. But on October 10, columnist Sidney Skolsky reported: "The reason there's so many good-looking chicks at 20th Century-Fox is because producer David Weisbard [*sic*] and Mark Robson are interviewing the dolls in *Valley of the Dolls.*" Likewise, *Variety* reporter Army Archerd's column a week later featured an item about Robson and Weisbart's setting up shop in Manhattan "on the hunt for new faces for *Valley of the Dolls.* Both feel a newcomer should get the role of Neely." Playing Neely, Weisbart added, "will make a star out of someone."

Even then the pursuit of Candice Bergen persisted. On October 27, Owen McLean cabled producer Edward Leggewie, Darryl F. Zanuck's right-hand production aide in his Paris office, assuring him that they were actively pursuing Bergen, as the "Zanucks"—translation: Darryl—had insisted. Four days later, 20th's London office wired McLean, Weisbart, and Robson that a "highly promising" conversation had just taken place directly with Bergen, who was en route to New York and promised to notify her agent to contact 20th's New York casting director, Linda Schreiber. But internal 20th memos for the next few months document that Bergen was proving hard to pin down.

On October 28, Hank Grant of the *Hollywood Reporter* instead confirmed the casting of lovely blonde Jill Ireland (a 20th TV series staple) as Anne Welles but this had to be someone's wishful thinking. As Hollywood correspondent Dick Kleiner of the *Citizen-News* reported on December 27, the public should disregard the casting rumors because the studio had to delay the start of production for a month or more and because the script wasn't ready. The "juicy roles," he wrote, were still very much "up for grabs." Oscar winner

Julie Christie, another Darryl Zanuck favorite, was aggressively pursued to play Anne or Jennifer, but when the casting team suggested Faye Dunaway for Anne, Robson's reaction to her was, like his reaction to Barbara Harris, "negative."

Casting an even wider net to find the right Neely, the moviemakers considered massively popular singer Petula Clark, Helen Mirren, Liza Minnelli, and Andy Warhol "superstar" Baby Jane Holzer. The pregnancy of Streisand—*still* Weisbart's first choice for Neely—also paved the way for the moviemakers to consider another actress who'd played Fanny Brice. Composer Jule Styne had handpicked twenty-two-year-old Marilyn Michaels, making a big splash as a singer, comic, celebrity impersonator, and stage star, for the *Funny Girl* national touring company. Michaels recalls, "Publicity-wise, *Valley of the Dolls* was a very happening thing. The book was a satire in some ways, but it also reflected what was happening at the time with pill-taking. Especially in show business, you have to rev up in order to do what we do, particularly if you're working in Las Vegas as I did. By the time of the second show of the night, I'd be so up from the experience and the audience that you couldn't just put your head on the pillow and go to sleep. So we took pills— Nembutal, Seconal, barbiturates that were extremely intense and hypnotic. Jacqueline Susann knew what she was writing about. One irony was that her husband, Irving Mansfield, this sweet little Jewish talent agent and producer, had given me my first break in variety show TV in 1964 on the weekly CBS show he was producing called *On Broadway Tonight* hosted by Rudy Vallee. So, imagine two years later when I'm reading *Valley of the Dolls*—very much a roman à clef—and here's Neely O'Hara marrying a sweet little Jewish talent agent described as being very good at oral sex. *Very* shocking stuff at the time. Everyone knows how writers always get their best stuff from what really went down, and Jackie wasn't *that* creative, so I always wondered how I'd react if I ever ran into Irving again in a dark alley or anywhere else."

Said Michaels, "My manager was Jerry Weintraub, and I was with the William Morris office, so I wasn't surprised when I was sent up to meet for Neely with Mark Robson, who seemed very nice, laid back, with an almost nondescript personality. Don't get me wrong, that was exciting, but compared to what was going on with *Funny Girl*, it was anticlimactic. I'm going to be bitchy now, but I've been waiting for years to say this: Mark Robson was wrong. I was perfect for Neely and I should have done it. I would have been better on every level. When I heard much, much later that Patty Duke had been cast, I knew it was wrong, but I understood. Mark Robson made the safe choice—casting a wonderful actress who was young, paid her dues, who'd been borderline genius in *The Miracle Worker* and had success in that TV series where she played twin sisters or whatever the hell it was. The director could have discovered someone new, someone who had a shot at batting that role out of the park, like what Mr. Coppola did with Pacino in *The Godfather*. As neurotic and crummy as Neely is, you need to embrace her, feel sorry for her. As Neely, Patty, rest her soul, was a good actress encouraged to over-act beyond anything I've ever seen."

Concurrently Weisbart and Robson continued the search for the perfect Jennifer North. On November 1, twenty-six-year-old Jill St. John told columnist Herb Lyon, "Of course I would like the role of Jennifer in *Valley of the Dolls*. I think I can play the hell out of it. . . . I'm at the point where I can understand a girl like that. Don't get me wrong, though. The only kind of pills I take are iron pills. They give me energy." Alex Freeman in his November 2 column carried by the *Detroit Free Press* announced a tantalizing item about how Tuesday Weld was "glowing" after being informed that she is "a dark horse candidate for the Neely role that both Natalie Wood and Shirley MacLaine were also after."

But it was Raquel Welch's name that kept coming up again and again. In 1965, journalist and game show panelist Dorothy Kilgallen reported on Welch that "executives at 20th-Century Fox, feeling she's a real discovery, have not only locked her into a multiple-picture contract but have assigned her to the female lead in their

$5-million film, *The Fantastic Voyage* [sic]. They will fly her out to New York for the all-out treatment." Although hyped to the heavens by the Zanucks, it is debatable whether Welch got "the all-out treatment," considering that all that publicity hoop-dee-do had only resulted in 20th's farming her out to cheesy Italian-made productions and to Hammer-Seven Arts to play the fur bikini–clad cave girl in the campy *One Million Years B.C.*, a remake of *One Million B.C.* (Ironically that 1940 hit starred Carole Landis, one of Susann's inspirations for the character of Jennifer.) At the time, though, Welch's personal career aspirations were more ambitious. Shooting a film in London in January and February, she spent off-hours meeting with director Michelangelo Antonioni about doing *Blow-Up*, with Claude Lelouch for *Live for Life*, and François Truffaut for *Fahrenheit 451*; the latter two gigs went to other stars pursued for *Valley of the Dolls*, respectively Candice Bergen and Julie Christie.

Still, as a 20th contract actress, Welch agreed to test for Robson during his and Weisbart's London casting excursion. To prepare for her test, scheduled for 2:00 p.m. on Sunday, February 5, Welch and Robson met for a few hours daily for several days. She tested using the makeup and hair team for *Fathom*, a full crew, simple background sets of a hotel/rooming house and a park with two street lamps and two benches, and a female stand-in to play Anne and a male stand-in to play Tony. Her lengthy romantic, self-revelatory park bench scene and a telephone monologue with her mother convinced Robson and Weisbart to offer her the role. Private documents confirm that Weisbart offered Welch the role at a proposed weekly salary of $4,167 (roughly $33,000 today). Her decision to turn it down—it was Neely she wanted to play—made headlines. Susann, never the biggest Welch booster, took it upon herself to tell reporters, "She wanted to play Jennifer very badly and she started a campaign to play her by saying she'd been asked but refused. Believe me, she was never even considered for it. She has many assets, but talent is not one of them."

Thirty-five years later Welch recalled, "When I hit the white heat of stardom and was called this big sex symbol, I felt very uncomfortable all the time. You either get over it, change your head, or go into the drinking and snorting." Her misgivings about making *Valley* also stemmed from Jennifer North's similarities to Marilyn Monroe. "Back then I admired and wanted to emulate Marilyn Monroe. She was so unlike me in so many ways—physically, mentally. The only thing we had in common was the need to please and receive some kind of echo of acceptance. I loved her in her comedies and musicals. In her other things, though, you just felt her kind of fragility was so close to her being the victim if not actually being the victim. Who wants to aspire to being a victim? In retrospect, *Valley of the Dolls* could have been a step up from some of the things I ended up doing. I had a big argument with the studio about it. I felt it was just tacky, just another version of the one-dimensional stuff I'd had plenty of. I don't think now it was particularly smart to turn that down." The "big argument" led to 20th's threatening her with suspension. Still, the moviemakers didn't fully give up on trying to persuade her to do the movie, but other performers kept coming to the fore.

Enter another contract knockout—"liquid-lipped Jean Hale, a blonde cross between Virna Lisi and Ursula Andress," as a Hollywood columnist described her. By the time of the *Valley of the Dolls* casting frenzy, the independent, highly principled twenty-eight-year-old Salt Lake City–born debutante and former model had already turned down a role in *Butterfield 8*, had been a finalist to costar with Warren Beatty in *Bonnie and Clyde*, and had completed a key role opposite Stephen Boyd in the ludicrous, wondrous Harlan Ellison–scripted *The Oscar*. Although Hale was under contract to the Zanucks, Francophile Darryl F. Zanuck wanted Catherine Deneuve, not Hale, for the role Hale eventually played in *In Like Flint*. (Deneuve didn't like making movies in Hollywood, where, she said, "It's all about the hair.") Weisbart and Robson tested Hale several times, but when offered the role of Jennifer, Hale, a Mormon, refused to do the semi-nudity required. The filmmakers also considered other 20th contract players, including Cristina Ferrare, Linda Harrison (later Mrs. Richard Zanuck), and Edy Williams. The spectacularly endowed Williams, signed to a 20th contract at age twenty-two, reportedly went all in to pursue the role. She has said, "When I was under contract to Fox, they wanted me to be another Marilyn Monroe. They made my hair platinum blonde and they asked me to do things like her." The young Williams possessed the looks, body, and even some of the desperation the role required, but internal studio notes indicate a no-confidence vote in her ability to carry off its acting demands. Along came a rush of new candidates, including Howard Hawks's discovery Michele Carey (*El Dorado*), Sharon Tate (*The Fearless Vampire Killers*, and heavily touted by producer Martin Ransohoff as Hollywood's new Marilyn Monroe–Kim Novak hybrid), Laura Devon (*The Richard Boone Show*), Celeste Yarnall, Warner Mary Tyler Moore (who was looking to shed her suburban wife and mother image after five seasons of *The Dick Van Dyke Show*).

While the filmmakers continued to agonize over the casting of Jennifer North, Joe Scully suggested a temporary pivot by focusing on casting Jennifer's grasping, mooching, round-heel mother. His November 29 list of recommendations numbered an impressive gallery of Broadway, TV, and Late, Late Show pros, including Joan Blondell, Audrey Christie, Glenda Farrell, Betty Field, Florida Friebus, Eileen Heckart, Celeste Holm, Audrey Meadows, Kay Medford, Agnes Moorehead, Jeanette Nolan, Bibi Osterwald, Maureen O'Sullivan, Lee Patrick, Kate Reid, Ruth Roman, Madeleine Sherwood, Katherine Squire, Jean Stapleton, Jo Van Fleet, Elizabeth Wilson, and Shelley Winters. Also topping Scully's list was Ann Sothern, but when Robson reduced the role to a voice-only role, Sothern—a brilliant comedienne who had a wicked way with a zinger—wrote David Weisbart asking, "Would you possibly consider my doing a test for the musical comedy star in *Valley of the Dolls*? I like that bitch dame and I did start in musical comedy." There is no record of whether Weisbart responded.

To play Miriam Polar, the filmmakers—who'd lost Carolyn Jones because of production delays—compiled a wish list consisting of many fine character actresses of their generation, including Colleen Dewhurst, Eileen Heckart, Julie Harris, Angela Lansbury, Kim Stanley, Maureen Stapleton, and Jo Van Fleet. Also considered was Broadway and television actress Hildy Brooks, whose agent described her as—ouch!—"a *pretty* Anne Bancroft." Weisbart interviewed and auditioned many of them, but the pick was the singular Lee Grant, who had caused a stir on Broadway in 1949 playing a twitchy shoplifter in *Detective Story* by Pulitzer Prize winner Sidney Kingsley (no relation to *Valley* screenwriter Dorothy). Twenty-four at the time and playing a fortysomething, Grant repeated her role in director William Wyler's multi-Oscar-nominated 1951 movie version and earned a Best Supporting Actress nomination, her first of four. Just as her career was gaining momentum, she got sidelined for the next twelve years—what should have been her prime earning period—when, as the new wife of screenwriter Arnold Manhoff, a Communist Party member, she was blacklisted by the House Un-American Activities Committee. Her offense? The casual mention of the Party during the 1951 funeral of Joe Bromberg, the stage and screen character actor hounded by right-wingers after director Elia Kazan accused him of being a Party member. At the time of Grant's casting in *Valley of the Dolls*, the forty-two-year-old was slowly battling her way back, riding the tailwind of her unmissable Emmy-winning performances on more than sixty *Peyton Place* episodes. With a commitment of work from April 10 through May 10, 1967, Grant signed for the thankless role, earning a weekly salary of $2,250, with a guaranteed total of more than $13,000 (approximately $102,000 today).

By the beginning of 1967, casting sessions had shifted into nonstop overdrive. On January 29, international newspapers reported 20th's official signing of Candice Bergen as star of the production that would begin filming on East Coast locations in late February. Around the same time, two intriguing "possible Neely O'Haras" came to the forefront. Elizabeth Hartman, a 1965 Best Actress Oscar nominee for starring as a sensitive young blind woman in her first film, *A Patch of Blue*, screen-tested for Neely. (Patty Duke had been unable to accept the role in *A Patch of Blue* because of her TV series commitments.) Hartman's *Valley* audition, on the heels of her provocative about-face as a sexy mantrap in Francis Ford Coppola's *You're a Big Boy Now*, convinced the moviemakers that they'd found what they were looking for—charisma, vulnerability, a capacity for turn-on-a-dime steeliness, and off-center charm. It didn't hurt that Hartman and Candice Bergen had appeared together in 1966 in director Sidney Lumet's sexually bold "women's picture" *The Group*. On January 12, Hearst Corporation syndicated columnist Dorothy Manners led with the story that Mark Robson himself had flagged down Hartman at her Ohio family home to tell her that she'd won the role. Manners reported several days later that Hartman had signed contracts to play Neely, but nothing ever came of it. (Plagued by psychiatric problems, Hartman took her own life in 1987.)

Internal studio memos indicate Joanna Pettet's emergence as a frontrunner beginning on January 20. Lovely, gifted Pettet had, like Elizabeth Hartman, impressed Robson and Weisbart in *The Group*, and her career was on the ascendant. The filmmakers thought that the versatile Pettet might work as either Neely or Jennifer and they assigned Linda Schreiber to discuss screen test options with her. Joe Scully reported that Pettet would not test for the Neely role because she "does not sing and does not feel that a role requiring a dubbed-in voice would be advantageous to her career." She would be available to test for Jennifer beginning January 27 when in town for the opening of her new picture, *The Night of the Generals*. How serious Team *Valley* was about Pettet can be inferred from Joe Scully's compiling information on the actress's salary for her last three movies and the details of her five-year nonexclusive United Artists contract. Still, Pettet's agents declined the offers for her to do *Valley of the Dolls*. Pettet today says, "I had no knowledge about even being considered for any of those roles. I believe I was working in London at the time."

Also on January 20, Robson and Weisbart brought in for meetings and screen tests another bumper crop of contenders including Laura Devon, Lauren Hutton, Judi West and Jennifer Warren (all for the Jennifer role), Millie Thom (aka Millie Perkins) for Anne, and, for Neely, Nancy Dussault, Anita Gillette, Susan Anspach, Kathryn Hays and—believe it or not—Marlo Thomas. Some of the actresses rated brutally sexist responses. One Jennifer contender, who went on to win several theater awards and also played the female lead in at least one of the most well-respected movies of the '70s, rated the comment "looks—only fair" while another, introduced by an iconic Hollywood pantheon-level director in one of his '60s comedies, rated the cryptic comment, "Uh-Oh!" A few days later, an ongoing debate over whether to test Jessica Walter as Neely or whether they should act on the "strong screen tests" delivered by Kathryn Hays and Marlo Thomas for Neely, Robson and Weisbart decided to see Patty Duke, whom Robson first met in 1966 and called a "preposterous" candidate. But in 1967, Robson told reporters that Duke re-emerged and "one day just walked in and asked for a screen test." He described her as "a girl whose nerve endings were exposed and ready to fry right before your eyes. Of course, I had known she was a remarkable young actress as a child. Now here, she was a girl in her early 20s."

As Duke recalled, "They were seeing big sexy girls with breasts. I don't have any breasts. Finally, they agreed to talk to me. I must have done something right because they wanted me to test for the role." Name checking Marlo Thomas and Kathryn Hays, Duke has said, "Several actresses of my generation were considered for the part. Everyone wanted to be Neely as she was the jazziest character in the novel, plus everyone wants to be the bad girl. They hadn't seen me in a year, so I begged them to see me as I am now. I had lost a lot of weight. I'd gotten married. I wanted that part and I went after it with everything I had. You see, I decided I wanted to do a movie, any movie, but particularly this one. I wanted a part where I was a mature woman." During the office meeting, Weisbart and Robson asked Duke to test for the role: "Hey, wait a minute, I thought, *Who, me test?* I've got an Oscar at home on my mantel. That proves I shouldn't have to test for roles. But then I realized they would never consider me for the picture unless I did the test. So I did. I thought it was for my acting ability, but they just wanted to see how I'd look in the part."

Duke came ready to rumble. She prepared herself by reading the novel, about which she said, "I'm certainly no great judge of great literature, but I must say I did enjoy the book. It's entertaining." Since ending her stint on *The Patty Duke Show*, she had spent over a year suffering what she described as "a difficult time." She said, "I felt I was fat and ugly and stupid. I wouldn't see anybody in the business. Sure, time hung heavy on my hands, but I got myself a hobby—making friends. I never had any friends, not really. Now I have some. Yes, I stopped working by choice, but then I got terribly sick and had to have three operations. I had been through analysis." She could not or would not reveal her devastation over learning that her talent representatives had sapped the earnings from the first three years of her TV series. Worse, her undiagnosed and unmanaged mental state—what we would today call bipolar disorder—revealed itself in terrifying mood swings, drug and alcohol abuse, several suicide attempts, and multiple psychiatric hospitalizations. An actress who knew Duke well during this time said, "You can almost say without exaggerating that Anna (her real name) was driven from a psych ward to the Fox studio gate on Pico Boulevard to do her screen test—and later, to begin filming *Valley of the Dolls*. She had been hospitalized twice before the movie began filming." Duke said, "I could identify with this girl Neely. I understood why she became so ill and was unable to cope with success."

To prepare for the screen test, Duke worked with a speech

coach to help lower the chirpy, girlish vocal register familiar to viewers of *The Patty Duke Show*, and with an acting coach to deconstruct the long monologue required of her. As with every serious candidate, she tested for the role with an eight-minute drunk scene set in Anne and Lyon's Malibu beach pad. Shot on January 23 on a fully dressed 20th soundstage, Duke was costumed, made up, and coiffed, she recalled, "to be twenty-six but look like I'm in my forties." She performed with blond 20th contract player Pat Becker, who would go on to play a small role in the movie but who voiced Anne Welles's lines in the test. Also part of the test was Asian American actor Ernest Harada as Lyon Burke's houseman (a role he later played in the film).

The cinematographer for the tests was William Daniels, legendary for his work on *Greed*, *Dinner at Eight*, and *Cat on a Hot Tin Roof*, and most of the signature films of Greta Garbo, whose favorite cameraman he became. Mark Robson, for whom Daniels had previously shot *The Prize* and *Von Ryan's Express*, declared he wanted "everyone and everything in *Valley of the Dolls* to be filmed in 'the grand Hollywood style.' No one can light or film more elegantly than 'Billy' Daniels. I knew I had to have him shoot the tests as well as the picture itself." Robson's first assistant director, Robert J. Koster, called Daniels "the cameraman of choice for many of Hollywood's more famous actresses because of his magnificent lighting ability. He was also a shameless tyrant to the production department and delighted in making us look foolish. One learns however to indulge the artist if the finished product reflects the effort, and that was the case with Bill."

Daniels, having worked with such powerful, demanding leading ladies of the '30s and '40s as Jean Harlow, Norma Shearer, Joan Crawford, Irene Dunne, Jeanette MacDonald, and Margaret Sullavan, had no trouble with the *Valley of the Dolls* cast, possibly because of his formidable demeanor and a manner that announced he would brook no interference. Ernest Harada recalled Patty Duke's being deferential to Daniels and the cameraman's picking up on her feverish intensity and desire to please. But Duke's behavior and stance were even more memorable than Daniels's. As Harada recalled, "Patty Duke was the star of the test, not me, of course, but her attitude toward anyone 'beneath her station' seemed dismissive. There was a moment during the screen test where I had a line about Lyon Burke not being home. She repeated my line in a mocking, stereotypical Asian way that, well . . . it told me a great deal."

Although in her screen test Duke makes too big a banquet of the monologue and covers her apparent nerves and small memory lapses by dragging out the dialogue, she is less shrill and strident than in the film itself. That subtler performance sheds light on why Duke considered the test "better than anything I did in the finished film." Said Jacqueline Susann of the casting, "I never would have dreamed of Patty Duke. She had that lovely, sweet image, but she wanted the part so badly, she even went to the hospital to take off 20 pounds. Then [contrary to Duke's account] she insisted on a screen test, even though she had already won an Oscar and a Tony [in fact, a nomination, not a win]. It was so perfect, she made everyone's blood run cold." Although Duke reported that she never actually saw Jacqueline Susann during the audition process, she felt certain that the author was reviewing the tests and knew that "she had apparently wanted Liza Minnelli to play Neely." Robson told Duke that if she were chosen, he would insist on her spending six weeks improving her singing voice under the tutelage of Barbra Streisand's rehearsal pianist (a then-unknown Marvin Hamlisch) and putting in an additional ten hours with vocal coach Jack Woodford to deepen and enrich her speaking voice. Still, despite lingering doubts on the filmmakers' parts, Duke joined the ranks of the "serious contenders" column, but she was not yet tendered an official offer.

Enter a shiny new candidate, twenty-four-year old Barbara Parkins, then riding the crest of popularity for torching it up as the sultry small-town bad girl Betty Anderson in her third season on ABC TV's *Peyton Place*. With *Valley of the Dolls* fever raging through

Hollywood at the time and the casting net being flung so far and wide, one would have expected the raven-haired, purry-voiced Parkins to have automatically been part of the casting conversation. "The era is past when studios molded stars," she said at the time, commenting in interviews that she felt "stifled, held back" by her TV series and, to push the boundaries, had agreed to a *Playboy* magazine shoot. "I wanted to show my body," she explained. "I don't think the viewers of *Peyton Place* even think that Betty Anderson has a body. I do, and I wanted to prove it." When it came to grabbing the attention of the makers of *Valley of the Dolls*, she took matters into her own hands—as well she should have. She explained back then: "I would sneak onto the soundstage to watch all these actresses being tested. And *I* wasn't being tested. I make it a point to see Dick Zanuck when there's something I want to do. I thought, 'I'm going up to Dick Zanuck's office and make a demand that I be tested.' It was very gutsy at the time. I'd only read little snippets of [the novel]. I heard that there were these three kinds of great roles being sought after. I wanted to test for Jennifer, the sex symbol." Why? "I was really interested in Jennifer, the Body Beautiful sexpot, because I wanted to get as far away from Betty Anderson as possible. Jennifer was the extreme—sexy, voluptuous, not much in the brain department. I was intrigued by the idea of doing sexy bedroom scenes. Do I consider myself sexy? I guess you could say I work on my curves." After hearing from Zanuck, Weisbart and Robson scheduled Parkins to test on the following day, January 27—but for Neely, not Jennifer. Once Parkins first scanned what was, in effect, an eight-page monologue, she requested an extra day to rehearse, but permission was denied.

Parkins has said that it "became an obsession with me, to achieve the dramatic aspect of Neely." So, decked out in full costume, hair, and makeup, and on a fully dressed set, Parkins (assisted by Harada, who said he "absolutely adored her") tested as if her career depended upon it. Looking self-assured and super glam while working the hell out of a black sable coat, Parkins made a startlingly different Neely. She may miss by a mile the character's guttersnipe, up-by-the-bootstraps quality, but she's a seething, calculating hot mess who, at one point, tosses in a hilarious "I'm a star—I'm a *big fucking* star!" She doesn't bat a false eyelash when her prop martini glass falls and clatters around on the floor. Photographing like a younger Elizabeth Taylor, she's too sensual, WASP-y, and self-composed to nail the demented, wrecked Neely. Harada considered Parkins "a marked contrast to Patty. She was the kind of person who says, 'I'm going to get a cup of coffee, can I get you some? What do you take in your coffee?' She was what she looked like—elegant, classy. I thought so highly of her."

Following the test, Parkins returned to emoting on *Peyton Place* and waited and waited for word . . . all the while reading in newspapers or hearing intrastudio scuttlebutt that this or that rival actress had been tested or had closed her deal. Parkins finally got hired to star, with top billing, in *Valley of the Dolls* during her yearly hiatus from filming *Peyton Place*—not to play Neely or Jennifer, though, but Anne. Soon after, Hollywood correspondent Dick Kleiner ran this little item: "Usually reliable busybodies tell me that director Mark Robson really didn't want Barbara Parkins, but the studio (20th Century Fox) insisted, and Robson really isn't gruntled." Parkins has admitted that she was "angry at first because I really wanted that juicy role." But when she asked Robson why he had chosen Duke over her, the director explained, "You're velvet. She's sandpaper." Said Parkins at the time, "When my agents came to the *Peyton Place* set one day and told me I'd been cast as Anne Welles, I thought, 'Well, I'm playing the bad girl on the TV show, now I'll get to play the nice girl in *Valley of the Dolls*.' We went out and celebrated. I didn't have any words. I couldn't believe it. To tell the truth, the thought of being magnified four times larger than life scares me to death. I've never been in a movie before. [Note: Except in 1961 in a bit role as "High School Girl" in 20th Century Fox's *20,000 Eyes*, that is.] There's a lot of Anne in me . . . mainly our experiences with men. No, we don't have similar backgrounds. I come from a modest family; she didn't. But we share the same situation of being vulnerable girls who came to the big city to make our way. I've also been involved with a Lyon Burke–type man who hurt me. One difference is that Anne went home and I'm not going to." Not for the first or last time, she raised eyebrows by telling a reporter, "I'm standing on the threshold of a glorious career. I'm wallowing in my own potential. . . . A lot of eyes are on me now." And a lot of ears would be on her, too; mandated by Robson, Parkins began preparing for her starting date by studying with voice coach Jack Woodford to help her strengthen and deepen her vocal delivery.

With the role of Anne finally cast, Weisbart returned to what they called "the Patty Duke question." After repeated viewings of Duke's screen test, Robson declared Duke too "remarkable to deny." 20th and Duke's agents closed her deal just before March 9, 1967. Her weekly salary was $7,500 (or $58,000 today) with a ten-week guarantee and an additional three-week living allowance of $500 per week. Her time commitment, between March 14 and June 1, would be the longest of any actor on the film. Weeks after her signing, she answered nationally syndicated Hollywood reporter Bob Thomas's question about how young fans of her TV series might react to her being cast in *Valley of the Dolls*: "I hope they won't see it." She told a *Los Angeles Times* reporter, "I'm now aiming for the adults, the young adults. This is no picture for any child to see—the pills, the sex, the language and everything. I'm hoping that adults will see a great change. I don't see how they can be really shocked. It's just a part. Even so, I believe in something called healthy self-interest. And it's Neely who's best for me right now."

The right Jennifer had to be found—and fast. Despite the many possibilities—likely and otherwise—Robson and Weisbart winnowed down the final three to Raquel Welch, Sharon Tate, and Karen Jensen. Finally, after many personal meetings, on March 8 Robson and Weisbart tested Tate, twenty-four, for the first time as Jennifer. Under a seven-year, $750-a-month contract to flashy, self-aggrandizing Filmways production company boss Martin Ranso-hoff, the ravishing, inexperienced Tate had been publicized to the hilt. Ransohoff built up Tate methodically over several years, letting her gain confidence and experience by appearing uncredited (and in a black wig) in his TV shows (including *The Beverly Hillbillies*) and then casting her in tiny roles in his feature films, including *The Americanization of Emily* and *Don't Make Waves*. In 1966, with the billing "and introducing Sharon Tate," she replaced an ailing Kim Novak in *Eye of the Devil*.

Tate was the daughter of a ramrod-strict army captain and a caring mother who, starting when Tate was six months old, entered her little girl in a succession of beauty contests, most of which she handily won. The beauty contest crowns—multinational due to her father's constant military reassignments—helped lead to Tate's getting bitten by the acting bug. Living with her family in Rome in 1961, and enjoying a romance with actor Richard Beymer, the seventeen-year-old Tate appeared in a crowd scene in the Anthony Quinn–Silvana Mangano biblical epic *Barabbas*. That same year, while on a date with a soldier, she was raped. After later becoming engaged to 20th Century Fox contract player and *Take Her, She's Mine* star Philippe Forquet, by 1966 Tate was fully in the thrall of director Roman Polanski. They began living together sometime around April of 1966, and according to many, Polanski, who reluctantly cast her in *The Fearless Vampire Killers* (he'd wanted Jill St. John), dominated her. Said her friend Joanna Pettet in 2016, "[Polanski] ruled her entire life from the moment she met him." According to others, including author Ed Sanders, Polanski told her what to read, how to dress, routinely demeaned her in public, kept her under his thumb, and pushed her into drugs, orgies, and private sex videos he shared at parties with friends.

It was no surprise, then, that Tate had felt a kinship with the Jennifer North character. She said at the time, "[Jennifer] strikes me as a very sympathetic role. Reading about this girl in the novel when it first came out broke my heart." On March 8, Mark Robson and cameraman Daniels captured Tate on the 20th test stage on two separate sets. One scene presents her in the character's cramped, threadbare apartment while doing her futile "I must, I must, I must increase my bust" exercises, only to be interrupted by a phone call from her mother hitting her up for cash. In another she played her death scene in bed. She comes across as the role demanded—lustrous, slightly vacant, lost, and a heartbreaker, never more so than when speaking her mother's cruel mantra, "I know I haven't got any talent. I know all I have is a body."

Robson also shot a park bench scene between Tate and Tony Scotti, a 20th contract actor the director had been considering to play singer Tony Polar. Delivering dialogue about their underprivileged childhoods and their checkered sexual pasts, Tate and Scotti spark nicely off each other and are more natural, relaxed, and appealing than in the final film. Robson, reviewing the screen test and bringing Tate back for another go-around, told David Weisbart, "She's not a sexpot. She's a very vulnerable girl." When you view the tests today, although some of Tate's limitations and inexperience may be painfully exposed, she also shows that she is more than a stunning beauty—she's touching, fresh, and sympathetic. David Weisbart delivered Tate the news that the role was hers and that she would be needed for nearly three months, until May 23.

But what about the potentially scene-stealing role of the no longer young show business hellcat, Helen Lawson? From December into March, several dozen plus-forty candidates stepped up to the plate, and several dozen more got mentioned. In early December of 1966, Pulitzer-nominated reporter Leonard Lyons confirmed in his "The Lyons Dens" column that Rita Hayworth had been offered the part, though nothing came of the offer. In January, Lucille Ball shouldered in, vaulting herself to the top of the list of contenders. The moviemakers sparked to the idea; signing Ball to *that* role would not only be a shocker but also a publicity windfall. Ball—with her singing voice dubbed, of course—certainly could have been a revelation playing the prickly, vengeful, but ultimately sympathetic grande dame and survivor. On December 24 nationally syndicated Hollywood columnist Alex Freeman reported that Ball was committed to the project so long as the script would be "padded a little to make it an even more important part." Apparently, Ball wanted more than a little padding, so the moviemakers kept dangling the carrot before Joan Crawford, Bette Davis, and Betty Hutton.

On February 20 columnist Earl Wilson swept aside all the daily pot-stirring about potential Helens by reporting that Judy Garland "wants the Helen Lawson role." Fox had proffered a tentative deal memo on February 15. On March 1, 1967, hundreds of national newspapers, including the *Chicago Tribune*, announced further that Garland was "homing-in" on the part, and, behind the headlines, on March 4, Garland's agents and 20th closed the deal, which required the forty-four-year-old star's services from somewhere near the end of April to mid-May. The financially and emotionally battered Garland was dutifully reported as "very anxious to work again" (read "contrite") and "excited" that André Previn and Dory Previn had written five songs from which she had her pick.

The signing of one of *the* great performers of the twentieth century was, to put it mildly, a major upgrade for the project. At Garland's best, her performances could ignite a range of emotional responses—joy, empathy, compassion, awe, adoration, love, heartbreak, inspiration—at a level of which most other entertainers could only dream. As actor Spencer Tracy once put it: "A Garland audience doesn't just listen. They feel. They have their arms around her when she works." But along with her blazing talent came a highly publicized history of emotional volatility, firings from movies, substance abuse, failed suicide attempts, lawsuits, unhappy marriages, canceled engagements, financial woes, umpteen "comebacks," and charges that she was too risky to be depended upon. In more recent years she'd performed brilliantly on her much-troubled CBS

TV series *The Judy Garland Show*, concertized, and showed off her skills as a witty, wicked raconteuse on talk shows hosted by Jack Paar and Mike Douglas. But she'd been off the big screen for four years, artfully dodging such iffy projects as the 1965 Carol Lynley–starring version of *Harlow*, in which Ginger Rogers replaced her.

20th laid out the terms of Garland's April 3 contract simply and succinctly: her guaranteed salary was $25,000 (about $191,000 in today's dollars) per week for three weeks. If reshoots were required, she would be paid an additional $25,000 per week. Two weeks prior to the start of her contractual term, she had to be available (without compensation) for photographic tests, costume fittings, and rehearsals. The studio would furnish a car and driver for the run of her contract.

Before the conclusion of Garland's official contract negotiations, she and an uncharacteristically tamped-down, somber-looking Jacqueline Susann appeared in a joint press conference on Thursday, March 2, at the St. Regis Hotel in New York. Hyperalert 20th publicists stood close by. Journalists were crammed wall to wall, some of them out for the kill, well aware that Susann had based some of Neely O'Hara's best and worst qualities on Garland. "Judy, why did you accept the role?" "Because they asked me." "How do you feel about playing the part of an older woman?" "I didn't necessarily think that Helen Lawson is supposed to be older than me. I don't think anyone *is* older than me." She elaborated, "I don't think an actress could get a better—a better role. It's a good chance to sing one song and yet I don't have to depend upon singing. I like to act, too. I think it's going to be good. I hope I'm good in it." "Do you identify with the role?" "Everybody gets upset if I'm happy. People don't know how to pencil me in any other way than miserable. Well, I'm glad about this part. The part is no more me than *Judgment at Nuremberg*. It doesn't pertain to me. But the character seems very real. I've known many actresses and they have to look out for themselves. If they seem a little rough, they have to protect themselves. The same applies to me—except that I usually get fired." "Do you find pill usage to be prevalent among show business people?" "Well, I find it prevalent around newspaper people, too," she said, getting laughs. "Let's face it," she added, "the role calls for an old pro over 40. That's for me. It's for sure I am no longer Dorothy in *The Wizard of Oz*." When another reporter asked, "Can the picture improve upon the 'trashy' book?" Garland deferred to Susann, who answered, "Right now, I think I'd like to have a gun," generating big laughs.

Garland also made a promotional appearance as the Mystery Guest on the March 5 episode of CBS's popular game show *What's My Line?* In preparing to make her exit, she gave a couple of nervous shrugs and a theatrical scratch to the top of her coiffure and said, "I think I'm supposed to mention a picture I'm going to do—*Valley of the Dolls*. I'm the only one in the book that doesn't take pills!" She also agreed to appear on the *Today* show on March 15.

In signing on to portray the movie's Ethel Merman–inspired character, was she exploiting her own life and career woes? Was she thumbing her nose at the Judy/Neely comparisons? Was she simply trying to get back to work and reestablish herself as employable? Hollywood-centric syndicated reporter Norma Lee Browning's March 28 column said: "Lots of luck to Judy Garland, 45, for her comeback in *Valley of the Dolls*. She'll need it. . . . Everyone's keeping his fingers crossed, hoping she'll make it thru the picture."

The confirmation of Garland's casting also opened the floodgates for her fans, who wrote Darryl F. Zanuck and other 20th executives to voice their approval and enthusiasm. In one such handwritten letter of March 11, a Fairfield, Illinois, man praised the moviemakers for casting "the greatest entertainer in the world today," adding, "I'm sure I speak for all of the millions of Garland fans the world over in thanking you for bringing her back to the screen. Please cast her in many more films." In another letter, dated March 30, a fan from Indiana wrote: "I hope you realize the great service you are performing by bringing Judy Garland back to the public via *Valley of the Dolls*. . . . As a producer, please try and build up the part of Helen Lawson to a point worthy of Miss Garland's talent. If you do, I know that [she] can win another Academy Award and will and I will see *Valley of the Dolls* many times."

In a final preproduction press commitment, Garland agreed to sit for a *New York World Journal Tribune* profile. In "Over the Rainbow and Into the Valley Goes Our Judy," writer, journalist, songwriter, and cultural critic John Gruen addresses Garland's less than ideal casting as "talon-y" Helen Lawson. In the star's St. Regis Hotel suite, Gruen encounters a "rail-thin . . . disconnected . . . cheerful . . . friendly . . . frantic" Garland, who tells him, "I'm delighted to be in *Valley of the Dolls*, although my slanderous press already has me walking off the set! Mind you, the set hasn't even been built, but already they have me walking off it! It's this kind of ugly slander that keeps me out of work. What am I supposed to do about it? I really need to work. I'm happiest when working, and when I work, I give a lot." She puts the bravest face possible on the recent bankruptcy that cost her and her fourteen-year-old Lorna and eleven-year-old Joey their Beverly Hills mansion, calling it "too big, too impractical. . . . I never really liked it. It looks like a [Gloria] Swanson reject. . . . If worse comes to worst, I can always pitch a tent in front of the Beverly Hilton and I can sing gospel hymns. That should see us through." Downing several vodka and tonics, Garland sounds exactly like a *Valley of the Dolls* character when she says, "If I'm such a legend, then why am I so lonely? If I'm such a legend, then why do I sit at home for hours staring at the damned telephone, hoping it's out of order, even calling the operator asking her if she's *sure* it's not out of order? Let me tell you, legends are all very well if you've got somebody around who loves you, some man who's not afraid to be in love with Judy Garland!" In retrospect, how could anyone involved with *Valley of the Dolls* read this interview and not see that Garland was flashing warning signs signaling panic, disarray, and personal chaos?

CHAPTER NINE

The Casting of the Dopes

E very actor, agent, and manager on the planet knew that the *Valley of the Dolls* movie would be female driven. The only meaty and memorable roles were written by and for women. But facing the facts was never Jacqueline Susann's strong suit, and so she presumed that big-name stars would line up to play Lyon, Tony, Mel, Ted, and Kevin. But in 1966, David Weisbart and Mark Robson's main focus was the signing of three lesser-known young women for the female leads and the biggest name possible to play Helen Lawson. Susann claimed she had no idea how drastically the male roles had been minimized and so, for Lyon Burke, the dashing, womanizing, would-be Hemingway, she proposed to the press such stars as Sean Connery, Paul Newman, Steve McQueen, Robert Redford, and Warren Beatty, among others. Similarly, her wish list for an actor to play cosmetics magnate Kevin Gillmore numbered Kirk Douglas, Cary Grant, William Holden, and David Niven; again, in fairness to Susann, the author had not been told that the later screenplays had reduced Gillmore to a relatively minor player. Once her expectations had been tempered and she learned that the movie would be made on a cost-conscious budget, she rethought her choices for Lyon, telling a reporter, "I'd love Richard Burton, of course, but that's impossible. Maybe George Peppard or Rod Taylor? What I really mean is someone who looks the way Stewart Granger looked 20 years ago."

When the dominoes fell, the real search for the *right* Lyon Burke played out from early December 1966 through February 1967. Casting department heads Owen McLean and Joe Scully had prepared a contingency list of second-string Lyons. One was Tony Curtis, to whom a twelve-year-old Canadian adoptee named Barbara Parkins had once sent a photo and fan letter asking for advice. Curtis had written back, "You look like a very lovely girl, but a little young for an acting career. I suggest you continue your schoolwork until you are 18 or 20. Then, if you are still interested and have studied for it and really want to be an actress, you'll find success." The casting department couldn't sell Weisbart or Robson on Curtis, whose career had begun a downturn.

Brought in for meetings and screen tests were Christopher Plummer (red hot after *The Sound of Music*), James Garner, Adam West (TV's *Batman*), Vince Edwards (TV's *Ben Casey*), James Franciscus, David Hedison, Jeffrey Hunter, Robert Lansing, Patrick O'Neal, Gig Young, and the Jackie-endorsed Rod Taylor (*The Birds*) and George Peppard (*Breakfast at Tiffany's*, *The Carpetbaggers*). When David Weisbart asked Robson to consider George Segal, admitting that "he might not be the ideal Lyon but he might bring his own values to the part," the director wouldn't hear of it. Frustrated by not finding the guy they were after, Robson and Weisbart got the greenlight from the Zanucks to make two separate London trips in January and February to headhunt Continental candidates. Joe Scully was assigned to coordinate Robson's interview requests with 20th's London offices, but the director suddenly changed tactics. Like Susann, he insisted on pursuing pie-in-the-sky choices of leading men. Few actors were willing to meet without having read the screenplay, especially one based on *that* book. Some were simply unavailable, including Peter O'Toole, Albert Finney, Alan Bates, and Terence Stamp (the latter two were busy filming *Far from the Madding Crowd*). Alerted that Peter Finch's schedule might be freeing up at just the right time for *Valley*, 20th arranged a private screening for Weisbart and Robson to eyeball Finch in the Jules Dassin–directed *10:30 P.M. Summer*; both thought he looked "too old." Kenneth Haigh (*Cleopatra*) screentested and was assessed as "80% right" for the role. Less so were such others as Patrick McGoohan (TV's *The Prisoner*), Michael Craig (*Modesty Blaise*), William Squire (Brit TV star), and Peter Wyngarde (*The Innocents*). (In between seeing potential Lyons, Robson and Weisbart rejected as "not right" for Tony Polar the pop singer–actor Jordan Christopher, the young husband of Sybil Burton, the ex–Mrs. Richard Burton.) Brian Bedford's test and interview made a strong enough impression to warrant a second meeting, especially with the actor's strong showing in director John Frankenheimer's just-released action movie *Grand Prix*. But when Weisbart offered Bedford the role on February 18, the actor passed.

Beginning at 10:00 a.m. on the morning of March 6 and extending into the late evening of March 7, with an (unspecified) female stand-in playing Anne, Robson screen-tested more than two dozen British and Irish actors aged twenty-five to thirty-five. On the rebound, Robson and Weisbart flew off to Paris to reconnect with Alain Delon. But as much as Robson had loved directing the Gallic dreamboat in the 1966 action thriller *Lost Command*, he just couldn't make him work as Lyon Burke.

With a production start date looming, the moviemakers had to pull the trigger. At the end of March, a casting scoop broke, courtesy of veteran Hollywood columnist Florabel Muir, famously shot in the keister in 1949 during an early morning Sunset Strip nightclub mob hit on her friend and confidant, Mickey Cohen. Muir announced the casting news as, to put it mildly, "a surprise choice . . . for a role every male film star in and out of Hollywood has been angling for"; Weisbart had signed Paul Burke to play Lyon Burke. The tall, dark, stolid, ruggedly attractive forty-one-year-old Burke was the New Orleans–born son of a prizefighter who had duked it out twice in the '20s with the heavyweight champion Gene Tunney; in the '40s, Burke and family ran a French Quarter club and restaurant in New Orleans. The half-Italian, half-Irish Burke had himself trained to become a prizefighter from age eleven but began working steadily in the early '50s as a guest star on a TV series. He won attention as star of the 1959 weekly spy adventure *Five Fingers*, after which he received two Emmy nominations for playing a detective on the critically praised cop drama *Naked City*, and then got tapped to replace actor Robert Lansing as an ace flyer in the World War II drama *12 O'Clock High* when 20th decided that Lansing was "too old"—even though Burke had a year on Lansing. Burke, an avid pilot who flew his own private plane, shared a '20s-era Spanish-style Palm Springs hacienda with his former showgirl wife, Peggy, and their three children.

Burke signed on to *Valley of the Dolls*—his first feature film—at a weekly salary of $5,000 (roughly $38,400 today), a full $3,000 more than the highest-paid female cast member. Robson required Burke's services from March 9 through May 25, after which the actor was set to report to Boston, Massachusetts, locations to join Steve McQueen and Faye Dunaway (who had won her role over Sharon Tate, Candice Bergen, and Raquel Welch, among others) in the stylish romantic caper thriller *Thomas Crown and Company*, released as *The Thomas Crown Affair*.

Jacqueline Susann based her novel's second most important male character, sexy, opportunistic, childlike singer Tony Polar, on several real-life counterparts. One of them was the phenomenally talented entertainer Bobby Darin, whose heart had been irreparably damaged by childhood rheumatic fever and was doted on by a fiercely protective older sister (later revealed to be his own mother). But Susann's most predominant model was singer-actor-comic and Rat Packer Dean Martin, for whom she harbored more than an innocent sexual crush. Despite Martin's suave, swaggering, self-effacing swinger image, offstage and off camera he was a reticent loner who hated parties, suffered from claustrophobia, and had reportedly read only one book in his entire life (*Black Beauty*) but was addicted to comic books. When Susann met Martin after a nightclub performance, her heart a-flutter, the singer barely tore himself away from the comic he was reading.

From the outset, Susann had stumped for Elvis Presley to play Polar. But by 1966 and 1967, thanks to the singer's mercenary manager Colonel Tom Parker, the ship had long ago sailed on Presley's doing anything in movies but teen-targeted fluff. With the nightclub and TV circuit offering Weisbart and Robson a bumper crop of photogenic crooners, one would have guessed that the moviemakers would have been all over such possible Polars as Robert Goulet, Sergio Franchi, Andy Williams, Tom Jones (just imagine *that*), and, obviously, Bobby Darin. Reported to have turned down the role are James Darren, Jack Jones, and George Maharis, as well as non-singers James Caan, Martin Sheen, Vince Edwards, and Robert Conrad.

On January 20 and 24, Weisbart and Robson met with Robert Forster, whom 20th had signed for a five-film deal sparked by his nude horseback ride as the object of Marlon Brando's erotic obsession in Warner Bros.' John Huston–directed *Reflections in a Golden Eye*. The casting notes indicate Forster impressed everyone, but, for unspecified reasons, the moviemakers kept shopping. Moving to the forefront, though, were two strikingly handsome newcomers, Clint Ritchie and Gil Peterson. Ritchie, a strapping, macho former truck driver, service station attendant, construction worker, and bartender, had recently signed a seven-year 20th contract. Ritchie's *Valley* screen test so wowed Weisbart and casting director Joe Scully that, for a time, he looked all but set—until Robson declared him "so good-looking, he could play Lyon but he's really too young and outdoorsy for either [the role of Lyon or Tony]." Blond Gil Peterson was a former letterman in four varsity sports at Mississippi State who had spent summers singing on the nightclub circuit throughout the South and had recorded with jazz guitarist Herb Ellis a 1962 album of standards, *Gil Peterson Sings "Our Last Goodbye."* Footage screened for the filmmakers at 20th showed Peterson singing and dancing as a washed-up pop music teen idol in *The Cool Ones*, his feature film debut after dramatic roles on TV series including *Combat!*, *Run for Your Life*, and *The F.B.I.* At the time of *Valley of the Dolls*, Peterson had declined a long-term TV contract with Universal to instead sign with Warner Bros.; then Seven Arts bought out Warner Bros. and invalidated all existing talent contracts.

Although Robson and Weisbart considered Peterson a viable choice, in the end they rolled the dice on an absolute screen novice. The 6-foot 2-inch Tony Scotti was a Long Branch, New Jersey–born former University of Maryland track star, wrestler, and basketball and football player. 20th launched Scotti with major fanfare, but his only post–*Valley of the Dolls* screen appearance was with Gena Rowlands in *Nick Quarry*, a never-aired 1968 20th TV pilot based on the Frank Sinatra detective flick *Tony Rome*. As children, Scotti and his older brother, Ben, had been dragged by their Teamsters' union business agent father to perform at local saloons. If the elder Scotti thought the union member bar patrons failed to show sufficient appreciation for his boys' vocal and instrumental talents, he'd ask, "What's the matter? You don't want to work tomorrow?" Scotti attended the University of Maryland on a football scholarship but quit in his junior year to launch a singing career. Brother Ben, who played for the Washington Redskins and got traded to the San Francisco 49ers, suggested that he become Scotti's full-time manager. Once Scotti decided to go all-in as a performer, he bartered with his grandmother: money and bus fare to New York in exchange for his painting the interiors of the apartment buildings she owned.

In New York, Scotti studied voice and movement, modeled, did TV commercials, and auditioned for Broadway roles, including the hip-swivelin' teen idol in *Bye Bye Birdie*, for which he reportedly emerged as a producers' favorite to play the showy character based on Elvis Presley and Conway Twitty. (The producers instead hired Dick Gautier.) Signed to a record deal, Scotti won moderate airplay attention with records including "Primrose Lane" and "I Just Haven't Got What It Takes" and played singing engagements, warbling among (barely) beaded-and-feathered showgirls in nightclubs in Canada and Las Vegas. While working in Vegas in 1965, he married dancer and *Playboy* Playmate-to-be Susan Denberg (née Dietlinde Zechner), the voluptuous Austrian-German beauty known for roles in the 1966 *Star Trek* episode "Mudd's Women" and in the 1967 Hammer horror film (and Martin Scorsese–lauded) *Frankenstein Created Woman*. Scotti's marriage to Denberg was as short-lived as Denberg's film career.

In 1966, 20th signed Scotti to a standard seven-year contract. "I've been one of those almost-made-it guys until now," he told a reporter, referring to his earlier brushes with near-stardom. He immediately earned a spot among the students of the studio's New Talent School. Richard D. Zanuck—eager to replicate, or *top*, his father's signing of such contract players of the palmy '30s and '40s as Tyrone Power, Alice Faye, Don Ameche, Betty Grable, and Gene Tierney—launched the New Talent program in June of 1966, budgeted it at $500,000 per year and housed it on an entire floor in the studio's mighty Executive Building. Zanuck appointed casting head Owen McLean to oversee the project, a competitor of the star-making finishing school concurrently being run by Lucille Ball as the Desilu Workshop, students of which included Tony Scotti's then-wife, Susan Denberg, Barbara Parkins, Carole Cook, and Robert Osborne, decades before the latter became the favorite host of Turner Classic Movies. Meanwhile, Monique James (vice president of West Coast Talent) and Eleanor Kilgallen (vice president of East Coast Talent and the younger sister of Dorothy Kilgallen) ran Universal's version of the program from 1962 to 1980, guiding the early careers of Robert Redford, George Peppard, and Harrison Ford, among others.

At 20th, young candidates who showed potential were required to be interviewed and approved by the studio's casting directors. If those interviews went well, the gauntlet next included filmed personality tests, script readings, and auditions with the school director, veteran actor Curt Conway, and talent coordinator, Pamela Danova. A personal meeting with Zanuck marked the final step. Candidates who made the cut were required to sign a seven-year contract at a frugal $65-a-week salary (about $515 today), with options renewed or dropped every six months, solely at the studio's discretion. 20th's roster of young hopefuls numbered Elizabeth Baur, Pat Becker, James Brolin, Sam Elliott, Cristina Ferrare, Linda Harrison, Karen Huston, Lara Lindsay, Clint Ritchie, Tony Scotti, Tom Selleck, Corinna Tsopei, Edy Williams, and, only *very* occasionally, Jacqueline Bisset and Raquel Welch, whose careers were already in takeoff mode. Students attended five-day-a-week, nine-to-five classes in acting (taught by Curt Conway), voice, diction, movement, personality, and handling the press. Much of the latter training was dispensed by former actress Pamela Danova, a prim, proper, demanding Brit and dialogue coach with a mile-wide bawdy streak. On day one, Danova, the wife of suave film and TV actor Cesare Danova, handed out this manifesto to every contract player:

WHAT IS EXPECTED OF YOU

The image of "the Star" is what has made Hollywood great. You will reflect that image constantly, whether at the studio, or shopping for groceries.

You are being groomed for stardom in every possible way. That means you must be a master of your craft, be able to walk with poise, speak with assurance and clarity, and behave with propriety. You will learn to be gracious to anyone and everyone in preparation for the day when you yourselves will have fans and admirers of your own.

The time has passed for stars to resemble the boy and girl next door and the beatniks. When someone pays money to go to the movies, they expect to see handsome, clean-looking healthy young people—not slovenly, mumbling, scratching delinquents. If a part calls for you to appear otherwise, then the Make-up Department, not nature, will prepare you for the role.

Contract players adjudged to be lazy, untidy or undisciplined will be eliminated from the Studio Roster.

Pamela Danova

• • •

Opinions vary as to the value of the program—deliberately and calculatedly dismantled circa 1970 by Darryl F. Zanuck while he forced his son's dismissal as production chief and reinstated himself as the studio head. Sam Elliott has shrugged off the school's effectiveness, saying: "Unlike the program at Universal, where those guys under contract really worked and did movies and television, this thing was primarily based on nepotism—not that a lot of it isn't—but because of that, I don't think a lot of the producers on the lot took it very seriously." But, asserts former 20th contractee Lara Lindsay (*The Boston Strangler*), "Dick [Zanuck] really believed in the studio system, believed in finding young actors and actresses with potential and grooming them for stardom."

As with other moviemakers on the lot, David Weisbart and Mark Robson kept an eye on the studio's roster of young hopefuls. Every six months, the students got showcased in stage shows—usually comprised of scenes from past and current 20th movies—created to give producers, directors, and casting people a chance to look over the possibilities. For a nanosecond, James Brolin and Tom Selleck—the latter of whom his classmates agreed was the One Most Likely to Succeed on the strength of his good looks alone— became possibilities for either Lyon Burke or Tony Polar. Neither stuck. Selleck's consolation prize: the studio reportedly pressed him into service as a photographer's beefcake model who appeared shirtless in *Valley of the Dolls* advertisements nuzzling Sharon Tate and Barbara Parkins. In the end, though, stunning contract player Corinna Tsopei, the Athens-born model and Miss Universe of 1964, was one of the few New Talent School students, aside from Tony Scotti, to win a spot in *Valley of the Dolls*. Tsopei (along with fellow contract player Pat Becker) got chosen as one of the highly decorative telephone volunteers in the film's charity telethon scene featuring Patty Duke and, in a special guest star appearance, the prickly, self-enchanted stand-up comic and talk show host Joey Bishop.

Weisbart and Robson screen-tested the twenty-seven-year-old Scotti several times, noting that he "came on strong." According to studio records, at 10:00 a.m. on both February 26 and March 8, Scotti first rehearsed with Robson and was then put on film. On Scotti's first day, on a nearly empty soundstage, he faced the deliberately tricky task of crooning live using a handheld microphone to a prerecorded instrumental track of Francis Lai and Pierre Barouh's theme from the popular French import *A Man and a Woman*. For reasons known only to Robson, the director preferred him to all the other candidates, including Neil Diamond, who had already hit the Billboard charts with "Solitary Man" and "Cherry, Cherry." Robson thought Diamond "all" wrong for the role and apparently refused to meet with him.

Finally, the moviemakers chose to roll the dice and signed Scotti to play Tony Polar at a salary of $400 weekly (about $3,100 today) with a guarantee of ten weeks' work. When asked by a reporter why Robson decided against casting any of the major male movie and recording stars mentioned as potential players, he answered, "A powerful best seller like this well-known novel doesn't require top box-office names necessarily to insure viewing of the film version. The book's exposure is so vast that there's a ready-made audience for [it]. Therefore, new faces can be introduced, bringing in a freshness, talent-wise, to the film. A case in point is Tony Scotti. I'm sure that filmgoers will exclaim, 'Who's that?' and thus establish an immediate following, perhaps even fan clubs, for a new personality. This is important for our business."

Scotti told veteran Hollywood reporter Vernon Scott at the time, "Somehow I always knew I'd be a success in this business. My first interview out here was at MGM where I told them I didn't come out here to be a working actor. I said I was going to be a star and make a million dollars for some studio. I believe in destiny. I turned down a lot of other jobs—singing engagements, not acting work—to be available when the right time came. This picture is it." The studio publicists began planting Scotti's name in gossip columns, one of which mentioned that he'd been "playing the dating game with a whole string of Hollywood lovelies," including brainy Leslie Parrish (*Li'l Abner*) and predictably, but perhaps not factually, his costar Sharon Tate. Although Scotti's on-camera career ultimately stalled, he later went on to major success in the music business, becoming MGM's record production department vice president in 1971 and three years later cofounding the Scotti Brothers record label with his brother. The pair helped make a recording star out of teen idol Leif Garrett and were key figures in boosting the early careers of "Weird Al" Yankovic, Felony, and Survivor. In the late eighties, the brothers later branched out into film production (*Lady Beware*, *He's My Girl*) as well as TV production with *America's Top 10* and, later still, into syndication with *Baywatch* and *Acapulco H.E.A.T.* (Since 1984, Scotti has been married to international singer-actress Sylvie Vartan).

While the Tony Polar casting conundrum was at its height, Robson and Weisbart were also busy reviewing a parade of actors for the other male roles. Among those considered to play well-intentioned, mellow, mediocre agent and Neely O'Hara punching bag Mel Anderson, aka Mel Harris in the novel, were Richard Benjamin, Bill Bixby, Dick Clark, Dennis Cole, Keir Dullea, Larry Hagman, Dean Jones, James MacArthur, Robert Reed, Wayne Rogers, Dick Sargent, Robert Walker Jr., and Richard Beymer (that old beau of Sharon Tate's who starred in *West Side Story*). Agents for Red Buttons even submitted his name. Robsons' choice was thirty-eight-year-old George Grizzard, whom he had directed in his movie debut six years earlier in *From the Terrace*. Critics praised Grizzard's Broadway performances in *The Glass Menagerie* and *Who's Afraid of Virginia Woolf?* and he looked all but set for *Valley of the Dolls*. But, in mid-January, Grizzard instead chose to return to Broadway for a role in Robert Anderson's collection of one-act comedies, *You Know I Can't Hear You When the Water's Running.*

In mid-March, Weisbart hired Martin Milner, who became a star with George Maharis for four seasons—and, later, with Glenn Corbett for one season—on the groundbreaking, shot-on-location TV series *Route 66*, created and written by Stirling Silliphant. Milner, thirty-six, signed at $2,500 a week for a guaranteed $21,000 ($166,000 today) for eight-plus weeks of work beginning March 16 through to May 15. The Detroit-born actor was the son of Paramount Theater circuit dancer Jerre Martin and film distributor Sam Milner, who relocated to Los Angeles when Milner was a baby. At age fifteen, in 1947, he was cast by Warner Bros. in the movie version of Clarence Day Jr.'s Broadway hit *Life with Father*, which led to subsequent roles in *Gunfight at the O.K. Corral*, *Marjorie Morningstar* (one of many influences on *Valley of the Dolls*), and *Sweet Smell of Success.*

For the remaining male roles, Joe Scully had been firing off casting memos about who might fill the roles of fashion designer Ted Casablanca and cosmetics magnate Kevin Gillmore. By late January and early February, proposed for the "double-gaited" and "over immaculately-dressed" Ted were George Chakiris, George Maharis, Richard Chamberlain, Anthony Perkins, Alain Delon, Keir Dullea, Ray Stricklyn, Anthony Franciosa, Sal Mineo, and Hampton Fancher (who went on to write *Blade Runner* and *Blade Runner 2049*).

By mid-April, Alexander Davion had won out over the competition with a guarantee of five and a half weeks of work at $1,500 per week (about $10,000 today). Robson declared the good-looking, dark-haired Parisian Davion "one of the best foreign imports to hit Hollywood in years." Customarily billed as "Alex," Davion was no newcomer. Since 1951, he had built up his TV dossier in the UK and United States by playing nameless, often perfidious, Native Americans, Spaniards, and Italians as well as unsavory upper-crust Brits before graduating to featured roles on popular '60s TV series, including *Have Gun—Will Travel* and *Thriller*. On the big screen in the '60s, he had played Frédéric Chopin in *Song Without End* opposite Dirk Bogarde and Capucine as well as a sadistic aristo in *The Plague of the Zombies*.

For the role of Kevin Gillmore, Weisbart and Robson tested such actors as David Brian, Sydney Chaplin, James Daly, Arthur Hill, Richard Kiley, Kevin McCarthy, Gary Merrill, Barry Nelson, Larry Parks, and Barry Sullivan. Their choice was the fifty-year-old Charles Drake, who had worked constantly since the late '30s in *The Hunchback of Notre Dame*; *The Maltese Falcon*; *Now, Voyager*; *Yankee Doodle Dandy*; and *Winchester '73*, as well as on TV in *The Fugitive* and *F Troop*. Drake earned his $2,500 weekly (about $20,000 today) with a one-and-three-fifths-week guarantee by looking unthreateningly attractive and maintaining his dignity.

To play talent agent Henry Bellamy, Joe Scully suggested James Gregory, Lloyd Nolan, John Marley, and Nehemiah Persoff. Robson gave the nod to Robert H. Harris, whom he had previously used in *Peyton Place* and who appeared regularly with Gertrude Berg on TV's *The Goldbergs* and *Alfred Hitchcock Presents*. The actor earned $3,000 (about $24,000 today) per week with a guaranteed six and three-fifths weeks of shooting.

Also in late '66, Weisbart set in motion negotiations with the representatives of talk show hosts Johnny Carson and Merv Griffin, and with the celebrity panel of *What's My Line?* for "inside show-biz" scenes dramatizing Neely O'Hara's rising fame. Weisbart sent a message to Owen McLean asking if he could provide direct personal contact with the movie-averse, notoriously prickly Carson; Carson and his producer of twenty-five years, Freddie de Cordova, made such onerous restrictions and demands that Weisbart and Robson had no alternative but to ax the scene. On February 13, Weisbart sent Joe Scully an urgent memo about another of Neely's talk show scenes on the assumption that Scully was "well into negotiations with the Merv Griffin people for his appearance in this picture. This is extremely important, Joe, as we do not have any other directions to go for the moment in the film. Please advise." The scene had been written to involve both Griffin and his curmudgeonly veteran film actor cohost, Arthur Treacher, and a panel of guest stars; Griffin's proposed salary for the single-day shoot was $7,500 ($60,000 today) with Treacher and the guest panelists each to be paid $1,000 ($7,750 today).

Negotiations with Griffin's William Morris Agency representative Murray Schwartz dragged on until mid-March. Griffin eventually balked at involving himself in a project that might lose him favor with stars of the type Jacqueline Susann wrote about in *Valley of the Dolls*. The production had better luck with tyrannical Broadway producer and shameless promoter-showman David Merrick. He had not been officially asked to appear in the movie (pending decisions to be on the final shooting screenplay), but on March 1, 1967, Frank H. Ferguson, of 20th's Legal Department, sent a letter to Robson, Weisbart, Owen McLean, and production manager Francisco "Chico" Day that the Abominable Showman had approved of characters referencing him in the dialogue.

March saw a number of last-minute casting additions. In smaller roles, thirty-year-old Ernest Harada, who had spent a week supporting Patty Duke, Barbara Parkins, and many other hopefuls in screen tests, was cast in an unbilled role as Lyon Burke's houseman. The gifted Harada, who later appeared on many TV series and in movies, including *Rosemary's Baby* and *Earthquake* (directed by Robson), also went on to stop the show singing "Welcome to Kanagawa" in the original Broadway cast of Stephen Sondheim's award-winning 1976 musical, *Pacific Overtures*.

On March 13, the day before the scheduled start of principal photography, Manhattan casting associate Linda Schreiber recommended rising TV actor Robert Viharo to Robson (Scully's note indicated Schreiber was "high on him"). Schreiber thought Viharo might bring something extra to the small role of the theater director seen early in the movie with Neely and Jennifer in the rehearsal hall with Helen Lawson, Anne Welles, and Mel Anderson in Lawson's theater dressing room and, later, with Helen Lawson and Neely during their powder room imbroglio. Robson approved, and Weisbart closed the deal at $1,000 a week for six and four-fifths weeks.

On March 15, Schreiber cleared with the Screen Actors Guild and finalized (for one week at $400) the deal for the services of *A Chorus Line* composer-to-be Marvin Hamlisch. Hamlisch, the younger brother of 20th's Casting Department associate Terry Liebling, would appear on-screen as Neely O'Hara's rehearsal pianist and would (for a separate fee) also accompany Duke's off-screen vocal rehearsals.

CHAPTER TEN

Preproduction— Gonna Dig a Valley

DOLLING IT UP, TRAVILLA STYLE

Back on January 23, the *Los Angeles Times* ran 20th's press announcement that producer David Weisbart's choice of costume designer was William "Bill" Travilla. Travilla won the assignment over tough competition, including Moss Mabry (*The Manchurian Candidate*), with whom Weisbart had worked on *Rebel Without a Cause*. Also considered were Oscar-nominated Donfeld (*Days of Wine and Roses, Robin and the 7 Hoods*) and the esteemed veteran Oscar winner Renié (*Cleopatra, The Sand Pebbles*).

The production's costume requirements—even on a whopping $350,000 budget (the equivalent of $2.7 million today)—were challenging but also a field day for the Catalina Island–born Travilla, a look-alike of actor Stuart Whitman. *Valley of the Dolls* marked his first motion picture costume design gig in four years. After completing his previous 20th assignments, *The Stripper* and *Take Her, She's Mine*, in 1963, he had stepped away from Hollywood to focus on creating his own retail fashion line sold at higher-end women's stores and department stores across the United States.

As a sixteen-year-old self-starter, Travilla launched his career by designing peekaboo outfits for Los Angeles–area showgirls and strippers. That led to his working at Western Costume as a sketch artist for established movie costume designers, which, in turn, brought him to the attention of 20th Century Fox ice-skating movie star Sonja Henie, for whom he created gowns and ice show dresses. From the '40s on, Travilla's name became associated with dressing beautiful Hollywood dames, including sexy, sloe-eyed Warner Bros. contract star Ann Sheridan. His working relationship with Sheridan, promoted by Warner Bros. as "the Oomph Girl," helped him land an exclusive arrangement with 20th Century Fox, where he designed gowns for such stars as Betty Grable, Jeanne Crain, Jane Russell, and Susan Hayward. But Travilla's most reputation-making creations adorned the astonishing peaks, curves, and valleys of Marilyn Monroe, the atomic blond sexpot, whom he dressed to dazzle during her peak '50s years in 20th's *There's No Business Like Show Business*, *Gentlemen Prefer Blondes*, *How to Marry a Million-aire*, *The Seven Year Itch*, and *Bus Stop*.

Before the mid-March kickoff of principal photography, the moviemakers and the Zanucks instructed 20th's publicity boss, James Denton, to line up a series of newspaper interviews for chatty and press-friendly Travilla. The studio was anxious to establish the movie in the collective public consciousness as a glitzy, high-style affair, one for which Travilla had already lavished three months conceiving, designing, and overseeing the fabrication of a parade of outfits. As Travilla had already announced that past January: "I'm designing all the costumes for the principals in *Valley*, which means accessories and every bit of apparel they have. And I'll watch over the men and the big scenes. It's hard to say now exactly how many costumes I'll have, but it will be a lot—a couple of hundred pieces or more. Much bigger than a couture collection. I'll probably take some costumes out of stock, buy others and redo

Jackie and Irving, two minds but with a single thought. Even their ankh pendants matched.

Valley editor Don Preston, publisher Bernard Geis, Irving, Jackie, and publicist Letty Cottin Pogrebin.

Jackie charmed the crew shipping her book by supplying free donuts and books.

20th studio mogul Darryl F. Zanuck, prodigious in talent, power, and sexual appetite.

Darryl Zanuck pushed for *Valley*, studio boss son Richard Zanuck resisted.

Tony Scotti, Sharon Tate, Patty Duke, Martin Milner, Barbara Parkins, Paul Burke, and director Mark Robson make nice—for the camera.

ABOVE: *Valley of the Dolls* publicity portrait attributed to glamour photographer George Hurrell.

LEFT: Helen Gurley Brown and 20th executive husband David Brown, to whom Robert Evans brought the *Valley* manuscript and whom Brown promptly kicked to the curb.

A

ABOVE: Travilla called the *Valley* girls the shortest for whom he'd ever designed costumes.

A. Travilla's first (unused) design for Neely's attempted seduction of Lyon Burke.

B. Travilla's alternate design for Anne Welles's attire when reporters question her after Jennifer's suicide.

C. Travilla designed this ensemble to help Fox court Candice Bergen to play Anne; note the DKE sorority pin.

D

G

H

B

C

E

F

I

J

D. One of Travilla's earliest costume options for Neely's final meltdown in a theater alley.

E. Travilla's gown in blue pleated Fortuny chiffon for Barbara Parkins's gaga Gillian Girl TV commercial.

F. This gold lamé nightclub attire showstopper, designed for Julie Christie to play Jennifer, got nixed by Fox as insufficiently sexy.

G. The 20th brass required Travilla to emphasize Jennifer's bosom, so out went this lounge pajama ensemble (created for Julie Christie).

H. A pink Champalal pinstripe coat was the original choice for the post-theater scene of Tony taking a tumble.

I. Travilla tried buying time for Judy Garland by spending a week creating maroon, orange, purple, and green versions of Helen Lawson's power suit, claiming that the original color didn't pop on camera.

J. Alternative wedding dress design, created for Natalie Wood when 20th sought her to play Neely.

Sharon Tate, backgrounded by 20th's executive building, poses for a costume test for the sanitarium scene.

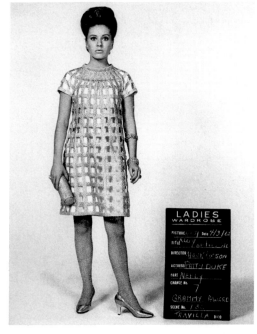

Patty Duke puts up with a costume test of Neely's very expensive, very heavy gold birdcage Grammy Award dress.

Barbara Parkins struts her stuff for a Gillian Girl hair and costume test.

Celebrity hairstylist Mr. Kenneth designed Barbara Parkins's pretzel 'do.

Sharon Tate had to be sewn into Travilla's clingy beaded nightclub gown.

Cameraman William Daniels and crew shoot Patty Duke for the Neely O'Hara career montage.

Despite early misgivings, director Mark Robson was won over by Barbara Parkins's professionalism after filming in freezing weather at Mt. Kisco's Leonard Park Ice Rink.

TOP: After filming Sharon Tate and Tony Scotti in Manhattan's Carl Schurz Park, Mark Robson told his producer and cameraman that the actors were much better in their screen test.

BOTTOM: Patty Duke raged when Robson was off during a press interview while she filmed the sanitarium freakout scene.

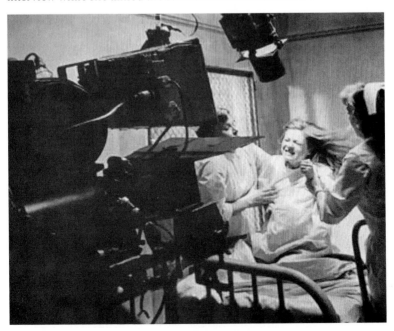

Preparing to shoot a movie-within-a-movie scene, is Patty Duke brooding that director Mark Robson is "crucifying" her?

Patty Duke, Mark Robson, Lee Grant, David Weisbart, and Barbara Parkins welcome Jacqueline Susann to 20th to film her cameo.

Patty Duke and Gil Peterson in one of the cut scenes from Neely O'Hara's flop movie *Love and Let Love*.

Every columnist jockeyed for access to the "troubled" *Valley* set. Patty Duke's expression and body language say it all.

Patty Duke counseled Sharon Tate on how to answer interviewers' questions without trashing *Valley of the Dolls*.

On location in New York, Patty Duke with husband Harry Falk. The wallflower in the jacket and tie is Marvin Hamlisch.

At a Manhattan preproduction press conference, Jacqueline Susann and Judy Garland pretend everything's just fine.

ABOVE LEFT: Travilla was saddened to see frail Judy Garland "literally wasting away" and did everything possible to keep her on the movie. ABOVE RIGHT: Barbara Parkins believes Judy Garland's take on Helen Lawson could have earned her an Oscar.

Producer David Weisbart, director Mark Robson, and cinematographer William Daniels welcome Oscar heavyweight Susan Hayward to the gladiatorial arena.

ABOVE LEFT: Judy Garland models Travilla's beaded pantsuit during costume tests. ABOVE RIGHT: Susan Hayward angered the costume designer by insisting he remove the costume's padding to disguise her weight gain.

Patty Duke vs. Susan Hayward. The fireworks weren't only on the screen.

Betty Rollin's deliciously dishy cover story sent shockwaves through showbiz.

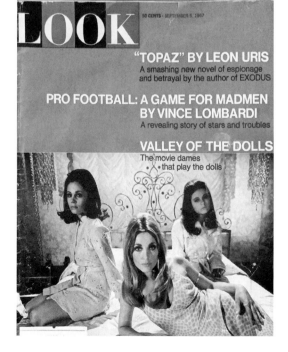

LOOK

50 CENTS · SEPTEMBER 5, 1967

"TOPAZ" BY LEON URIS
A smashing new novel of espionage
and betrayal by the author of EXODUS

PRO FOOTBALL: A GAME FOR MADMEN
BY VINCE LOMBARDI
A revealing story of stars and troubles

VALLEY OF THE DOLLS
The movie dames
that play the dolls

The original pressbook gave theater owners lessons in the fine old art: don't smell it, *sell* it.

Valley of the Dolls posters and ads featured key art by several photographers, with a young Tom Selleck one of several anonymous male scoundrels.

During the *Valley* luxury liner premiere, Travilla, Sharon Tate, and Tony Scotti look as if they know they're on the *Titanic*. Barbara Parkins keeps up appearances.

them but will design most of the costumes from scratch." He added, "Designing for movies is difficult. I am generally given the complete script and a list of the cast at the beginning. This time it is different, more difficult since I don't know who the actresses will be and only have thirty-eight pages of script so far. But I hope I will know the cast soon. . . . I *have* to."

Because of the many script and casting hurdles on the film, some of Travilla's earliest and most stunning "Anne Welles" sketches were designed expressly for Candice Bergen; in later drawings for the same character, the flair and influence of Jacqueline Kennedy are obvious. The designer said at the time, "Once the girls got cast, I met with them and asked what they liked and don't like. Then, I sat down and drew my feelings, capturing their feelings, too. I love the thinking that goes along with designing for a film. There is a reason for everything . . . the hows and whys are like a puzzle. I went to my office and thought the whole thing through. I consider the plot in its entirety, the sequence of actions and costume changes, the personality of each character, the physical appearance of each actress and how they act. Once I know their likes and dislikes, I create 'a wardrobe plot,' a catalogue of every scene and costume change. That's when I begin designing for the character(s). I always think of someone I know who is like that character. That way I can best figure out what the character would wear and the costumes are always true to life."

Travilla's earliest game plan for the four major female characters provides an insight into the designer's thinking process while also revealing how the script and production were still evolving to the point where scenes and locations were constantly being changed from the page to the screen.

ANNE WELLES:

When I met with Mark Robson and David Weisbart to discuss the characters, I saw Anne as a shy, clean-cut typical American girl

who comes to New York from a small New England town. Not interested in show business—all she wants is a job. Her entire manner,
her behavior, her very way of life must be exemplified as much by
the way she dresses as by the way she deports [*sic*] herself. She's
an honest, forthright human and that's the way I will design her
clothes—honestly, simply, attractively in the best of taste. In one of
Anne's opening scenes, she arrives at the office of theatrical attorneys for an interview. In real life she would probably be wearing a
double-breasted coat, boots, gloves and a headscarf and would remove these outer garments while she was talking to the receptionist. In the movie, the scene with the receptionist takes just a matter
of moments but I have to design costumes that make [Anne] look
different in each scene but yet like she is working with a limited
budget.

NEELY O'HARA:

In the opening sequences, the character appears as a youngster, the
ingénue, another of the thousands of hopefuls who dream of stardom.
She's rehearsing in a show and wearing hip-hugger, bell-bottom
slacks that lace up the front. She's a working showgirl, perfectly natural, full of zip, clawing her way to the top. At this point, she couldn't
care less what she's wearing. I think of Neely at the age of seventeen as a groovy Greenwich Village type who is "with it" but doesn't
really have good taste yet. It's a different story once she's made the
grade, and then it is that she's high fashion—stylish, a bit *avant-
garde* and kooky and disheveled and mismatched as she destroys
her relationships and career.

JENNIFER NORTH:

She's a flashy showgirl. A no-talent, statuesque, amply bosomed,
stunning girl whose only asset is the display of her body. She has an
enormous bust and this is important, but the actress who can best

play the part may not. In which case I would have to construct large bosoms for the actress and design her clothes so that they would look real. I dress her extravagantly, daringly. In one scene, we practically have to sew her into her gown. Jennifer reminds me of Marilyn Monroe. I always disapproved of what Marilyn wore. I thought it was bad taste. But she was right. She was building a career and the clothes she wore helped build the image she wanted to create. I think it was the same way with Jennifer.

HELEN LAWSON:

She's a crude, rough, selfish, hard-bitten woman who fights with every dirty trick she knows—and she knows them all. She is a foul-mouthed, ruthless woman, completely without taste or finesse. I think Helen would buy expensive, nice clothes but that her taste is wrong and that she would destroy a magnificent outfit with too many things. She might wear a bright red printed wool coat with a twin print dress in a sheer fabric. But it would look perfectly ghastly with her orange hair and all the accessories she would add. She comes on like gangbusters—like a scream—and I will dress her just that way.

• • •

In every interview, and with the endorsement of the Zanucks and the *Valley* moviemakers, Travilla revealed a major reason for his agreeing to do the movie in the first place: "The clothes the female leads wear in the film will be able to be duplicated in every budget shop and department store in America. I hope they will provide a guide for what the well-dressed woman would wear."

After Travilla's private consultation sessions at 20th with Patty Duke, Barbara Parkins, and Sharon Tate, he reported to Robson and Weisbart (and later, to the press) that he had "never worked with so many small girls." Duke stood just under 5 feet and Parkins was a shade over 5 feet 3 inches. Because each had very different proportions, each played dramatically different personality types, and each was required to look much taller on the screen, Travilla devised three distinct fashion silhouettes and costumes scaled appropriately. With this assignment especially, he insisted that he needed to "create an illusion; whether it be making the leading lady look more beautiful, more perfect by hiding her defects, or making the actress appear as if she has the physical attributes that the character she's playing has."

Patty Duke said, "When I knew Travilla was designing a wardrobe just for me, I got ambitious and reduced to eighty pounds." Returning the compliment, the designer created for Neely's Grammy Awards scene a leading-edge latticed "cage" dress fabricated from gold bullion costing $150 a yard, wholesale. (The same material today would cost $1,100 per yard.) In devising the costumes for Neely, Travilla had some clever tricks up his sleeve. The costumes Duke wears in Neely's first and last scenes are striped to suggest the character's imprisonment. The designer also indulged himself by weaving in a sly, subtle nod to a signature Judy Garland role. Virtually every pair of shoes worn by Duke as Neely are, like the famous ruby slippers from *The Wizard of Oz*, adorned with bows. In Neely's screaming-in-the-alley finale, the bowed slippers are even emerald green. The exceptions are the charity telethon scene and the scene at the Grammy Awards; in the latter it is Barbara Parkins who wears a pair of bowed shoes.

A costuming pièce de résistance for Parkins's character was a fur coat consisting of nutria squares applied to black leather. At wholesale in 1967, the materials alone cost a cool $6,000; today they would be well over $44,000 *before* labor. For Sharon Tate, Travilla pulled out all the stops, including a towering bejeweled forty-pound showgirl headdress with cascading purple feathers. As he and Tate began working together, Travilla, privately and in the press, began calling her his all-time favorite actress/model, replacing Marilyn Monroe. He rhapsodized about Tate's "amazing beauty—a more classical beauty than Marilyn's perfect beauty, a faultless, exciting figure, sex appeal, and with it the same defenseless childlike quality that Marilyn had. I dress her extravagantly, daringly." The big exception, he noted, was reserved for Jennifer's suicide scene, where he deliberately extracted color and simplified the line. He explained, "I think it's terribly important for a motion picture to be almost quiet, especially if you have an emotional scene. You can't take away from an actress's performance with a beautiful gown and expect to come up with a fine film. We play the clothes down in those scenes." Going so far as comparing Tate's "fascinating, yet wholly feminine strength" to Marlene Dietrich's and Greta Garbo's, he thought the newcomer possessed "the kind of sex appeal and personal appeal to become as glittering a star as Bette Davis, Joan Crawford, Rita Hayworth, Lana Turner, Elizabeth Taylor." Coworkers noted that Travilla became so fond of Tate that he spent much more time than usual on the set and frequently drove miles out of his way to drop her off at her home after work.

It was an entirely different story when Judy Garland reported to 20th on April 14 to complete camera tests and to model wardrobe, wigs, and makeup for Robson and cameraman William Daniels. On seeing Garland, Travilla was stunned, calling her "a tragic figure, so nervous and frail. She was literally wasting away. It was as if there was no life left in her skin; her body dissipated." The designer had deliberately created the star's costumes to help compensate for qualities she lacked—absolute authoritativeness, brassiness, and self-assurance. He was so respectful of Garland and her participation in the film that he worked overtime in the hope of wowing her. To finish that bejeweled, intricately detailed paisley pantsuit for Helen Lawson's opening night cocktail party—a heavily embellished dazzler that looks as weighty as armor—Travilla put two seamstresses to work for two weeks hand dying beads to match perfectly and then sewing them on, along with sequin borders to accent the paisley pattern. Garland told friends that she thought Travilla's work "lovely" and that she was looking forward to wearing "five beautiful outfits."

Although Barbara Parkins has called Travilla "a master at designing gowns" and has opined that some of Sharon Tate's dresses were "stunning," she was less enamored of most of her own wardrobe, except for some of her Gillian Girl TV commercial ensembles. During her March 3 costume fittings, she apparently expressed reservations about the unflatteringly "boxy" look created for her character and thought that Travilla had overloaded her with beige and earth tones. In recent years, Parkins has lamented the fashion designer's crowning her with a cashmere beret that she compared to a mushroom growing out of her head. Off-camera, Parkins was thoroughly modern, opting for cutting-edge American and European couture.

To complement Travilla's high-fashion profile, David Weisbart hired celebrity hair stylist Mr. Kenneth to create hair designs, falls, and wigs for Parkins throughout the movie, particularly for that wonderfully outré Gillian Girl TV commercial. It was as much a shrewd publicity move as it was an aesthetic choice. As mid-twentieth century's first superstar celebrity haircutter, Mr. Kenneth, whose name was frequently dropped in the press, also became familiar to the public because of his guest appearances on TV's *What's My Line?*, *I've Got a Secret*, and *The Mike Douglas Show*. The Syracuse, New York–born Kenneth Everette Battelle was known for creating famous "looks" for socialites Brooke Astor and Margaretta "Happy" Rockefeller and had risen to international prominence while working for five years in the early '50s at the flagship Helena Rubinstein salon in Manhattan. At Rubinstein's—and this was a major deciding factor in his being chosen to tress up Parkins for *Valley of the Dolls*—Kenneth first came into the orbit of Jacqueline Kennedy, for whom he created a much imitated full-headed, softer hairstyle to replace the stiff, short, and lacquered look she had been sporting. Continuing to build bridges between high society and show business, by 1956 Kenneth was running the hair salon for milliner Lilly Daché, where client Lucille Ball called him God, where Audrey Hepburn became a regular client, where his short haircut for redheaded actress Kay Kendall sparked a major style trend, and where he unleashed Marilyn

Monroe's tresses from constant bleaching and the tight, constricting hairdos inflicted on her by 20th Century Fox.

At the time of his efforts at making Barbara Parkins as Jacqueline Kennedy–like and elegantly fashion forward as possible, Kenneth ruled the roost at his own luxurious pamper palace salon at 19 East Fifty-fourth Street. In contrast to the stark, imposing granite exterior of the multistory former town house built in 1900, legendary decorator Billy Baldwin was hired by Kenneth to create a hectic, lively interior space. 20th paid Mr. Kenneth $7,000 (about $53,000 in today's economy) for his tonsorial razzmatazz and for the sheen that they expected his name to lend to the film.

LOCATIONS, LOCATIONS, LOCATIONS

On January 2, Mark Robson and his wife, Sara, jetted via American Airlines from Los Angeles to New York to begin location scouting. Joining Robson immediately after was production designer Richard Day, a seven-time Oscar winner and twenty-time nominee, whose '20s credits began on the extraordinarily high note of his work on Erich von Stroheim's *Merry-Go-Round*, *Greed*, and *The Wedding March*. Completing the advance location scouting team were producer David Weisbart, cameraman William Daniels, and production manager Francisco "Chico" Day. Darryl F. Zanuck pushed for Day, the brother of dashing movie actor Gilbert Roland, having been impressed by his work on several of the mogul's pet projects, including *The Grapes of Wrath*, *The Mark of Zorro*, and *The Ghost and Mrs. Muir*, as well as his work for producer Walter Mirisch on *The Magnificent Seven*. The group's first task was to choose from one of Day's preselected locations meant to serve as Anne Welles's first New York residence. They considered the Barbizon Hotel (140 East Sixty-third Street) and the Webster Apartments (419 West Thirty-fourth Street) before opting for another historic "for women only" residence, the 1903 Renaissance Revival–style Martha Washington (known today as The Redbury) at 29 East Twenty-ninth Street.

For the theater rehearsal scenes involving Neely, Jennifer, and Anne, Day proposed and Robson approved the look and feel of the interiors of the Variety Arts Studios at 225 West Forty-sixth Street, with its fifteen differently configured studio spaces from which to choose. Robson sent emphatic memos about the location to Richard Day; the multi-Oscar-winning art director Jack Martin Smith (*The Wizard of Oz, Madame Bovary, Peyton Place*); and set decorators Philip M. Jefferies (*The Manchurian Candidate*), Raphaël G. Bretton (*Hush . . . Hush, Sweet Charlotte*), and Walter M. Scott (*The King and I, The Sound of Music*). The director wanted the Variety Arts Studios' painted signs—reading, variously, "Watch Your Step—Step Up," "Step Down," and "One Step Down Outside Door"—replicated and placed conspicuously in the theater's interiors reproduced on the 20th soundstages back in Los Angeles. "Those signs speak to themes in our picture, in a way," Robson wrote. (So much for themes. The signs are virtually invisible in the movie.)

The team assessed the exterior and interior of the Alvin Theater (today the Neil Simon Theater) at 250 West Fifty-second Street for scenes depicting Neely O'Hara's disastrous Broadway opening night in *Tell Me, Darling* (the title a spin on *Say, Darling*, the 1958 comedy by Abe Burrows and Richard and Marian Bissell, with songs by Jule Styne, Betty Comden, and Adolph Green); additionally, for a Neely bar scene after the curtain falls on her show, they liked the lounge at the Hotel Piccadilly, a now-demolished Forty-fifth Street art deco show crowd haunt west of Broadway. For the theater itself, though, Robson chose the Playhouse Theater at 137 West Forty-eighth Street, knowing full well that Patty Duke had performed there more than seven hundred times in the acclaimed *The Miracle Worker.* Day proposed using the alleys of the Plymouth, Biltmore, and Belasco theaters as on-location backdrops for Neely's final breakdown; Robson instead shot the scene on a 20th soundstage. For Helen Lawson's big opening night, Robson endorsed the Shubert Theater at 247 College Street, New Haven, Connecticut.

While in New York, as inspiration and reference for Helen Lawson's penthouse apartment, William Daniels's assistants shot translucent plates of a thirty-second floor unit at the swank St. Moritz Hotel at 50 Central Park South (today it's the Ritz-Carlton New York, Central Park). For Neely O'Hara's guest appearance with Johnny Carson, Chico Day sought permission to shoot interiors and exteriors of NBC Studios at 30 Rockefeller Plaza, but the plans got scrapped when Carson vetoed the *Tonight Show* scene. A unit at 350 West Forty-sixth Street served as a visual reference for a scene in the interior of the young, struggling Neely's apartment, shot later on a 20th soundstage.

Anne and Lyon's post-theater drinks and conversation were to be filmed in the old-school wood-paneled interiors of either the Hofbräuhaus or the Taft Tap Room. Meanwhile, Tony and Jennifer's walk was scheduled to be shot near the big rock at Eighty-fourth Street and Riverside Drive; alternates included Gracie Mansion, Carl Schurz Park (between Eighty-sixth and Eighty-fifth Streets), the Children's Zoo (Sixty-fourth Street and Fifth Avenue), and an apparent Robson obsession, considering the number of times it is mentioned in memos, the then-current Pepsi-Cola exhibit at 500 Park Avenue. (It never made it into the final film.) Scenes of the interior and exterior of Lyon Burke's apartment were set to be filmed at the historic block-long Apthorp, between Broadway and West End Avenue and between West Seventy-eighth and West Seventy-ninth Streets; shots were planned (but dropped) showing Anne Welles leaving Lyon's apartment and exiting the fabulous Italian Renaissance Revival building built between 1906 and 1908. Richard Day had always set Helen Lawson's hair-raising ladies' lounge humiliation to be shot on a set at 20th, but based upon photos to be taken at a number of potential locations—the interior of the Blue Angel at 152 East Fifty-fifth Street, the Copacabana at 10 East Sixtieth Street, and the Persian Room at the Plaza Hotel—Robson liked the Copa best, and on January 18, representatives for the film got the okay from the nightclub's infamous operator, Jules Podell, to

shoot reference photographs of the club to serve as guides for rep-
licating elements of the club on a 20th soundstage.

Their New York work completed, the preproduction team decamped to New England. There, for long days by helicopter and
car, they searched for what Robson called "locations very different
from but as fine as we had in Maine for *Peyton Place*"—meaning,
picturesque streets, colonial-style homes, farms, churches, a frozen pond, and other environmental attributes to best represent
Anne Welles's halcyon, postcard-perfect fictional hometown, Lawrenceville. The director and his advance team required a frozen
pond for what was described as a "Currier and Ives–type skating
scene." They also needed shots from Anne's point of view as her
train passed homes with classic weather vanes, a cemetery, a
quaint covered bridge, and snug houses lining a river. By mid-
January, after rejecting Ridgefield, Connecticut ("beautiful but we
will need snow conditions to match"), Robson, Weisbart, and
Chico Day scoured Route 58 from Redding to New Haven, noting
buildings and natural elements they liked, including First Church of
Christ Congregational, a golf club, a red barn, and a large frozen
pond and reservoir; studio notes recorded that Bedford Village offered "virtually ideal" roadside signs, farms, "good houses, small
Square, churches, and a cemetery on a hill." All were photographed;
few made the final cut. Robson planned to shoot exteriors repre-
senting Anne's storybook New England family home in Redding
Center, Connecticut. The crews of 20th duplicated the home's interior to scale on a Los Angeles soundstage; this would prove to be an
annoyance to Paul Burke, forced to crouch in certain scenes so that
he wouldn't bump his head on the ceiling. The company earmarked
a number of shots to be captured in historic Bedford Village.

SLIGHTLY OUT OF TUNE

Months before the production's March start date, David Weisbart
signed the songwriting team of gifted composer André Previn and

the lyricist Dory Previn. Their assignment: write a theme song as well as eight or ten diegetic songs (later whittled down to five) to be sung by Neely O'Hara, Tony Polar, and Helen Lawson. Although the Previns, married since 1959, were on a creative high, irreparable fractures were eroding their personal lives.

Dory Previn (née Langan), born in 1925, grew up the eldest daughter of a hardscrabble, almost militarily regimented Irish Catholic family in New Jersey. The psychic wounds and repercussions of her relationship with her father, Michael, an emotionally volatile, troubled World War I veteran, set the stage for a lifetime of disorder and anguish. Michael Langan, firmly convinced that he was sterile, claimed from the beginning that Dory was not his child. When Dory was eight, her father boarded up the dining room, and for four months he kept her, her mother, and her infant sister captive. Previn would later undergo decades of psychoanalysis and suffer a series of nervous collapses and psychiatric hospitalizations. Still, as a young girl and teenager, she did her best to sparkle and help keep her family afloat; she sang, danced, modeled, acted, and held down a string of odd jobs. She also wrote songs on the side. A chance 1958 encounter with *Singin' in the Rain* and *An American in Paris* producer Arthur Freed won her a junior lyricist job at MGM, where she met and began collaborating with pianist André Previn (né Priwin).

Born in 1929, Previn was a bona fide child prodigy. He had studied for five years at the Berlin Conservatory of Music beginning at age nine, financed by his wealthy lawyer father, an intimate of Arturo Toscanini and Jascha Heifetz, who were among the dinner guests at their frequent glittering parties. In 1945, the Priwins—renaming themselves Previn so that their son wouldn't be called "André Prune"—fled Germany for California. Aided by his uncle, Charles Previn, the head of music at Universal, André came to the attention of MGM at fifteen and was signed to a long-term contract. By 1946 he had recorded his debut piano jazz album, and that same year was appointed as the (uncredited) music supervisor on a Katharine Hepburn–Robert Taylor movie, *Undercurrent*, directed by Vincente Minnelli. Of his fourteen years at MGM, "a demented conservatory" as he described it, Previn said: "I loved the studio. I loved the way it smelled. I was crazy about the Indians in the lunchroom, and Romans making phone calls, and the highly charged and technically dazzling music-making on the recording stage. Most of all, I loved being a part of it, a part of a peculiar fraternity, belittled and superior at the same time, envied for all the wrong reasons and commiserated with for the stuff we all took in our stride." For Previn, the run-up to *Valley of the Dolls* included his winning four Oscars for Best Adapted Score for *Gigi, Porgy and Bess, Irma La Douce,* and *My Fair Lady.*

Before Dory, Previn was married for five years to Betty Bennett, whom he divorced in 1957 while she was pregnant with their second child. Once he and Dory wed in 1960, they began writing original songs for movies such as *Pepe,* for which Judy Garland crooned the Oscar-nominated "The Faraway Part of Town." Two years later, they earned another Oscar nomination for "Second Chance," for the Robert Mitchum–Shirley MacLaine movie *Two for the Seesaw.* On her own, Dory wrote lyrics for songs for *Tall Story* and *Goodbye Again,* both starring Anthony Perkins. Although the Previns were in demand and their tunes got recorded by major artists of the era, including Bobby Darin, Sammy Davis Jr., Rosemary Clooney, Nancy Wilson, Vic Damone, Doris Day, and Jack Jones, by 1965 their marriage was imploding. Still, they continued to collaborate on such movies as *Inside Daisy Clover*—another Judy Garland–esque, *ain't-Hollywood-awful?* assignment that led most directly to their being hired for *Valley of the Dolls.* That same year Dory was briefly hospitalized for a psychological collapse; surely she could identify with the turbulence of Neely O'Hara just as surely as she could empathize with the slow-moving tragedy that was Judy Garland's life.

After long discussions with Weisbart and Robson, it was decided that they would pen five original songs for *Valley,* the most music they had cowritten for a film to date. Those pastiche-type tunes were meant to be the calling card for a much bigger prize: an eighteen-song assignment on MGM's musical version of the beloved 1939 Oscar winner *Goodbye, Mr. Chips*, which, after losing two big directors, two major leading men, and three leading ladies, proved to be an ill-fated project in every respect. Asked about collaborating with his spouse, Previn said, "You must be able to argue with your collaborator. You can't be afraid to say, 'That stinks.' But you have to remember it's your working partner talking, not a husband or wife." On the evidence of the songs André and Dory Previn concocted for *Valley of the Dolls*, the two should have said "That stinks" more often. But one fact is indisputable: André Previn's championing of another young musician made a major contribution to *Valley of the Dolls*. Long before composer John Williams became known as "the world's most successful film composer," with fifty-one Oscar nominations, five Oscars, seven British Academy Film Awards, and twenty-four Grammy Awards for credits including *Star Wars*, *Jaws*, *E.T.*, *Schindler's List*, and *Close Encounters of the Third Kind*, he was still climbing Hollywood's Mount Everest. Williams, thirty-five at the time, had been a friend of André Previn's for years, and remained so until Previn's 2019 death.

The prodigiously talented Williams was the Manhattan-born son of percussionist Johnny Williams Sr., who played in the Raymond Scott Quintette, the CBS Radio Orchestra, and other radio show house bands. Right after one of radio's biggest hit shows, Lucky Strike's *Your Hit Parade*, became an NBC TV show, the senior Williams moved to Los Angeles with his wife, curly-haired and red-headed sixteen-year-old John, and younger son, Jerry, in tow. Williams Sr. played on several dozen movie and television scores as part of the staff orchestra at Columbia Pictures. When he and his fellow musicians would jam together off-hours, the piano chops of sixteen-year-old John, who had begun studying piano at seven, impressed the veteran pro musicians. At both UCLA and Los Angeles

City College, Williams studied with a number of teachers, including Robert Van Eps, a classical composer who'd been a music arranger at MGM since *The Wizard of Oz*. With fellow North Hollywood High School students, Williams launched a jazz quintet—called by *Time* in 1948 "the hottest band in Hollywood"—featuring young musicians skilled enough to jam at hip clubs with some of the town's best musicians. Williams himself wrote the quintet's charts and was so obviously talented that it wasn't long before he was playing solo at the legendary Cocoanut Grove.

At twenty-four, "Johnny Williams" joined the staff at Columbia Pictures as an arranger, and not long afterward he was lured by 20th, where he orchestrated motion picture scores for giants including Dimitri Tiomkin, Franz Waxman, Alfred Newman, and Lionel Newman. He married actress Barbara Ruick (daughter of actors Mel Ruick and Lurene Tuttle) in 1956, the year she played Carrie Pipperidge in 20th's movie version of *Carousel*, on the score of which Williams played piano. (They were together until Ruick's untimely death from a brain hemorrhage in 1974.) His impressive credentials and his connection with Previn set him up perfectly for the *Valley of the Dolls* gig, which he won over several other composers, including Jerry Goldsmith (Robson's *Von Ryan's Express*, *Our Man Flint*), Frank De Vol (*Hush . . . Hush, Sweet Charlotte*, *Cat Ballou*), Lionel Newman (*Gentlemen Prefer Blondes*, *The Pleasure Seekers*), and Franz Waxman (*Sunset Boulevard*, *Peyton Place*). The studio budgeted the combined costs for the Previns' songs and for John Williams's original score and orchestrations at $103,288.

THE LOOK

From the outset the Zanucks, producer Weisbart, and director Robson's mandate for production designer Richard Day was to give *Valley of the Dolls* visual opulence and scope—on a budget. Guided first by Harlan Ellison's 1966 screenplay draft, production designer

Day devised almost seventy different sets. Working with set decorators Walter M. Scott and Raphaël G. Bretton, Day was particularly enthusiastic about the designs for the sets backgrounding Neely O'Hara at her drunkest, most disorderly, and pathetic. For two barroom scenes, one in New York's theater district, the other in San Francisco, Day envisioned the character hemmed in by "dark, decadent reds" to underscore her anguish and to emphasize how fast and far she'd fallen. Day's production sketches are most attuned to the earliest screenplay attempts—particularly Harlan Ellison's. They envision a visually bolder, more ambitious, subjective, even arty movie—and, probably, a higher-budgeted one. Viewed years later, the production sketches and storyboards impress. Neely's barroom binge scene and breakdown in an alley by the theater are deliberately impressionistic, stylized, and meant to immerse the audience in her drug- and booze-addled perceptions. One storyboarded sequence begins on Neely's hand clutching a bottle of dolls in the unnatural glare of an overhead light. The camera would loosen to reveal her in her opening-number stage costume. She stares at the pill bottle while a solitary man watches her from the end of the bar. Over a close-up of the bartender's hand cleaning and stacking wineglasses would come the man's disembodied voice saying, "We're closing, Miss O'Hara," followed by an extreme close shot of Neely's bleary, unfocused eyes as she reacts. Then: a nightmarishly distorted point-of-view shot of the deserted theater alleyway across the street; giant overlapping close-ups of Neely's mouth crying out for help; one tear-filled eye and, superimposed in the eye, an image of her collapsing onto the pavement, and through special optical effects, her body appears to tumble and fall into the pupil of the eye; then a low-angle view of Neely sprawled across the wet pavement and her red, yellow, and blue pills spilling out of her prescription bottle and their colors running into a puddle. Finally, there would be a long, slow pullback as Neely struggles to pull herself back up against the brick wall as she cries out.

Other sketches suggest that Day, cinematographer William Daniels, and Travilla may have been in synch on taking a similarly skewed, subjective approach to the look of the film—offbeat camera angles, special effects, garish colors—as well as a mocking, judgmental stance toward the characters' idea of the Kennedy era, Camelot-glamorous "good life" of the '60s. Shades of Douglas Sirk and Michelangelo Antonioni, in fact. Director Mark Robson, alas, had a more obvious and conventional movie in mind.

CHAPTER ELEVEN

Feuding, Fighting, Fussing:
The Filming of the Dolls

With four hundred thousand English-language *Valley of the Dolls* hardcover copies in print, not counting one hundred thousand book club copies, and with the film's budget refined to slightly under $5 million (roughly $38 million today), the stage was set for the crew to capture the first footage for Production A 871. On East Coast locations with assistant directors Eli Dunn, Richard Kobritz, and Robert J. Koster, Mark Robson eased into things by filming exclusively with Barbara Parkins, who, limited to her brief eight-week hiatus from *Peyton Place*, needed to complete her movie chores as soon as possible. The film's shooting schedule required Parkins's availability from February 16 through 25, then from March 8 through May 15.

And so, in near-zero temperatures, Robson and cinematographer William Daniels captured Parkins and a hundred extras (recruited by area radio stations) doing their Currier and Ives–influenced best as they skated at Mount Kisco's Leonard Park ice rink. Local newspapers quoted one resident onlooker describing Robson as "focused, serious" while Parkins seemed "excited, very pretty and pleasant"; another noted how she never once heard the actress "complain about how awfully cold it was." For his part, Robson remarked to the crew how "fast and agile" Parkins was, after having had so much television experience. Assistant Director Koster, working with the director for the first time, was impressed by how "wonderful, intuitive" Robson was.

From Mount Kisco, with snow falling nearly the entire time, the company decamped to Katonah, New York, where they spent much of the following day filming Anne Welles's train departure to Manhattan, involving Parkins and actors Margot Stevenson (Mother), Judith Lowry (Aunt Amy), and Darryl Wells (Willy, Anne's soon-to-be-dumped hometown boyfriend). A day later, in atmospheric Redding Center, Connecticut, they captured Anne (in two changes of costume) entering and leaving her New England childhood home and walking in the nearby woods, as well as some background shots of church and other home exteriors. Leon Fitzgerald and Ed Longo, doubles for actor Paul Burke, were filmed at that same time, and the village green at Bedford Village, New York, supplied the backdrop for exteriors depicting Anne walking in Lawrenceville and entering and exiting the Lawrenceville Inn.

During the company's stint in Redding Center, local resident Edward Steichen, the world-renowned eighty-eight-year-old photographer known for his fatally glamorous portraits of the beautiful and not so beautiful, stopped by to visit his old friend and fellow painter with light, William Daniels. The two artists had, separately, created some of *the* definitive images of Greta Garbo in photographic portraits and on the movie screen. While on the *Valley of the Dolls* set, Steichen is not known to have taken any photos of Barbara Parkins, who confided to interviewer Peer Oppenheimer and others, "I don't want just to be compared with Marilyn Monroe or Joan Crawford. I want to be a real star, another Garbo."

On to the official start of production in New York City, where the script called for a city to be blanketed in snow, but where skies were gray and rainy with only occasional flurries. Production manager Chico Day had to arrange for truckloads of fake snow (composed of crushed gypsum and lime) to be shipped to the city, where it would then be sprayed and spread around the shooting locations. With the convoy en route, a full-scale blizzard struck, stranding the trucks midtrip and leaving Parkins, forty paid extras, and the crew helpless while more than a foot of snow fell on the city.

For public consumption, though, everything related to *Valley of the Dolls* was upbeat. To mark the start date of principal photography, the March 9 edition of the *New York Times* carried a splashy full-page ad bankrolled by 20th Century Fox. Considering the movie that was eventually made from *Valley of the Dolls*, it's hard not to laugh when reading the flagrantly purple copy issued by the studio's chief publicist, James Denton:

NO AMBER LIGHTS, PLEASE. NO GAUZE ON THE CAMERAS. JUST THE HOT, WHITE LIGHT OF TRUTH. TODAY, THE KLIEG LIGHTS GO ON AS *VALLEY OF THE DOLLS* GOES BEFORE THE MOTION PICTURE CAMERAS. Now, production is beginning on Jacqueline Susann's novel while it is still high on the best-seller lists after more than a year. In order to recapture all the vividness and excitement which has made "Valley" such an all-time favorite, many of the New York locations described in the book will be used as actual shooting sites.

Now too, the women of *Valley of the Dolls* come alive. Neely O'Hara—to her, stardom was too many minks, martinis and men. Jennifer North—she gave all she had to a world that gave nothing in return. Anne Welles—who saw them all for what they were but couldn't help becoming a part of it.

Valley of the Dolls boldly breaks into the playground of Broadway and Hollywood—where the games are rough, but open to all aspirants who want to play.

Director Mark Robson—whose credits include *Von Ryan's Express* and *Peyton Place*—will bring to life the places and people from the story that is already being called "the *Peyton Place* of show business." And you know who put *Peyton Place* on the screen. 20th Century Fox.

Mark Robson acknowledged the showy publicity by writing to Jonas Rosenfield Jr., 20th Century Fox vice president and director of Advertising, Publicity, and Exploitation: "Saw the ad in the *Times* and on behalf of the whole company of *Valley of the Dolls*, we thank you. It's great." Meanwhile, Robson, staying at the Sherry-Netherland, received this telegram from Darryl F. Zanuck almost forty-eight hours *before* the director got a congratulatory telegram from Richard D. Zanuck: "Dear Mark, Best of luck on the start of *Valley of the Dolls*, what I know will be a real winner. Fond good wishes. D.Z." The senior Zanuck also cabled Patty Duke, staying at Alrae Hotel and Apartments (today the Hotel Plaza Athenée): "Know you will be great as Neely. Stay well. Best of luck, D.Z." Although Zanuck still lamented Candice Bergen's and Julie Christie's turning down the role of Anne, he wired Barbara Parkins, somewhat ambiguously: "Hope *Valley* does as much for you as you do for it. Best, D.Z." while he cabled Sharon Tate, about whose abilities he expressed doubts: "Know you will be an excellent Jennifer. D.Z." Richard Zanuck telegrammed Paul Burke: "Good luck, Paul. Lyon will be an exciting character in your hands."

Most of the other acting talent and some crew members were ensconced by 20th at the venerable St. Moritz. Joining the team was former dancer Robert Sidney, who choreographed the 1949 Broadway musical *Along Fifth Avenue*, featuring Jackie Gleason, Nancy Walker, and (close friend of Jacqueline Susann's) Joyce Mathews. In 1950, Sidney choreographed the young Broadway fireballs (and wife and husband-to-be) Joan McCracken and Bob Fosse in *Dance Me a Song*; in Hollywood, he choreographed Susan Hayward's hootchy-kootchy dance in the ill-fated 1956 costume epic *The Conqueror*, and also worked on *The Opposite Sex* and *Where the Boys Are.* David Weisbart had flown in Sidney from LA to coach Patty Duke in movements and gestures that might help her be more convincing as a rising singing superstar while performing "Give a Little More" and "It's Impossible"; later, when back in Los Angeles, Sidney would be tasked with staging Helen Lawson's song numbers for Judy Garland.

Sharon Tate and Tony Scotti flew from LA to New York on Wednesday, March 15, in order to wrap their scenes by the seventeenth and loop back to Los Angeles that same night. On the sixteenth, Paul Burke and Martin Milner flew from Los Angeles to New York along with David Weisbart's frequent music editor, Kenneth Wannberg (who later went on to do *Hello, Dolly!* and later still, extensive work for Steven Spielberg and George Lucas), and makeup man Ernie Parks, known for his contributions to such 20th Century Fox movies of the '40s and '50s as *The Snake Pit* and *American Guerrilla in the Philippines.*

On March 16, Robson began the morning's shooting with a romantic walk and park bench interlude between Sharon Tate and Tony Scotti filmed in Carl Schurz Park. The picturesque park, named for the soldier, statesman, and journalist, runs along the East River from East Eighty-fourth Street to East Ninetieth Street, near Gracie Mansion. During shooting, bitter winds whipped off the river, making the ten-degree temperatures feel even colder. As with most actors—especially newcomers fearful of being fired at any moment—the shivering Tate and Scotti did not complain and shared warmed-up gloves between takes. Robson dispensed cigarettes and Napoleon brandy to his cast and crew. And although he preferred the looser, more offhanded performances the actors had given in their screen tests, for the sake of staying on schedule, and before his actors' teeth began chattering, he moved on, holding out the option of later reshooting all or part of the scene on the set.

That same day, as snow pelted the city, the company made short work of a series of (subsequently cut) establishing shots of Barbara

Parkins arriving at Grand Central Station and hailing a cab. During his first assignment as an assistant director, Robert J. Koster, who recalled thousands of tourists and locals watching the filming from behind police lines, grew fond of actor Paul Burke. Koster, whose father, Henry Koster, directed such films as *The Bishop's Wife* and *The Robe*, thought of Burke as a brother "under the skin." Koster recalled in 2013 how the actor preferred to sleep overnight in his trailer on location rather than at a hotel and how, like Lyon Burke, he rarely spent the night alone: "Every morning he and I had the same routine. I knocked on his door and identified myself. He asked me in. He was in the back bedroom, always attended, usually with a different lady every day. As the two looked up sleepily from the bed he would say, 'Bob, I want you to meet my new secretary (insert name here).' I paid the lady her due respect, even if she was stark naked, and left the motor home confident that Paul would be on set in a half hour. He always was." Apparently, the married Burke—like Lyon Burke—didn't pull well in double harness.

The night before Patty Duke's first day of filming, she woke up screaming. It wasn't the first time that had happened; it wouldn't be the last. Still, on March 16, she and a limo driver braved the snowstorm and Duke climbed out at the Playhouse Theater, where from 1959 to 1961, she had starred in *The Miracle Worker*. Along with her considerable talent, in those days Duke brought major issues to the set. Her obsessive fear of death, for instance. For another, seething resentment for ex–guardian/managers John and Ethel Ross, opportunistic leeches who put her to work at age seven; changed her name; kept her away from other children; micromanaged her diet, grooming, and wardrobe; plied her as a child with alcohol and barbiturates; sexually molested her; and swindled her out of $1 million in earnings. Then there were the effects of Duke's chronic drug and alcohol use, her alarming mood swings, and the multiple suicide attempts that led to psychiatric hospitalizations. Daily production notes indicate that makeup artists needed extra time to camouflage her bottom lip, broken out in an angry fever blister. Duke said,

"One side of the lip was so much more voluptuous than the other, it looked dreadful."

Her first shots required her to lurch and stagger from a bar to the theater across the street. Robson called for a couple of retakes for technical glitches, and Duke mock-complained to him that as she stood in the bar awaiting her cue to exit, a horny male customer persistently kept trying to ply her with booze. At the time of filming, the featured production at the Playhouse was the generation gap comedy *The Impossible Years*; it was the final production to play there. Patrons pouring out after seeing the show might have been confused by the marquee and lobby posters that had been changed from "Alan King in *The Impossible Years*" to "Neely O'Hara in *Tell Me, Darling*." (Note: The poster lists one of O'Hara's costars as "Chico Dayson," an inside joke on the nickname of the movie's production manager Francisco "Chico" Day.)

Duke got through the silent scene just fine. But she knew that the rest of the day and into the evening would be spent capturing moments that are among the few featuring all three young heroines together, despite how so much of the novel's power and appeal stemmed from Jacqueline Susann's interweaving of the lives of friends and frenemies. Coming out of makeup, it would be Duke's first time being confronted by the movie star sheen of two stunners, the sweet, beguiling Sharon Tate and the cool, reserved Barbara Parkins. Harboring deep insecurities about her diminutive height and physical appearance, how could Duke not feel a bit like teenage Judy Garland had while making *Ziegfeld Girl*, getting hit daily with double doses of the dazzle and lollapalooza of costars Lana Turner *and* Hedy Lamarr?

As if Duke's plate weren't already overflowing, after a decade of film and TV performances, a blockbuster run on Broadway, an Oscar win, and fronting three seasons of her self-titled TV series, she was receiving second billing under newcomer Barbara Parkins, whose major claims to fame were sultry good looks, a knack for self-promotion, and her well-earned popularity as the hottest thing on the TV pop culture phenomenon that was *Peyton Place*. That said, Duke had nabbed the film's juiciest, showiest role, one for which Parkins herself had gone all out. For their part, how could Parkins and Sharon Tate not feel slightly apprehensive about sharing scenes with such an experienced, trained, and acclaimed actor? As Cary Grant put it, in the sexist mind-set of his era, "Women who want to be actresses have a disease. Wanting to be a star is all-enveloping. It's not a very feminine pursuit." These factors and more laid the groundwork for crackling tensions and insecurities that would play out throughout the filming, as each actress, in her own way, came out swinging.

On March 16, Parkins breezed through silent shots depicting Anne Welles walking into the theater hall, asking for directions from the receptionist, played by scene-stealer Thelma (*The Pajama Game*) Pelish, making her way past several rehearsal spaces, and watching from the balcony as Duke as Neely sings for her fellow gypsies André and Dory Previn's ballad meant to be in the Garland style, "Give a Little More."

Duke considered herself an able vocalist. In 1965, during the run of ABC's *The Patty Duke Show*, she had scored a top-ten hit on the Billboard Hot 100 with "Don't Just Stand There," a Lesley Gore–style "You Don't Own Me" type of ballad written by Lor Crane and Bernice Ross. Three other (less popular) Billboard Hot 100 entries, "Say Something Funny," "Funny Little Butterflies," and "Whenever He Holds You," followed, as well as several albums, all recorded for the United Artists label.

Duke resented Mark Robson's forcing her to mime to a pre-recorded music track. She was also anxious that, despite her sessions with choreographer Robert Sidney, she might not move like a singer, let alone one who is supposed to be phenomenally talented. She believed she had made big gains in her preproduction classes in singing, diction, and voice deepening, so much so that she had told coworkers and the press about her plans to create a Vegas (and beyond) nightclub act that would include "It's Impossible" and "Give a Little More." (In the words of Holly Golightly, the mind reels.)

"I knew I couldn't sing like a trained singer, but I wanted to do the songs," Duke said. "They wanted someone with a fantastic voice. I thought it was important for Neely maybe to be pretty good in the beginning, but the deterioration should be that raw, nerve-ending kind of the thing. And I couldn't convince the director." Duke persisted in thinking that her own singing voice—or at least some electronically sweetened version of it—would be heard in the final movie. But when she realized that was not going to happen, she was bitterly disappointed. Said Marni Nixon, the brilliantly talented lyric soprano and "ghost singer" for Deborah Kerr in *The King and I*, Natalie Wood in *West Side Story*, and Audrey Hepburn in *My Fair Lady*, "Non-singers can't hear themselves accurately. Even if an actress works hard and studies with a coach before making a movie, if their singing is weak, flat, or sharp, they just won't know it. It can be difficult for actors getting the news that someone else is going to sing for them, even worse if they only find out when they see the finished picture."

And so Duke performed the scene along with several musicians (including rehearsal pianist Marvin Hamlisch) and extras posing as Broadway "gypsies," miming to the track recorded by a session singer. Duke said, "I don't know who the girl is they used. The first girl was fired and I never met the second girl." The second girl was singer Gail Heideman (sometimes billed as Gaille Heidemann), who went on to success as a songwriter recorded by Dusty Springfield and Ann-Margret and as a voice actor for TV's *Kung Fu Panda: Legends of Awesomeness* and video games including *World of Warcraft: Legion*. Although Heideman convincingly matched Duke's vocal tone and diction, she had neither the right material nor projected the unmistakable star quality that might have helped Duke convincingly portray a meteoric talent. By comparison, imagine the difference if the moviemakers had been successful in casting, say, Barbra Streisand as Neely.

With Duke and Parkins finished for the day but remaining on the set, along with actors Martin Milner and Robert Viharo, things grew tense when it came time for Robson to work with Sharon Tate. For Tate's big entrance—scripted, storyboarded, and preplanned in elaborate detail by the production designer and the cinematographer—her character was to have risen up, Ziegfeld Girl–style, from the stage below, a Venus on the half shell sporting a weighty, towering royal blue feathered headdress. But Robson scuttled the idea for something simpler and more economical but painful for the actress. Instead, he required Tate to descend one of the West Forty-fifth Street theater's wooden staircases to applause, catcalls, and bawdy stripper music—and in heels, yet.

One or two takes should have been sufficient for the usually perfunctory, five-takes-*tops* Robson, yet the director obsessively reshot the scene, requiring Tate to climb and descend the dozen or so stairs again and again. Duke, who thought Tate "a divine creature," observed to her friend and coauthor William J. Jankowski in their 2018 book, "[Robson] didn't say, 'Could you hold your hands a different way this time?' In my interpretation, he just wanted to watch her dwindle and get tired. There finally came a point where it was obvious to everyone that there was no need to do take twenty-seven and we finished that portion of the scene." Robson's battering baffled other actors on the set, particularly when his aggression was directed at Tate, whom actor Robert Viharo called "the sweetest, purest, most open spirit." With Duke and Robson already oil and water, when the scene wrapped, the actress approached Tate and commiserated, calling the director "that fucking bastard." Though Tate refused to verbally bash Robson, she gained Duke's instant admiration for never giving the director the satisfaction of letting him break her stride. Recalled a crew member, "[Robson] never communicated what he wanted, just that Sharon should do the same things over and over. She wanted to please him, but it seemed like he singled her out and was trying to break her or kind of make her an example or something. Once I heard him mutter and call her 'hippy-dippy,' which surprised me because it was cruel but also because Robson was such a square that I couldn't imagine him even knowing about George Carlin and his 'hippy-dippy' weatherman thing. Anyway, seeing a director treat someone as sensitive as Sharon like that was uncomfortable to be around. I noticed that he was fine on the set with the guys who were there, like Martin Milner and Robert Viharo. I only got to observe Sharon Tate in person that one time, but she was like a ray of sunlight, full of life, good-natured, friendly to everyone, not just the 'important' people. That poor girl, though, I thought the director got really mean about it."

Robson was hardly the only prickly pear on the set. His and Patty Duke's clashes became the stuff of legend. But was their conflict strictly a matter of Method in her madness? Madness in her Method? Or a complex mix of both? In any case, Patty Duke's whiplash mood pockets and oddities had become common knowledge around Hollywood, and as misunderstood as those symptoms were at the time, blind items and carefully couched references began appearing in print long before the film's release. "Patty Duke was a little twit," said actress Patricia Winters, a red-haired Rita Hayworth look-alike and beauty contest winner who had earlier appeared in *Jeanne Eagels* and *Marjorie Morningstar*. In *Valley of the Dolls*, Winters played a beautiful redheaded client and dinner date of Lyon Burke's. Winters recalled, "She made it unpleasant for everybody and was so moody and strange, playing up the 'star' bit to the hilt. She had absolutely no interest in being the least bit kind or friendly to anyone she didn't think was on her level. What she had to do should have taken hours, not days. To be honest, though, we secretly thanked her for making so many mistakes and being so demanding because it meant we got paid for extra days. She didn't seem to like anybody on that movie—certainly not Mark Robson."

Before the company packed up and traveled to the West Coast to continue filming, Robson captured outdoor footage of Patty Duke bouncing on a trampoline for a montage sequence. Actress-singer Suze Lanier-Bramlett, known for playing John Travolta's girlfriend on *Welcome Back, Kotter* and for being among the terrified in Wes Craven's *The Hills Have Eyes*, recalls observing the filming.

"I had just arrived in New York and was all excited to see a real movie star," says Lanier-Bramlett. "I was a fan of Patty Duke. I just happened to run into an area where they were filming and everything was very brightly lit. The first thing that struck me was, 'Patty Duke is so tiny.' But that quickly went out of my mind because she was out of control, yelling at a few bystanders. *What are you looking at? Quit staring at me!* She was also quite belligerent to the crew. I remember saying to the friend I was with, 'What a bitch!' After I saw her behaving that way, I have to say I *was* a fan of Patty Duke."

Assistant director Robert J. Koster, in contrast, called Duke "surprising." He noted her "reputation for being temperamental and eccentric" and yet judged her to be "professional in every respect, worked well with the crew, and generally belied all the rumors. Good actress, too." In any case, Duke's aforementioned trampoline and touch-your-toes stuff—some of which was later reshot at 20th and optically superimposed over an orange backdrop using a Duke double—were incorporated into a clumsy, poor man's version of *A Star Is Born*–type montage, this one only suitable for a cheesy '60s TV special. The footage, cut to a jazzy, up-tempo John Williams arrangement combining "It's Impossible" and "Give a Little More," depicts Neely awakening, showering, exercising, walking on the 20th lot, being put through her paces by a vocal coach (played by prolific character actress Peggy Rea, whose credits include an episode of *The Patty Duke Show*) and a choreographer (Robert Street, who danced in *Gentlemen Prefer Blondes*) who shares his bottle of dolls, as Mel watches disapprovingly.

When the time came for the three stars of *Valley of the Dolls* to interact, the absence of significant scenes together might have blunted the movie's impact but also might have been a blessing for the production. A supporting actor on the picture observed, "Duke, Parkins, and Tate—those girls came out of their corners with their dukes up, wanting to be major stars. Who could blame them? But it was really something to watch." With the New York leg of the shooting wrapped, the company flew back west to begin filming on the 20th lot. Days later, an overheated Hollywood columnist predicted: "After *Valley of the Dolls*, Patty Duke will become the next Bette Davis and Barbara Parkins the new Joan Crawford."

From a career résumé standpoint, that Hollywood insider's prediction didn't pan out. Though Parkins's on-set relationship with Duke started uneventfully, it would soon emanate fire and ice reminiscent of Davis and Crawford's raging professional animosity. The studio, Weisbart, and Robson hosted a social gathering for the key players—nothing too fancy by Hollywood standards, just a nice catered, open-bar, meet-mix-and-mingle affair. It soon became apparent, though, that Duke and Parkins might not often be hanging out together any more than they had to. Although completely professional, Parkins was cordial and frosty, and Duke only slightly less so. Tate, on the other hand, magnetized everyone with her unassuming charm and likability. She struck Duke as "a nymph" with a penchant for bawdiness and mischief—a knockout with a knockabout knack for playfulness: "If there was some fun to be had or harmless trouble to get into, she was first in line," Duke told her coauthor Jankowski in 2018.

That gathering, Patty Duke also recalled, was where she "first met Jackie [Susann]." Despite Duke's finding the novelist to be "super-duper glamorous and gracious" and someone who "carried herself in those Pucci dresses like someone to be reckoned with," Duke apparently learned at that party—through crew scuttlebutt—that she was *not* Susann's first choice to play Neely. By a mile. Duke said years later, "From the way Jackie acted toward me, though, I never would have known." Had this been a less important movie for Duke, had Duke been in a better place emotionally, she might have shrugged it off. Instead, the knowledge helped goad her into acting the living hell out of the role, to prove the doubters how wrong they were—one or two of whom just might have been working alongside her. Duke, decades later, recalled, "I know that soon after I auditioned, Barbara Parkins had also auditioned for the role of Neely. I got the part of Neely, and Barbara wound up with the far less interesting role of Anne Welles. This might shed some light on feelings Barbara may have had about me that were less than friendly. Perhaps she had resented me, since I got the role she had so coveted. Barbara was a bit aloof on the set, and I don't remember being anything but nice to her, and why would I treat her differently than I had treated any other person on that film? Now that I am thinking of it, to have to act with me where I was getting to chew up the scenery as Neely—and she *really* wanted that part— must have been devastating to her. Bless your heart, Barbara."

Unlike the success-driven Duke or Parkins, Sharon Tate said, "What I want out of life is happiness. I don't want money. I drive a Buick Riviera. I have all the clothes I want. I like myself. I'm glad I'm me. I'd like to have a baby." Everyone seemed smitten with Tate. Well, almost everyone. As Duke recalled, "I was crazy about her and I don't know anyone but our director who wasn't crazy about her." Tate's fellow actors and crew members noted director Robson treating her as if she were the gorgeous, not especially bright Jennifer North and not the lovely, kind, anxious-to-please Sharon Tate. One of Tate's *Valley* coworkers recalled her as "one part flower child, one part aspiring Encino housewife, she was so trusting, good-hearted, nurturing, and sweet that it was too easy for the wrong kind of person to use her or sell her short." Robson frequently treated her, in Duke's estimation, as if she were "an imbecile." If one believes Roman Polanski's detractors, Tate hardly needed to leave home to get similar treatment.

One case in point: the company spent several days on location at 22470 Pacific Coast Highway, Malibu, California, a 4,800-square-foot private home built in the late '40s and owned by a prominent lawyer. The property was expensively rented to the production to serve as the unhappy homestead of Mel and the by now out-of-control bitch on wheels movie queen Neely. The director seemed to be more excited about the casting of the house than of his actors. As Robson said, "This house, perfect for Neely—everything is a bit too much";

as for the homeowner's existing furnishings and decor, he called it "the kind of stuff that shrieks, 'I am very *expensive.*'" There to document the shooting was the esteemed Italian movie set and portrait photographer Pierluigi Praturlon, a favorite of Federico Fellini's who had also became close friends with Sharon Tate.

Now might be the time to talk about the controversial stopwatch, the one Robson almost always used whenever he was shooting. On *Valley of the Dolls* the director demanded his actors move and speak their lines within a prescribed amount of time—usually much, much faster. And they had to do it again and again until they got it right—or at least according to Robson's concept of right. Patty Duke railed, "He literally used a stopwatch in his hand during filming and he was not even embarrassed about it. He was cutting the film as they went along. Even if you do that, you don't admit it."

As Robson filmed Tate and Martin Milner in the poolside scene, he held that stopwatch in plain sight, clocking Tate as if she were being paid by the hour and demanding the exact timing of her movements. Again, she couldn't seem to please him, and the filming dragged on. Martin Milner thought Robson's method "not necessarily the way to get someone's best work." Duke, calling the director's behavior "inexplicable," said, "Robson told Sharon she was to enter on a certain line, which is nothing unusual. Then he told her she was to sit down on a certain word, unbutton her top button on another word, and so on until the jacket was open. What was that all about? What does it matter when the button was open? It's not as if they were shooting some sex scene where he wanted her beautiful breasts revealed at a certain time. He just tortured her with it. 'No, no, Sharon. Not like that! I told you, the first button should be on the word "the"'! This went on for well over an hour. Again, her inner strength would not allow him to see that she was humiliated, but we were all humiliated for her. I don't know what he thought he was proving, because he was the only one who wound up looking like an asshole." The essentially powerless cast members took out their anger and frustrations in the tiny, passive-aggressive ways they could. Duke recalled how she and Tate "were always making faces at Robson and giving the evil eye behind his back, but he had the last laugh. We were the ones who ended up looking ridiculous."

Robson printed several of the dozens of takes he extracted from Tate; later, he had her repeat the scene, matching it in close-up. Duke and Tate wandered off together out of earshot. Tate rolled her eyes and replied, "I got so tired but I wasn't going to complain and fall on my sword." Duke has said, "She wouldn't cry [in front of Robson] because she was such a pro and didn't want to mess up her makeup. She asked me what she did wrong, as she assumed it was she who had the problem. I told her nothing was wrong with her, but that the man doesn't have a clue as to what he was doing. I told her he just wanted to make the pretty girl look stupid. That helped reinforce what she already knew. She never retaliated, but she never gave him what he wanted, which, I believe, was to make Sharon cry or have a tantrum on the set. I am the one who gave him that."

Barbara Parkins said, "He was always trying to make Sharon cry, which would bring up emotion. He was always having her in tears. He wanted her to *emote*." Duke said she could tell Tate was a good actress because in her scenes as Jennifer, she completely switched off the distinctive, fun-loving "twinkle" she had offscreen: "Instead, she went to her ultimate vulnerable place for that role." But Duke came to regret that neither she nor any of her fellow actors truly stood up for Tate in the moment: "Actors are chickenshits. It has to be something dangerous before we will speak up about it. Sharon was afraid of hurting someone's feelings, and that was why she didn't speak up. People don't like ugly people, and they don't like pretty people, and when you couple beauty with intelligence, you have a big firecracker."

With Tate and Milner released for the day, Robson's focus turned to the scene dramatizing Neely's finding her live-in lover Ted Casablanca (played by Alex Davion) cavorting in their swimming pool with his new young playmate. To play Casablanca's side chick—the one Neely calls a "little tramp"—the moviemakers had chosen Leslie McRay, an eighteen-year-old international cover girl and model who came to the attention of the 20th casting directors in an episode of *The Man from U.N.C.L.E.* and from recent newspaper photos of her winning the latest of her California beauty pageant titles. McRay, a former schoolmate of Darryl F. Zanuck's children Richard and Darrilyn, called making her film debut in this particularly memorable scene "a complete turnaround for someone so terribly shy, I could barely walk across a stage in a beauty contest, let alone say 'Thank you' when I won. Everyone I knew was excited when I got cast. I mean, this was a big, important movie everyone was talking about. The whole thing was a Hollywood education for me."

Given the loosening of Hollywood censorship restrictions after the heated legal battles over groundbreakers like *The Moon Is Blue*, *The Pawnbroker*, and *Blow-Up*, Robson decided to exploit the new permissiveness. For the nighttime pool escapade, the director wanted McRay and Davion to expose as much bare flesh as possible. McRay admitted reporting for the Malibu location night shoot feeling "really scared about what we might be asked to do—until they brought out these rubber pieces that covered up the particular parts." A strapless rubber bra protected McCray's upper torso; a rubber bikini bottom covered her below the waist. Recalled McRay, "Luckily, Alex Davion, who I'd never met before, was not only really handsome but a very classy guy. And Mark Robson? A consummate professional, knew what he wanted and was just the greatest gentleman. He was so nice that I just wanted to please him. He made it an adventure for me."

The temperature had dropped to thirty degrees by the time the crew was ready for the first take, but Robson took Davion aside and tried persuading him to dive into the pool stark naked. He apparently intended to shoot the actor's backside for the movie's release in countries with more relaxed attitudes toward nudity. Davion refused—even for art's sake. On Robson's signal, a production assistant rolled out a cart bearing Napoleon brandy and crystal snifters to warm up and relax his cast, and in the end, Davion performed one take au naturel. McRay, who completed her brief role in the wee small hours, recalled, "Mark Robson shot a lot of my backside as I climbed out of the pool but there was much less in the movie as it was released, which I was glad about. The nicest person to me on that set was Patty Duke. When I jumped out of the pool and ran, I was freezing cold. Patty ran right over and put a robe around me. She was so nice and sympathetic. You don't forget something that nice." McRay, who denied detecting any tension between director Robson and Duke during her brief time on set, observed, "What struck me about Patty Duke was her baby face and, at first, I thought they'd been wrong about casting her. But, whatever [Robson] must have done, he got a really good performance out of her. People don't talk much about how courageous it was of those actors—and everyone—to make that movie. 1967 was only the beginning of the drug generation. Today, drugs are common, but it wasn't so talked about then."

Much of Friday, April 14, was devoted to capturing the film-within-a-film "French nudie" footage of Sharon Tate and actor Philippe Auber tangling in the sheets. Under the gaze of William Daniels's camera, as well as that of a studio-hired still photographer snapping away at Tate and Auber, Robson rarely directed the actors beyond "Roll over and over and over." Later, producer David Weisbart watched as 20th publicist extraordinaire Regina Gruss showed Tate the photographer's publicity photos of herself scantily clad. Tate—whose contract guaranteed her photo approval—studied the images and said, "I want none of these to go out. None, none, none." Weisbart whispered: "Sharon's very sensitive."

On April 17, Barbara Parkins filmed her own "nude scene" with Paul Burke. Although slightly daring for Hollywood films at the time, the flesh exposed in both the Anne and Jennifer scenes is almost laughably coy and puritanical by contemporary standards.

Back then, though, even the suggestion of nudity in an American movie could spark a hullabaloo in the press. Army Archerd's *Daily Variety* column for April 17 excitedly reported how Sharon Tate had spent an entire day filming her French "nudie," that Duke had completed a pool scene half-clad and that Parkins had shot her nude silhouette moment. Parkins told a *Vancouver Sun* reporter, "I have this nude scene, but there is nothing more beautiful than a nude scene if it is done in good taste. In the film, you have innocence and you have womanhood. The transition is just beautiful. But, you know, I used to have fantasies about what was ahead for me. Now they're beginning to come true. It's exciting and exhausting. It's not at all like television. You look on the big screen and you see yourself in super-human form. And in the movies, they treat you like a personality. You're not just somebody working there. There are so many preparations to be made, so much planning. And you know people are saying, 'Can she do it? Can she *really* do it?' And you know that now you're facing the real test."

In the days following, Parkins proved herself masterful in whipping up publicity. She teased Jack Bradford of the *Hollywood Reporter* with the promise of her having done "not one, but two nude scenes and one semi-nude scene in slow motion!!" The hype was effective, but little of that footage turned up in the finished movie. She told another columnist: "People say, 'How could you do it? Don't you have any morals?' But they can't wait to see it. I was embarrassed because lots of people were standing around watching. I had to tell myself it wasn't for the sake of prurience, it was about a woman's first love affair, which should be a beautiful thing. My first love affair was miserable. When I did the bed scene with Paul Burke, I remembered all of it. I was twenty-two and very naïve. You know what it is? It's been made easy for men in this town. So many beautiful girls, they can have their pick. You have to go through a few love affairs to find a sensitive man."

One actress who worked briefly on the picture said, "Sharon Tate, Barbara Parkins, and Patty Duke reminded me of the three most beautiful girls in a sorority. They were competitors, sure, but they were also so kind of fun to watch—especially from a distance. I remember how interested they were in each other's makeup tricks. I was, too. I watched them like a hawk." Sharon Tate, for instance, kept a tiny mirror in her cleavage to check herself out before each take—for self-protection, not vanity. Duke concurred: "Sharon rarely looked at her face in the mirror. She must have known she didn't have to. However, just before a shot, she would use that small mirror and check her lips and make sure they were okay. I would usually look for a split second, for the same reason. Often, I would get mascara under my eye, because back then when I smiled, my cheeks came up very far. There are makeup people to do touchups, but I felt it was my responsibility since I was the one making it do that." Barbara Parkins has said that she believed that Tate did her own makeup: "She was gorgeous anyway, but the style of makeup she chose for herself—well, she glowed, she was so perfect."

Apparently, though, it wasn't a glow Robson was after. He consulted with the film's stellar makeup artist, Ben Nye, who helped glorify 20th Century Fox glamour-pusses Gene Tierney, Betty Grable, Susan Hayward, Marilyn Monroe, and Candice Bergen. Robson—never one to avoid a cliché—wanted Tate to look less dewy and more hardened, "like a showgirl," but she adamantly refused, and Nye helped talk Robson out of the idea. Starlet Patricia Winters said, "Anyone would have been crazy to try and think that they could improve on that makeup. Sharon was perfect. When she and I made up in the ladies' dressing room across from the set, I was fascinated that she brushed her eyebrows up. She was so sweet, she showed me how, and shared her makeup tips." Several women making the film recall Tate's taking pains to point out her imperfections. She'd display a diagonal scar under her left eye (the result of a fall onto a shard of corrugated tin at age five), another scar to the left side of her eye, and a chicken pox scar on her forehead. She told Robson and her coworkers that she wouldn't dream of having her scars removed. "I'm very proud of them," she said, "They're me." But Duke gives the crown to Barbara Parkins for being "the best at fixing her makeup. Barbara knew what she was looking for, and what she was looking at, and it didn't make her self-conscious."

The absence of warmth between Patty Duke and Barbara Parkins became increasingly apparent to their coworkers, especially in contrast with the obvious affection in the separate friendships of Parkins and Tate and Duke and Tate. An actor who worked with them recalls, "There was big, heavy competition with those girls, especially between Patty and Barbara, a lot of posturing going on and a lot of currying for favor, jockeying to be top dog. They put tons of pressure on themselves to make sure this movie was their *big* break. They wanted to be huge movie stars and they worked at it. It was obvious they didn't like each other. Barbara would polish off her scenes so professionally and just glide away from the set, cool as a cucumber. Patty would go full tilt in her scenes, then hit the crafts service table and eat, eat, eat."

Actress Patricia Winters was on Team Parkins, at least on this score: "Where Barbara Parkins was professional and competitive, Sharon Tate was so beautiful and sweet to everybody; with Patty Duke, everything she did, she made into a problem. Everything was a negotiation, an argument. It had to be her way. I didn't think she was worth the trouble because you could tell she was going to be so bad in the role. After a while, I'd just stand back and marvel at how unpleasant she made things for us all and how much time she wasted."

Parkins and Tate would often stand on the sidelines and watch Duke work because, as Parkins later said, "[she] had won an Oscar at something like seven years old and she was the pro and we thought, 'This is pretty amazing.'" Parkins once described Duke as "somewhat of a recluse" who "stayed off to the side when filming wasn't being done." She added, "But contrary to popular belief,

Patty and I were not enemies. We were not friends. But we were not enemies."

The same went for Parkins and her on-screen lover, actor Paul Burke. Robson and Weisbart paired them hoping they'd throw romantic sparks, but they fizzled. Burke appeared to be game; Parkins decidedly not. Citing their twenty-year age difference as one reason for the disconnect, Parkins would prepare herself for her romantic scenes with Burke by staring at a photo of singer-songwriter Cat Stevens in her dressing room. (Who says wishing won't make it so? A few years later, Parkins and Stevens became romantically involved.) Patricia Winters experienced Paul Burke completely differently. She said, "He was a dream—so kind. He was just beginning to have a movie career, and *Valley of the Dolls* was an important step for him. Yet when we rehearsed a kissing scene, he stopped us and said, 'Pat, when we shoot this scene, make sure you put that beautiful face in front of mine. Don't hide it.'"

Unlike the uneasy undercurrents in Duke and Parkins's relationship, the tensions between Duke and Robson only grew stronger and more obvious during the course of the shoot. According to Duke, the director "complained about everything I did and when he did, I'd just go to the crafts service table and put on weight." Things came to a head more than once, but especially during a particularly grueling week of filming. On Monday, Robson shot Duke's character being violently attacked and pummeled by another sanatorium patient. (Duke and Donna Mantoan filmed a longish scene, with dialogue, but it was trimmed to the bone before release.) On Tuesday, psychiatric hospital nurses played by the single-named Ellaraino (billed sometimes as Ella Raino Edwards) and Darlene Conley (decades before her seven-year stint on *The Bold and the Beautiful*) forcibly restrained her in a hydrotherapy tub. Duke, armed with firsthand experience of the horrors and abuses sometimes inflicted on patients in such hospitals, spent the day emoting at fever pitch. But instead of Robson working closely with his keyed-up leading lady on a scene front-loaded with potential psychological triggers, the director delegated most of the filming to his assistant director, Eli Dunn (*Von Ryan's Express*). While Dunn put Duke through her paces on the soundstage, Robson was being interviewed in a nearby office by Michael Scott, the director-host of the Granada TV series *Cinema*.

Scott, who described Robson as the "perpetrator" of *Valley of the Dolls*, recalled, "[Duke] had to scream and scream in the bath and every time we were set to interview Robson, he had to rush out of the room to make sure she was screaming 'properly.'" Eyewitnesses recall Robson later chiding Duke about playing the scene at half-mast: "You may have been able to do that when you had your TV show, but we're really *working* here." Duke fired back: "One of us *is* really working here and it sure as hell isn't you."

On Wednesday of that week Duke was filmed being accosted by a panhandler and on Thursday and Friday, she had to weep for hours. Although she kept trying to assure Robson that the "good instincts" that guided her as a child actor were still in play, the director was dubious. Duke said, "[Robson's] mentality was, 'I have to get a performance out of these girls.' I don't know about anybody else, but you don't have to get a performance out of me. I'll give it to you. You can help me or you can hinder me, but you certainly don't have to go get it." In a burst of humor and generosity, Robson extended Duke an olive branch by having the prop department fabricate a "Most Enduring Actress Award" statuette, presenting it to her and declaring a "Patty Duke Week." All of it was witnessed—and dutifully reported—by invited members of the press, of course. But word was leaking out. On April 21, Walter Winchell's nationally syndicated column reported: "Mark Robson, directing *Valley of the **Pills***, is having problems with one of the leads. Not Judy."

Barbara Parkins acknowledged how Patty Duke "had her own very strong ideas about how she wanted to play the role. So did the director. They weren't the same ideas." But Parkins didn't necessarily think that Robson's ideas were right for the material, either, especially when he appeared to lavish more care and concern on how he and William Daniels photographed loving close-ups of the heroines' bottles of pharmaceuticals, for instance, than on exploring the characters' emotions. "Got to get that cap off and get those pills down!" she observed. Calling Robson's approach to the material strictly "surface level," Parkins said, "Why were the girls taking those pills? What impact did they have on us? I didn't take drugs and I had no idea how I was supposed to look. Imagine how a director like Martin Scorsese would have dug in and almost given you the experience of taking drugs yourself? Well, our director didn't talk about any of that. We never sat down at a table and had a read-through. He never discussed things like 'When you take these pills, this is the effect that's going to happen. This is how I want you to feel in your body, in your head.' I found him very clinical and technical, 'Walk here, look up at her, then go over there.' In the scene when I wander out onto the beach and fall into the water, all he kept saying was 'Keep your face down! Keep your face down!' I was swallowing dirty Malibu water. He didn't care. His main focus was on showing the pills and the bottle, like when there is a big close-up of my hand reaching out and knocking over pill bottles and the pills rolling onto the tray. That was where Mark Robson shows 'The bottle, the pills falling onto the tray,' 'Valley of the Dolls actress taking pills,' and that's it!"

Ideally, the audience should feel pathos and empathy for the characters—"My God, these girls are losing it," as Parkins described it. Though, according to Parkins, Duke performing her scenes on the soundstage seemed so "amazing" that "none of us found it over the top at the time." She added, "But the way the director directed it probably was over the top."

When the formidably great Lee Grant began filming her role as Tony Polar's compellingly odd and controlling older sister, she proclaimed herself happy to be reunited with Barbara Parkins, "my sweet girlfriend from *Peyton Place*." But Grant harbored no illusions about anyone's making art out of *Valley of the Dolls* and has candidly called the acting gig strictly "a money job." In her autobiography, she described herself, at forty-two, being perceived—by the unapologetically ageist and sexist criteria of late 1960s Hollywood— as "no longer young enough or pretty enough for my next job, I was hungry to act, hungry to work, as hungry as a rabid dog. . . . By Hollywood standards, I was already over the hill."

Barbara Parkins called Grant "mysterious" and mostly recalled her on the *Valley* set "sitting in chairs in corners, usually with her arms folded." Duke, who carefully studied the Method actress from afar, recalled watching Grant film a moment in which she simply sits alone watching her brother perform onstage. Duke has said, "There were so many layers of what this woman was thinking. She allowed you to endow her with anything you wanted, but she made them all totally legit. I would watch [Grant] when we came back from lunch, say, and I could track her transformation back into her character. There was always some sort of interesting physicality she would do. Lee went somewhere in her psyche for every role she played, and it was almost as if when she had it perfect, she invited you in."

Grant shared a number of scenes with Sharon Tate, whom she has described as "shockingly beautiful" and "charming and mysterious," praising her work as "very sensitive." She recalled being struck by Tate's work as she listens to a doctor (played by William Wintersole) explaining Tony Polar's degenerative disease; she conveyed an "element of victimhood that was right for the part. She sank like a woman drowning in her role." Citing Tate as "lovely in the part, the only one I really believed on-screen, including myself," she described Tate, Duke, and Parkins as "actresses breathing the golden breath of success and impending stardom, as if to say, *This is it. Don't you wish you were me?* I never wanted the leaden, overwhelming responsibility of carrying a film or a budget."

Grant, who had studied and worked with some of the best, including legendary acting coach Sanford Meisner and director William Wyler, thought Robson "basically an editor." After shooting the earlier-mentioned scene with Tate, Scotti, and Wintersole, Grant recalls Robson approaching her with his trusty stopwatch. Informing her that the scene had run three minutes and forty-two seconds, he asked a jaw-dropping question: "Do you think you could do it in two minutes and thirty-four seconds?" Robson informed Grant that since he was already editing the movie as they were filming, he had only allotted that amount of time to the scene. From the first weeks of production, the daily footage was being turned over to four-time Oscar nominated Dorothy "Dot" Spencer, who had cut films for Ernst Lubitsch, John Ford, Alfred Hitchcock, Joseph L. Mankiewicz, and Elia Kazan; she had also edited eight of Robson's movies.

Grant has recalled that on Friday, Robson had been unable to wrap one of her more emotional scenes. When they resumed filming on the following Monday, Grant, naturally, brought the same level of intensity as she had the previous week. Robson led her away from the set and into his trailer, asking how she had been able to accomplish that. She replied, "I'd found something real for me and I could leave it on Friday and find it again when I came back into the situation." *Yeah*, he asked, *but how?* Grant thought to herself, *Does he* mean *it?* "It's called acting," she replied. Although Grant avoided speaking publicly about *Valley of the Dolls* for decades after the film's release, she has since, with admirable candor, called it "an unbelievable, laugh-out-loud disaster." But by comparison with her role in Irving Allen's 1978 killer bee disaster, *The Swarm*, which marked a reunion with Patty Duke, she called *Valley* a work of "genius."

From Patty Duke's standpoint, Robson continued to be "nasty and unkind." Duke had invested time and effort preparing for her role, altering her voice and walk, penciling red along the base of her eyelids until, she said, "it ran into my eyes and they were bloodshot." She said, "I went to bars and watched confused, tormented people full of self-pity and wondered how they got to be that way. I thought of my own life, how I used to feel sorry for myself. Self-pity is a dangerous pitfall." By her own admission, Duke became "miserable" making the movie. She said, "It was unfortunate that the realities of the circumstances that the characters were experiencing were not explored in the script, instead of the film going for the quick buck. At first, I thought I was being really good and serious in the role. I wasn't. I gave up early on. I gave up on the character and on participating once I saw the way they were headed with handling the production."

Aside from verbally zinging Robson, Duke manifested her anger and frustration in a number of ways, many of them self-defeating. As she recalled, "I don't know if the role was rubbing off on me or I was rubbing off on the role, but the meaner he got, the more frustrated I got. I was too afraid to fight back . . . in anything but little sneaky ways." Said a coworker with a ringside view, "I didn't want to be mean—and, look, it wasn't my place to say anything—but she was gaining so much weight. One day I said, 'I notice you like donuts, Patty. Why don't you tell me which ones you like the best, so I'll choose something else?' She said, 'Donuts? I don't even like donuts. But what I really don't like is that fucking Robson.' I couldn't even repeat some of the language she used talking about him but I also don't think she was wrong." Although Duke freely admitted, "I gained 30 pounds during that picture," it wasn't only the donuts that contributed; Robson required multiple takes of her gulping sugar-filled "dolls" and then chasing them with the tea-and-Coke mixture that stood in for booze.

Duke's weight fluctuations required Travilla and his assistants to let out her costumes. Meanwhile, Robson, cameraman William Daniels, and film editor Dorothy Spencer agonized over how difficult it was to match shots of Duke, whose weight sometimes varied by ten or more pounds during the same scene. One of the usual visual distractions? Pile taller wigs atop Duke's head. (Looking at *you*, poolside fight between Duke and Alex Davion.)

As for Barbara Parkins, she has never publicly complained of Robson's treatment toward her. But neither has she ever accused him of being the right person to direct *Valley*. She said, "I have to be honest and say that I had fun making it. It was exciting for me to be starring in a big film." And then, for Parkins, Duke, and other members of the company, came the biggest excitement of them all—the much-heralded arrival of Judy Garland.

CHAPTER TWELVE

It's Judy!

Judy Garland reported for preproduction meetings early on the morning of March 27. Despite being emotionally depleted, reeling from messed-up marriage number four with gay actor–tour promoter Mark Herron, the recent loss of her eight-bedroom Brentwood neighborhood home at 129 Rockingham Avenue, and being what daughter Lorna Luft (then virtually her caretaker) called "homeless broke," Garland appeared lively, enthusiastic, and gracious during a day devoted to makeup tests and costume and wig fittings with, respectively, Ben Nye and Ernie Parks, Travilla, and Kaye Pownall.

For Garland's introductory backstage dressing room scene as Helen Lawson, Travilla had created a white and red swirly-patterned ensemble featuring oversize culotte-style leg panels over matching red slacks; that costume was rejected but modified subsequently and sported by Barbara Parkins in Anne Welles's Gillian Girl TV commercial. As an alternative, Travilla had also created the "power suit" costume seen in the film, having it fabricated in five different solid colors, including forest green and tangerine. But before Garland's arrival, Weisbart, Robson, and Travilla had already opted for the visual exclamation point they hoped the crimson version would deliver.

David Weisbart casually introduced Garland to some of the key crew members, and she was shown to her dressing room on the set, positioned—who knows if deliberately?—directly across from Patty Duke's identical one, which Duke described as "doghouse-sized." Duke, "thrilled beyond imagination" by Garland's casting, said, "The first time Judy arrived, it was like going to Mecca. She was charming and, oh, very funny. We had a few days where we had gotten to know each other. She made me laugh every time she looked at me. I worshipped her." Reporting back to the 20th lot on April 14, Garland appeared playful, nervous, and self-conscious while filming further wardrobe and wig tests with designer Travilla and Robson. As the surviving footage shows, at least her sense of humor hadn't failed her. For Scene 24, set in Helen Lawson's theater dressing room, Garland, sporting a smart red jacket and skirt accessorized with a gold chain belt with suede ankle boots, gets asked by Robson to turn her face to the wall. "Without a cigarette and a blindfold?" she quips, to little audible response. She appears to be trying to personally engage the crew, but although they were polite, the mood seems strictly business, as if she and her coworkers are not exactly on the same wavelength. When the camera moves in for a closer view, she laughs, "You'll pardon me but I do get the giggles." For a scene set in Lawson's apartment, Garland models a shimmery iridescent caftan accessorized with a gold bracelet and matching lavalier earrings; she wonders whether she resembles "a fiery, burning monk." Holding a cigarette, she models the beaded paisley emerald and coppery pantsuit for Scenes 229–237, the scenes culminating in the wig-pulling blowout in the powder room of a New York restaurant.

Garland got through these preliminaries well enough, but as her filming start date approached, her old demons began pitchforking her. Patty Duke clocked Garland as "insecure" and "not in very good shape" but "so sweet, cute, and funny, you wanted to hug her all the time." When Garland confessed to Duke how nervous she was about the work to come, her younger costar "tried to reassure her" that all would be well. She also appreciated David Weisbart's spiffing up her larger, formal dressing room, housed in a special building away from the set. The company outfitted Garland's quarters with a piano, the latest-model portable record player, dozens of her favorite albums ("Judy must have music wherever she is," her agent stipulated), sterling silver–framed photos of her kids, and—a nod to the pastime she and her costar and fellow survivor Mickey Rooney first shared at MGM in the '40s—a handsome new Brunswick pool table.

Not necessarily evident in the costume tests or in her interactions with cast and crew was Garland's deep ambivalence about making the movie. She disliked the novel, a tome she described to an ardent fan who appeared to be lending a sympathetic ear as "the most miserably written book. [Susann] can't put more than eight words in a sentence. It's filthy. I even liked *The Carpetbaggers*, which was bawdy, at least—well-written, I thought. I didn't see the movie. But that was a good, racy book about Hollywood." She also thought the Deutsch-Kingsley screenplay leaned too hard on characterizing Helen Lawson as a clichéd, one-note, expletive-spouting harpy. According to Garland, David Weisbart never made good on his promises that the subsequent script rewrites would deepen and add complexity to the character. What's more, she didn't find Robson warm or simpatico in the least.

As for the movie's musical elements, Garland was offered her choice of singing any of Dory and André Previn's songs, including the title tune. The exception was "Come Live With Me"; that Tin Pan Alley riff on Christopher Marlowe's "The Passionate Shepherd to His Love." That one was always intended to be the signature romantic ballad of the Tony Polar character, reprised later in the narrative as a Polar–Neely O'Hara psychiatric hospital duet. It was no loss to Garland, who seemed to hate all the songs equally. She wasn't alone. "Everyone knew that those songs were mediocre at best," said performer Marilyn Michaels. "Come on, this movie was supposed to feature two 'Judy Garlands'—Neely and Judy herself—belting Judy Garland–type songs." When all the musical numbers were auditioned for Garland, the Previns raised the possibility of her singing "Give a Little More," naturally not informing her that the faintly Garland-ish ditty had been earmarked as Neely O'Hara's first song in the movie—the one she's rehearsing when Helen Lawson hears her and gets her fired from the show *Hit the Sky*. But after hearing the opening lyric, "Try, my friend, to face yourself with all you have in store," Garland dismissed the song as "sad, dreary," and "disastrous." "If I'm supposed to be the greatest star," she asked a friend, "why the hell should I have to try again?"

After hearing "I'll Plant My Own Tree," Garland privately lobbied Weisbart and Robson to switch it out for "Get Off Looking Good," a newly written hard-knocks anthem vocally and tonally tailored to help her bring to Helen Lawson touches of gallantry, pathos, humanity. Bobby Cole, Mel Tormé's replacement as the musical arranger for *The Judy Garland Show* and the man Frank Sinatra called "my favorite saloon entertainer," composed "Get Off Looking Good" when Garland complained to him and others that the Previns simply didn't know how to write for her. But Weisbart held firm and Garland was disheartened by even having to rehearse the inferior "I'll Plant My Own Tree." Choreographer Robert Sidney stood alone in saying, "She liked it. She liked the excitement of it."

Anxious to avoid being labeled "difficult" yet again, Garland kept quiet and gutted her way through a drama-free recording session conducted and arranged by John Williams. Sidney also said, "We had the [music] chart done in Judy's key. . . . Poor Judy. The first time I sang the song for her, I had to get under the table. She did the most outlandish things. Then I had to do it for her and Roger Edens." [Did Sidney actually mean Bobby Cole?] Veteran actor and *Valley* participant Kenneth DuMain told author Gene Arceri, "They knew right away Judy was having problems, because she recorded the big number 'I'll Plant My Own Tree,' and, a few days later, they had her back to redo a few bars that were not too good in the playback. They told her on that Friday that they were shooting the actual number the following Monday. She said, 'Oh, we must have a playback [track] before we can do it.' She didn't even remember having done it."

Nevertheless, Earl Wilson played cheerleader for Garland in his nationally syndicated column by reporting how on the fourteenth, between Garland's costume tests, the singer "in excellent voice" had "breezed so beautifully" through her prerecording session for "I'll Plant My Own Tree" that Weisbart predicted the song "will become one of her all-time standards." Wilson's and Weisbart's boosterism aside, listening today to Garland's recorded track, she sounds a bit sloshed and she lacks the electrifying emotive power and brilliance of her *A Star Is Born* days, let alone the gale-force delivery and aching throb of her '40s-era pipes. Still, despite her dislike of the lousy song, despite the audible wear and tear on her voice, and despite the track's not yet having been electronically "sweetened" by 20th's formidable sound techs—let alone the possibility that she would rerecord all or part of it—Garland didn't come to play. Hers is the performance of a once-in-a-lifetime talent.

Prolific Broadway producer and stage manager Albert Poland, the founder of the Judy Garland Fan Club in 1955 who became a friend and colleague of the entertainer's, offers his take on the song and on Garland's hiring: "If you ask me, Judy Garland was offered the role to buy her off. The Neely O'Hara character was so obviously patterned after her that [20th] was willing to pay her $100,000 to gain all that publicity. Now, I don't think the buyoff was ever articulated by Fox or by Judy; it was just quietly understood by both parties. She just went through the motions and the emotions. I don't think she ever intended to do the movie and I don't think Fox ever intended her to do it." Poland's version of the Garland fiasco is backed by a veteran celebrity agent–representative who asserts that a 20th higher-up in the '60s confirmed how "Garland's 'hiring' was a calculated publicity stunt. They were betting that she was in no shape to play even a supporting role. But the publicity was—or so they gambled—worth the risk. It was very sad and callous." But what about Bobby Cole's writing her a special song for the film?

Poland said, "Cole's song was touching, a *real* Judy Garland song, the lyrics of which basically say, if they're shoving you off the stage because you're too old, too *whatever*, at least quit with style while looking great. I mean, 'I'll Plant My Own Tree'? Really? She asked Cole to write 'Get Off Looking Good' to lend reality to the illusion that she really was going to do the movie. Judy had to get out of *Valley of the Dolls* just as she knew she was wrong for *Annie Get Your Gun* and had to get out of that one, too." After the theatrical release of *Valley of the Dolls*, Garland eventually sang "Get Off Looking Good" a cappella, during her 1968 concert appearances.

Whatever the truth about Garland's casting, the moment she stepped onto the 20th lot, she generated a publicity cyclone for the movie that was already the talk of Hollywood. On April 30, *Boston Globe* staff writer Percy Shain quoted Patty Duke as being so excited that she unwittingly put her foot in her mouth when discussing Neely O'Hara: "You know, in the scuttlebutt, they say this role is the prototype of Judy Garland. Judy Garland is in the picture—but she plays Ethel Merman!" Studio publicist Regina Gruss gave Duke and several of her costars a firm, gentle reminder of the studio's official directive, as guided by the Legal Department: if asked about Jacqueline Susann's real or assumed character inspirations, reply with a vague, disingenuous "Oh, there are similarities, but . . ."; most of all, *never* discuss the topic with Garland herself.

Before Garland began filming, Jacqueline Susann returned to the studio to help welcome the star and to shoot a (contractually guaranteed) cameo as a reporter interviewing Anne Welles after Jennifer North's death. Irving Mansfield quipped that in making the cameo appearance, Susann was "sort of a skinny Hitchcock with hair." On Susann's shooting day, the limo driver who picked her up at her hotel asked who she was to warrant such deluxe treatment, noting that both Patty Duke and Barbara Parkins drove themselves to the set, while the studio insisted on sending a driver for Judy Garland, "to make sure she gets there." Along with a limo, the novelist, who'd always wanted to be a star, was allotted a special parking space for her limo and, on the set, a canvas director's chair with her name stenciled on it. "I will play a cameo . . . and by a cameo, I mean more than just a walk-on," Susann crowed. "I have to have at least two lines. If I'm going to be in the movie, I want people to know where I was. Originally, I had four lines but ended up with three. Did you ever know of an actress who gave away a line? I was supposed to say, 'What were [Jennifer North's] measurements?,' but I felt that a male reporter would have asked that. A man is interested in the big bazoom thing."

The female cast members, said Patty Duke, "bowed down to her." Duke, who had been getting positive feedback from David Weisbart, said, "there was acknowledgment throughout the filming that [Jacqueline Susann] was really pleased with what I was doing with the role of Neely." The actress found the writer's on-set behavior "cute, actually, she was so naïve and giddy, just like a kid on Christmas morning." Duke found it especially delightful that Susann "went to makeup at least four times before she ever went on camera." Barbara Parkins called her "just so happy to be included and appreciative of the process. She wasn't in the movie a long time, but we all loved having her there, and behind that big hair and her Pucci dresses and attitude, underneath, her enthusiasm was just so childlike and infectious. She was having a good time." When asked by a reporter, Susann said, "I haven't seen a single day's rushes so far. I got the idea that they didn't want me to, so I didn't want to put them against the wall." She admitted that Judy Garland asked her what she thought of the screenplay. "I told her I hadn't seen it. She had a copy with her, and I started thumbing through it. David [Weisbart] rushed over and took it away and said, 'We'll send you a revised copy, Jacqueline.'" Susann said that they never did.

From Garland's own first days of shooting, pretty much everything was "off." She arrived with her onetime publicist/house manager/on-again, off-again, decades-younger fiancé, Tom Green, who would months later tell *Boston Globe* critic Kevin Kelly, "It was just terrible. You know, the first day we got to the *Dolls* set, they were shooting a nude scene. A nude scene! Right then, at that very first moment, I knew it wasn't the kind of film for Judy, not the kind of thing for America's Sweetheart. I mean, there's a long reputation here. She just can't be a glittering bitch in a Hollywood film."

As if that weren't a rocky enough start, many cast and crew members noted peculiarities—if not outright cruelties—in Robson's handling of the movie's most prestigious player. Patty Duke, who called Robson "the meanest son of a bitch I ever met in my life," recalled the director requiring Garland to report to the studio at 6:30 a.m., "knowing he wouldn't even plan to get to her until 4:30 in the afternoon. He kept this icon waiting the whole day. She was very down to earth. She didn't mind waiting. What I mind was the gentlemen around her who supplied her with wine and other things. And so, when she finally did get called to the set, she couldn't function very well."

An actor familiar with the circumstances said, "Liebfraumilch by the ton got stocked in her dressing room. In those days, no one thought it was doing her all that much harm. I mean, there were so many other things going on with poor Judy that Liebfraumilch would hardly be the thing that would do her in." Duke has recalled, "I'll never remember the young man's name that was her assistant or companion or whatever, but he would occasionally pour her a glass of wine, which would worry me. It wasn't so much that I was being judgmental of her for drinking the wine, it just worried me that it would undermine her and people would have that thing to hang it on if she wasn't performing to their expectations."

When Duke visited Garland's dressing room to wish her luck on that first day, she found her "in abject terror." She kept waiting for her director to do what directors traditionally do—especially one dealing with an emotionally volatile diva who hadn't faced a movie camera in four years—visit her dressing room, chat about the day's work, and ease her onto a set where everyone else already knew one another and had established a rhythm. Instead, Robson merely informed her through an assistant that he, the crew, and actors

Barbara Parkins, Martin Milner, and Robert Viharo awaited her on the set. Garland sent back word that she needed forty-five minutes more. "It's not as if anyone asked something exceptional of the guy," Patty Duke said about Robson's behavior. Garland did not "want her ass kissed," but that "part of her that had grown up being *Judy Garland*, superstar of MGM, was completely accustomed to have respect paid to her." Doubling back to the star's dressing room, Duke listened sympathetically when Garland told her that if only Robson would come and escort her to the set, her nerves might quiet down. Robson sent an assistant director. Said Duke, "It was like the director decided that some guy from the delicatessen on 33rd Street should talk to her. She crumbled."

Meanwhile, Barbara Parkins had been keyed up about working with Garland. Not only was her casting "the talk of the town," but Parkins also thought "having her sing those songs would have made the film even 'bigger' and more dynamic. Anyway, I was so nervous." Parkins turned to Jacqueline Susann in hopes of calming herself: "The night before the filming, I called up Jackie Susann, who I'd become close to—I didn't call up the director, strangely enough—I called her up and said, 'What do I do? I'm nervous about going on the set with Judy Garland and I might get lost in this scene because she knows how to chew up the screen.'" Susann counseled, "Honey, just go onto that set and enjoy working with that dame! Take her out for lunch. Just have fun." Of coming face-to-face with Garland on the set not long before the director was ready to perfunctorily rehearse them, Parkins has said, "I was in awe, just so caught up in her—I thought, 'I'm working with a legend. She's beautiful and she has a charisma about her'—even if she was dynamic but looked fragile. I couldn't take my eyes off her. Judy knew I was nervous. She would often come over and give me big hugs."

Theirs was supposed to have been a relatively simple scene. In her theater dressing room, Helen Lawson kicks press agent Mel out of her dressing room, grabs some contracts from Anne Welles, barks for a fountain pen, signs the papers, and orders the nervous

Anne to sit down and wait. Neely O'Hara is heard distantly warbling "Give a Little More," and when Anne makes nervous small
talk by making an offhand comment about how good Neely is,
Helen demands that the director cut the song and fire the newcomer, and she tears up the contracts. To protect the star (and themselves), the studio bosses had issued a directive: "Miss Garland is
not to be approached for any kind of publicity interviews or picture
taking during her actual acting days in the film." Despite that edict,
Robert "Bob" Freund, the longtime *Fort Lauderdale News* entertainment editor, was granted set access that day. Having attended
many of Garland's concerts, Freund commented on the star's "nervous electricity" and her looking "great, very slim." Garland and
cinematographer William Daniels shared a warm moment remi-
niscing about having last worked together at MGM in the '40s on
For Me and My Gal and *Girl Crazy*. Robson rehearsed the actors
several times before attempting several takes. Garland and Parkins
talked briefly, and Garland wrapped her arms around her warmly.

From the start, Parkins was "letter-perfect," while Garland was "a
bundle of nerves." She'd forget her lines entirely. Or flub them. Or
scramble their order. Or say them correctly but without the right ac-
companying physical actions. Garland tried defusing the situation
with self-deprecating humor, but Freund described her as "boiling
at her ineptness." She wailed, "I don't know about this picture business. Maybe I've been away too long." Imagine the showbiz trouper
being shown up by a newcomer who'd only been in front of the
cameras for six years; imagine how that newcomer might have felt
watching a show business trouper's embarrassment at being shown
up by a relative newcomer; imagine how that newcomer might have
felt watching a show business icon come undone. And, meanwhile,
a reporter witnessed the whole thing. Patty Duke recalled standing
out of sight on the soundstage, "just cringing, willing each word to
come out the way it was supposed to, and it never did." Parkins, describing Garland as "an emotional roller coaster," said, "I saw her go
through so many different types of emotions—angry, happy, sad."

Robson called for a break. David Weisbart (who had been summoned to the set) went over to Garland, who "glowed" and said,
"David, how nice of you to be here." The producer watched encour-
agingly as Garland and Parkins ran their lines to prepare for another take. When Robson called, "Action!" Garland mangled her
dialogue. Another try. Garland forgot to ask Parkins for the fountain pen. On the next take, Garland neglected to drop the contracts
in her lap. Do it again. Garland skipped the line "Sit down, you're
making me nervous," leaving Parkins stranded. The director and
his coproducer looked on "tolerantly."

When Robson finally got a decent take, the reporter wrote: "The
old Garland magic was evident. She put all the familiar pizazz into
the shot—and it worked." Not according to Weisbart or Robson,
though. Patty Duke observed, "There was no sense of tragedy on the
set, just that this was going to be a long haul." But nationally syndicated columnist Marilyn Beck reported more humiliations from
days two and three of shooting. Citing but not naming one of Garland's costars as her source, Beck reported how the star fell apart
when a dental crown wriggled loose and required her to be rushed
off to a dentist. Beck's on-set informant opined that the star's problems weren't being helped by "well-meaning people" on and off the
20th lot asking whether she identified with Helen Lawson, "an aging,
one-time great star on the skids."

Parkins has recalled, "As we worked, she kept losing her lines,
asking for her lines. Something was wrong. They gave her a week.
By the third day, Judy was flipping out. She stormed off the set and
locked herself in the dressing room." Not long after Garland's dental mishap, she learned during a shooting break that one of her
friends had attempted suicide; she refused to return to the set after
lunch. Duke believed that Robson was further undercutting Garland by ignoring the ideas she brought and not allowing her "to
make decisions about her character." As one crew member observed, "Robson had this hard-line, simple approach to the characters. The only way he wanted [Garland] to play it was like a tough,

snarling monster. Judy wanted to make her more of a person. He treated her like a prop or some stick figure or something. He wasn't letting her play to her strengths. He didn't seem to value her."

Patty Duke said, "Now [Judy] knew that she was not functioning up to par. She wasn't out in space somewhere, but she knew she couldn't do the work unless there was more kindness given to her." Bypassing Robson entirely, Duke went straight to David Weisbart and told him, "I'm not suggesting you kiss her ass or treat her any differently than the rest of us, but it seems she's not being treated even as nicely as the rest of us." Apparently goaded by the Zanucks and Weisbart, Robson began acting so much more deferentially toward Garland that, said Duke, he all but "kissed her ass in Macy's window."

But no matter how many of her colleagues stood up for Garland, her problems were spiraling out of control. Duke has said that it became abundantly clear from Garland's slurring delivery and unsteadiness on and off the set that she "was under the influence of something." It got worse and worse. Garland's chronic lateness fully manifested itself as it had decades earlier during her days at MGM and later at Warner Bros. during filming of *A Star Is Born*. "Each morning that [Garland] was due at the studio, they had a driver go over to her apartment to call for her," said actor Ken DuMain in a biography of Susan Hayward. "He would arrive there at 6:30 a.m. to pick Judy up at 7 a.m. and he'd wait throughout the morning, sometimes up to 12 noon, before he could even get to her and bring her back to the studio." Choreographer Robert Sidney recalled, "We had five days of her locking herself in her trailer and not coming out till 6 p.m. They had people there just to see she had no booze. [Her daughter] Lorna was a teenager then. She came running out of the room one day saying, 'Mommy was strange. Mommy was taking something. . . .' Nobody could handle her." Memos flew back and forth among Robson, Weisbart, and the Zanucks about how ten days with Garland had only yielded a minute and a half of (marginally) usable footage. Emerging from the screening room after viewing editor Dorothy Spencer's valiant attempts to cut together a

Garland performance in the dressing room scene, the filmmakers and executives uttered terms like "unfocused" and "lifeless."

When several actors and crew members asked why the star's name was missing from the shooting schedule for the next ten days, Robson replied that Garland and Parkins's scene together was to be reshot once Travilla and Kaye Pownall had made his requested wardrobe and wig changes. But with Garland costing the production $25,000 daily, something had to give. On April 27, Richard Zanuck descended on Garland's dressing room to deliver the news that she was fired, an act he called in 2013 "one of the toughest things I had to do." He elaborated, "After about the third day, she just wasn't doing it properly. There was [sic] no drugs involved or anything like that. But she was just—her acting ability had faded and she just wasn't getting it. So I went into her dressing room. She, of course, pleaded and asked if she could have more of a chance and everything and I just said, 'Judy this is for your sake, actually, as well as the picture. And it's better that we just call it a day today.' That was a very tough one. But those are the kind of sad and tough, sometimes ugly, things that someone who's in charge has to do. And you can't—or at least *I* couldn't—send a subordinate down to do those kinds of things."

For the sake of Garland and the picture, though, Zanuck brought along an intimidating group of subordinates/witnesses, including a 20th Century Fox attorney and casting executive Owen McLean. According to Garland, McLean said, "We're tired of your foolishness. We're just not going to put up with it anymore." "What foolishness?" Garland asked. She told a reporter that McLean "looked at me as if I were a child. 'We can't use you,' he said. 'You're through. And you're not going to get a cent.' I was stunned. 'Would you please repeat that slowly?' I asked. He did. I had signed a contract. I was doing a good job. But I was still O-U-T. Before long the nasty rumors began to drift around again. 'Judy Garland blew another big chance.' Blew another big chance? I did not! I will not believe it till I hear just what the studio says I did, and what terrible crimes I committed against their movie. Maybe young Zanuck wanted to show he was just as tough as his old man, Darryl. All right, they convinced me."

Sometime after Zanuck's departure from Garland's formal dressing room, recalled Duke, "I heard quite a commotion going on. She had a pool table in there and some of the noises sounded like pool sticks being broken and things like that. I called Judy on the phone and asked if she was okay. She said, 'Yeah, I guess so.' I told her I was going to the commissary to get a tuna sandwich and asked if she wanted me to bring her back anything. She said she'd love a Hershey bar. I brought her the candy, which was also my sneaky way to get the door to her dressing room open." When Duke returned less than twenty minutes later, she failed to gain access to Garland in person or by phone; she returned to her own dressing room, dozed off, and was awakened by a phone call from Garland.

Once Garland opened the door, it was clear to Duke that "whatever had been going on in her dressing room had escalated and she was beyond upset and sobbing." Shattered glass littered the floor. The pool table top was shredded. A broken ceiling light dangled. She kept repeating, "Those sons-of-bitches fired me! I've been fired!" Duke recalled her saying, "I don't know what to do. Nothing I do seems to please that man!" Duke continued, "Since I'd had my own run-ins with our director, I knew whom she was talking about. The two of us cried. My heart was broken, as I believe hers was as well." For decades Duke blamed Robson's behavior for Garland's unraveling: "I truly believe if Robson had the simple courtesy to say hello to Judy and to treat her with respect that she wouldn't have fallen apart. Judy would have done the part and she would have been wonderful. I believe that she also would have found a way to make a whole character out of Helen Lawson so she wasn't just a bitch. . . . To lose her was devastating. It stunned and shocked us all. It was tough to recover. We saw a scared, frightened lady fighting for her life." Parkins said, "Here was this great lady, this incredible star and we watched helpless as everything unraveled. It was heartbreaking. She would have *made* the movie. She would have won an Academy Award." Years later Duke remarked: "I thought it was cheap and tawdry to ask her to play the part. And it made me sad that she had reached the point of having to take this stupid role, playing opposite someone who was reputedly playing her. It's tacky, it's degrading, and it's undignified to have to do such a thing." In the end, though, she concluded, "I realized another month into the filming that Judy was the one who got off easy, as it was the rest of us who were stuck being in this turkey."

On April 29, two days after Richard Zanuck and company fired Garland, the studio filed with Garland's representatives a legal document labeled "Contract Canceled and Terminated by Agreement." The same day, international newspapers reported that the star had withdrawn from the production for "personal reasons." The studio-friendly press swung into action. Dorothy Manners's May gossip column sounded the note parroted from then on by most of the press: 20th was beyond reproach. Garland was beyond help. "Seems to be the old trouble: Panicsville sets in at the thought of stepping in front of the cameras again," Manners reported. "The chore of memorizing pages and pages of script seems to throw her. Producer David Weisbart and the 20th Century Fox Company were very patient with Judy. There were too many [mornings] when the assistant director would knock on the door of her elaborate dressing room and call, 'Miss Garland . . . They're waiting for you on the set. Rehearsals are starting. . . .' No answer from within. 'Judy! Are you all right?,' he'd call again. No answer. The assistant would try the door. It was locked. Yet the workers at 20th Century Fox knew she was there. She had been checked through the car entrance perhaps hours before. Puzzled, bewildered, the assistant would report back to the *Valley of the Dolls* company that Judy was 'unavailable.' She was given two or three weeks to pull herself together and didn't seem able to. The situation became intolerable and very costly. At last, there was no more going on like this. Again, even in despair, the studio protected the 'little girl' whose heart belonged over the rainbow. She was permitted to resign from the production."

Garland fired back: "I have not withdrawn. How dare they say I've withdrawn? I've done my work. I was up at six o'clock this morning to go to work. They simply didn't call me to go to work. . . . I was thrown out—and I don't like it. It's a shocking thing. Why? That's what I want to know."

Another columnist reported how Garland was seen "arriving and departing the studio at outrageous hours of the day and night. But during the vital working hours—where was she?" Yet another dredged up rumors that her being "unreliable" had in the past few years lost her roles in *Inside Daisy Clover* and *This Property Is Condemned* (as Natalie Wood's mother in both) and gotten her knocked out of the running to play Mrs. Robinson (!) in *The Graduate*. Because of the *Valley* fallout, she would no longer be in first position to play Edith Piaf in a George Cukor–directed project being shopped around town—a *highly* suspect rumor on its face, especially for anyone who ever heard Cukor's scathing private rants about Garland's behavior during their contentious, if stunning, *A Star Is Born* collaboration. In his *Hollywood Citizen-News* "Voice of Hollywood" column, Abe Greenberg touted that the newly available role of Helen Lawson "could result in as dramatic a bit of casting as movieland has seen since Bette Davis virtually came out of retirement to make the offbeat *Whatever Happened to Baby Jane?* . . . which rocketed her back to the top."

Several Hollywood columnists floated "fantasy lists" of potential Helen Lawsons that included Joan Crawford, Shelley Winters, Eleanor Parker, Ginger Rogers, Maureen O'Hara, Geraldine Page, Jane Wyman, Paulette Goddard, and Deborah Kerr. Dorothy Manners's May 7 column reported that Bette Davis—the young Judy Garland's acting idol—would not be pinch-hitting as Helen Lawson after all, due to scheduling conflicts with her latest exercise in "hag horror," *The Anniversary*, released by 20th Century Fox. Manners wrote that Weisbart and Robson would instead sign elfin, smoky-voiced Tammy Grimes, the Tony Award–winning Broadway star of *The Unsinkable Molly Brown* and *High Spirits*. In 1964 the talented, idiosyncratic

Grimes had thumbed her bobbed nose at ABC's offer to star her in *Bewitched*, believing that the special effects–heavy new sitcom would be a short-lived bomb. She instead chose to star with Dick Sargent in her own ABC sitcom, *The Tammy Grimes Show*, a full-on calamity. Of the ten episodes shot, four were aired. Out went Grimes.

Oscar-winning Ginger Rogers told reporter Jack O'Brian why she had rejected Weisbart and Robson's offer to play the hellacious Helen: "I simply couldn't stand having my ears hear that kind of language coming out of my mouth and I don't think anyone else could either." Rogers may also have been hesitant about taking another role from Garland, who in 1965 had left the cast of *Harlow* after working a single day, telling star Carol Lynley, "Honey, I'm not drunk. I'm not on drugs. And I'm telling you this is a piece of junk and I'm getting out." Rogers, like Garland, never made another film.

Meanwhile, on the subject of Garland's firing, David Weisbart told a reporter how the whole *Valley* crew felt "sick at heart. Prop boys, camera assistants, even the stars would say, 'Can't we shoot around her a little longer? Maybe she'll get to feeling better.' We went as far as we could, believe me." Dorothy Manners similarly reported "a silence of sadness" that "pervaded the troupe from the stagehands and cameramen up to the head of the studio." It was a sad and unfortunate episode in Garland's career, but at least 20th backed down from their threat to sue her. And though it makes a good story, let's not print the legend this time: Garland did not abscond with the Travilla-designed beaded-and-sequined pantsuit she later wore in her concert dates. The designer himself went on record as stating that he, with the studio's approval, made an outright gift of the outfit to Garland; some Garland aficionados say that Travilla personally boxed it, wrapped it, and had it sent to her. (Garland liked the pantsuit so much that she had her own New York seamstress whip up simplified, less ornamented and weighty copies in red and in white.)

Garland's army of ardent fans buried Darryl F. Zanuck, Robson, and Weisbart in letters. Some of them, according to the latter, were "vindictive." One such ended with an underlined "Bad luck to you and *Valley of the Dolls*." Others threatened boycotts unless Garland got rehired. Another apologist berated the moviemakers for firing his "star of stars" who deserved "another chance to redeem herself" and reestablish her status as "a top showstopper." Speaking to syndicated Hollywood correspondent Norma Lee Browning, Weisbart bemoaned the "volley of blasts" coming from "armchair casting directors." He said, "God knows I'm sorry the whole thing happened. We would have been much happier and it would have cost us a lot less money if it had worked out. She had every chance. Everyone was rooting for her." Asked to pinpoint the cause of Garland's problems on the movie, he said, "I would have to be a psychiatrist to answer that." He added, "It should pull Judy together to know how much she is loved by the public. Whatever her problems, a lot of help is being held out to her."

Sensing the potential for nasty blowback from the public, the Zanucks urged Weisbart and publicist Regina Gruss to invite top Hollywood journalists for set visits to help shift the focus away from Garland and back to the movie. In an April 30 *Los Angeles Herald-Examiner* piece, reporter Harrison Carroll described watching Robson direct Patty Duke as the druggy, out-of-control Neely storming off the set of an Old West movie set—the Old West of, oh, say, Judy Garland's stint in *The Harvey Girls* or in the aborted version of *Annie Get Your Gun*, from which she was fired? When the journalist asked if Duke had ever stormed off a set, she quipped, laughing—and absolutely, positively *not* referring to Barbara Parkins—"Of course not. There are always too many people nearby who could replace me." But by inviting Carroll to the set, the moviemakers had miscalculated. A childhood friend of Frances Gumm's and a Garland loyalist, Carroll filed a second piece the following week giving the actress her chance to sound off. "I had recorded the songs," Garland said. "I had the beautiful clothes. I had a heart flutter on the set. I was tired. I hadn't been sleeping. But it really was indigestion."

As usual, privately with intimates, Garland's mood swings could be titanic. Mere hours after her firing, in the Polo Lounge of the

Beverly Hills Hotel, she was seen out with her old pals, talk show host Jack Paar and James Mason, her *A Star Is Born* costar. Imagine the shade these three might have thrown over a long lunch and many drinks? And if only cell phones had been around back then, someone could have recorded the moment when Jacqueline Susann entered the lounge, spotted Garland and company, and turned on her heels and walked out. To further prove herself unsinkable, Garland put in a call to *Chicago Tribune* columnist Herb Lyon, who wrote, "Judy Garland, in amazingly good spirits . . . despite being fired from *Valley of the Dolls* movie cast, told us she was heading to N.Y.C. to set a quick deal: Judy and her three kids (including Liza) in an hour network TV all-family spectac[ular]."

Finally, both Liza Minnelli and Jacqueline Susann had their say. On June 4, in Sheilah Graham's newspaper column, the Hollywood insider reported that Minnelli—who had once claimed that her mother's great piece of advice was: To truly know someone, first study his medicine cabinet—when asked if she was upset about her mother's firing, answered: "No, I'm glad and so is she. She's too good for that sort of thing. My mother is a strong woman. She's not the tragic figure people make her out to be. When things get hard, she gets upset, then it's over and she's back on her feet. She's built up resilience." Meanwhile, Jacqueline Susann told a reporter that a bewildered Garland had called her, insisting that she thought she was doing well in the movie and added, "Where did everyone go? I can't get anybody on the phone." Susann told Roger Ebert in a July 18 interview: "It's too bad about Judy Garland. Everybody keeps asking me why she was fired from the movie, as if it was my fault or something. You know what I think? Here she was, raised in the great tradition of the studio stars, where they make 30 takes of every scene to get it right, and the other girls in the picture were all raised as television actresses. So they're used to doing it right the first time. Judy got rattled, that's all. It was so pitiful. The role of Helen Lawson has to have strength and Judy had gotten thinner than I had ever seen her. There was a scene in a powder room where Patty is supposed to grab her hair. If she had done it, it looked like Judy would have crumbled. I don't think Judy is through at all. But in every picture she's made, she's been used to be[ing] the star. Now, she walked on the set and saw three girls who had no hang-ups yet and who needed only one take to make a scene. There was also fear. People kept saying, 'You've got a chance to win an Oscar with this part.' There was so much riding on it. She'd be fine in the morning—until she got in front of the cameras." In an August 27 *Chicago Tribune* feature story by Clifford Terry, Susann said about the casting of the movie: "No writer ever thinks it's exactly like he or she envisions it. Two things can happen—the actor can be terrible or can bring something new to the character. I felt that Judy was not really right for the part."

Two months before *Valley of the Dolls* opened in theaters, Garland made an attempt to save face as best she could. In a self-signed feature article titled "The Plot Against Judy Garland" published in *Ladies' Home Journal* and syndicated in newspapers internationally, she wrote: "I got fired again. Oh, I know the studio says I 'withdrew for personal reasons.' But don't believe a word of it. Judy Garland was fired, canned. Why, I don't know. I had been working smoothly and hard. And nobody had complained that I wasn't." She told another journalist: "It was a terrible part. I played a dirty old lady. My first line was, 'Who the hell are you?' . . . I found the part difficult because the woman I was to play was coarse and shouting all the time. I was brought up to be polite and not raise my voice—except in song. I didn't like the role. I thought I could do it, but I couldn't—I couldn't force myself to use that kind of language. . . . I was fired. I'm undependable. Independable? Which is it? Anyway, I'm irresponsible. Isn't that the story about me? I'm 102 years old and it's been the same story about me almost from the beginning. Hollywood is cruel and not wise now. When they made fine pictures, it was hard work but fun. Now they make dirty pictures."

On May 24, 1968, wearing a Helen Lawson beaded pantsuit while concertizing at the opulent Back Bay Theater in Boston, Massachusetts, she asked the adoring audience if they had seen the movie. "Isn't it an *awful* picture?" she said to applause and laughter, calling the film "*Valley of the Hoo-hah*." Garland wowed her audience that night; she was a no-show the following night.

Disgruntled Garland fans kept pummeling 20th. Although the missives came in daily by the hundreds, Mark Robson responded to at least one: "At this stage it is too late to do anything further in the direction that you had hoped for. We have already committed ourselves to Miss Susan Hayward who we expect will do a magnificent job in the role." The official announcement of Hayward's casting came less than a week after Garland's dismissal.

CHAPTER THIRTEEN

(Not So) Suddenly Susan

Up against the wall, Mark Robson rejected all other Helen Lawson casting suggestions and placed a personal phone call to Susan Hayward. A decade before, the redheaded Hayward was *the* reigning diva of 20th Century Fox—tempestuous, ferociously competitive, icy, emotionally aloof, utterly professional. The spirited Hayward and Robson had last worked together in 1949 on the soggy and sentimental *My Foolish Heart*. Hayward's performance as an unhappily married woman recalling her first love earned her a Best Actress Oscar nomination, but the movie bore so little resemblance to its source material, J. D. Salinger's critique of American suburban life "Uncle Wiggily in Connecticut," that the writer never again allowed a mainstream filmmaker to officially adapt his work.

Before *My Foolish Heart*, Hayward had been plugging away in Hollywood since the late '30s. She finally hit her stride and also copped her first Oscar nomination in 1947, starring as a tragic songbird in *Smash-Up: The Story of a Woman*, itself such a blatant *movie à clef* that Bing Crosby reportedly considered suing Walter Wanger for producing a film that all Hollywood knew was based on his rocky relationship with his hard-drinking singer wife, Dixie Lee.

Two years later, Hayward earned yet another Oscar nomination playing tragic real-life songbird Jane Froman in *With a Song in My Heart*. 20th paired her with some of the top leading men of the era—including Gregory Peck in *David and Bathsheba*, Robert Mitchum in *The Lusty Men*, Clark Gable in *Soldier of Fortune*—and made Hayward such a major moneymaker that Darryl F. Zanuck declared, "The studio is basically hers now."

Often earning top billing over her male costars, Hayward was so big that MGM bypassed their own contract stars to borrow her from Zanuck for *I'll Cry Tomorrow*, based on the harrowing autobiography of alcoholic, mother-dominated Broadway star Lillian Roth and scripted by Helen Deutsch. Not only did Deutsch draw more than a bit of inspiration from Roth's decline when dramatizing Neely O'Hara's, but *I'll Cry Tomorrow* also features an appearance by the young, big-screen Neely-to-be, Patty Duke. Hayward's gritty performance netted another Oscar nomination and a Best Actress win at Cannes. She surprised audiences with her more than passable singing voice on such American Songbook standards as "I'm Sitting on Top of the World."

While ticket buyers couldn't get enough of her, some who worked with her were less enchanted. She was a tough cookie who had come up hard through an impoverished childhood. "A bitch," declared Henry Hathaway, who directed Hayward and Gary Cooper in *Garden of Evil*. "Anyone who is a bitch to work with has got to be a bitch to live with. That's an inherent thing, a part of your makeup, to be an obstruction to everything. She was a little twisted. She was twisted in her walk. She always walked a little sideways, stood a little sideways. It's a thing that was in her nature. It was in her head, her look, her walk, in the way she stood. That girl was twisted." If she moved awkwardly, she had good reason. Being struck by a car at age seven and confined for months to a body cast left her with a limp as a result of one leg being an inch and a half shorter than the other. And if her especially brutal climb to the top of the Hollywood heap didn't already make her seem an obvious candidate to play Helen Lawson, there were personal quotes like this: "You aim at all the things you have been told that stardom means—the rich life, the applause, the parties cluttered with celebrities. Then you find you have it all. And it is nothing, really nothing. It is like a drug that lasts just a few hours, a sleeping pill. When it wears off, you have to live without its help."

When Robson put in a panicky call to Hayward about stepping into the movie, the actress wasn't sure she was willing to return to the fray. She said she considered herself a working girl, not a movie star. As she put it: "I had to slug my way up in a town called Hollywood, where people love to trample you to death." Weary of the Hollywood rat race, she left it behind for a massive cattle ranch and a Florida beachfront spread that she had shared with her husband of nine years, former FBI agent Floyd Eaton Chalkley, who had died the previous January. She told reporters that she had lost her taste for the limelight and now preferred to spend hours "stretching out and looking at the sky." She chose not to mention the hours she also spent stretched out smoking five daily packs of cigarettes and downing alarming measures of Jack Daniel's, Johnnie Walker Black Label, and Beefeater martinis while also converting to Catholicism. Hayward had reportedly passed on several "comeback" proposals, including playing Mrs. Robinson for Mike Nichols in *The Graduate*, a project (as with Judy Garland) for which the director had also paged Patty Duke to play Hayward's daughter. (Duke never bothered to read Buck Henry's screenplay and later admitted, "I could kill myself.")

With Hayward keeping Robson and company guessing for several days, David Weisbart, hoping to woo her, got Richard Zanuck to spring for a Fort Lauderdale trip for Travilla, who had previously costumed Hayward in the aforementioned *Garden of Evil*, to let the star preview the costume sketches on her own turf. Her mid-May reunion with Travilla was anything but warm and friendly, as many have said about *any* personal encounter with Hayward. The costume designer recalled watching Hayward riffle through his sketches to the tune of tinkling ice and through a low-hanging haze of cigarette smoke as she made comments like "I wouldn't be caught dead in this." No wonder Robson figured Hayward had the brass—and the famous shock of red hair—to play Helen Lawson.

The actress ended the suspense by signaling that if—and only if—20th paid Judy Garland the full salary she had been promised, then Hayward would sign on. Garland got paid. "I'm doing it for you, Mark," she told Robson. "The terms are secondary." Secondary maybe, but none too shabby nevertheless: $50,000 (approximately $340,000 today) for four scenes, two weeks at the studio, and special billing on the ads, posters, and credits reading "Susan Hayward as Helen Lawson." She assured the Florida press that her return to Hollywood would be "strictly temporary" and explained: "I was getting restless and a little fat. It's good for me to work, it's good discipline. Nowadays, I simply won't do a picture unless I know the director and his work. Mark Robson is directing it. I first worked with him 24 years ago. We did *My Foolish Heart* together. Another reason is that the part's short, it's good, and the salary's terrific." Mark Robson observed of the no-nonsense Hayward, "I think she didn't trust actors or actresses. She had a few directors at the beginning of her career who were out-and-out bastards and gave her no help at all. But once she felt she could trust a director, she'd work her ass to the bone for him. She trusted me."

Meanwhile, with Hayward's deal set, Dick Kleiner reported in his nationally syndicated "Hollywood Showbeat" column how he and other journalists were the recipients of "tearful, tragic telephone calls." The caller? Judy Garland. The called? Anyone who might have influence with *Valley* producer David Weisbart. Before Hayward departed for Los Angeles, she agreed to an interview with the *Fort Lauderdale News* arts editor Bob Freund, the same journalist who had witnessed the beginning of Garland's meltdown on her very first day of filming. When asked about Garland, Hayward said, "She's such a talent, such a fine actress. I guess I don't understand these things, though. I've enjoyed every minute of my career. It isn't art to me. It's work and darn good work. But it's never been my life. There are other things vastly more important to me."

In contrast to the reception given to Judy Garland, the ceremonious arrival of Hayward's limousine early on Monday morning, May 15, was all pomp, deference, and, well, kissing her ass in Macy's window. Fresh from her luxe Beverly Wilshire Hotel suite, Hayward stepped onto the 20th lot to work for the first time since making *The Marriage-Go-Round* in 1960 and was royally welcomed by Richard Zanuck, Weisbart, Robson, and cinematographer William Daniels. Also, unlike on Garland's arrival, select reporters and photographers were invited to document Hayward's return to her former home studio. "I thought this part might be interesting, something different," Hayward told Associated Press correspondent Gene Handsaker, choosing to forget that she'd already done in 1964 the tawdry roman à clef movie version of Harold Robbins's *Where Love Has Gone*, in which overheated sex kitten Joey Heatherton (as a Cheryl Crane type) stabs the new stud bedded by her glam, self-absorbed Lana Turner–type mother, played by Hayward. To another reporter Hayward enthused, "It's fun doing a small part, two weeks in Hollywood and then back to my lovely house in Fort Lauderdale. It's great to be here again, as long as I know I can go home again. The strangest thing's happened. I've learned I love to fish." Helen Lawson, she joked, would never go fishing. "She's not exactly a person you'd take home to mother. She's a woman with a backbone of steel. Will I do another film after this one? An actress should never say, 'Never.' She never knows when she'll get the urge."

When a *Los Angeles Times* staff writer asked about taking over for Judy Garland, the star pivoted like an old pro at the publicity game: "Don't know the circumstances of Miss Garland's leaving the part, so I can't tell you. We don't read the columns down there in Fort Lauderdale. We're just plain people. Nowadays I work only when I get restless—itchy feet. Somebody had to take [the role]—may as well be me." Plus, she may have even identified with the role. As she explained, "Helen's not typical. Most women are much more soft. They're only hard till they meet the right man and fall in love. Then, it all changes. Any woman would put true love before a career. Helen never finds that."

After Hayward finished running the press gauntlet, Weisbart and Robson whisked her off to a dressing room crammed with flower arrangements and congratulatory telegrams from Darryl F. Zanuck and others. From there, she went straight to hair and makeup and finally to a wardrobe session with Travilla, on whose nerves she continued to grate. Because Hayward had four inches of height on the 4-foot 11-inch Garland, Travilla's Helen Lawson outfits had required either fabrication from scratch or had to undergo major alterations. This was especially true of the costly beaded pantsuit earmarked for the catfight confrontation between Helen Lawson and Neely O'Hara. To accent Hayward's coloring and more voluptuous contours, Travilla modified the costume, putting an emphasis on darker, wine-colored embellishments. Still, Hayward, self-conscious about her weight, further locked horns with the costume designer. "She made me take everything out—the lining, pads, everything," said Travilla. "That way, she thought she'd look thinner. I argued that the gowns would fall out of shape. In the end, I had no choice but to take it all out; only the beads stayed."

Hayward also insisted on accessorizing the pantsuit with bling from her own wardrobe: a starburst diamond brooch with a cabochon emerald she had previously sported in *Ada*, a 1961 melodrama costarring Dean Martin. As one *Valley* crew member assessed Hayward's fashion sense, "I wanted to think Susan was trying to emphasize Helen Lawson's vulgarity. But, no, it was her own taste. She thought it looked good, but it was just too much of a muchness." With the press, Hayward went for roses and lollipops: "The outfits for us girls in this show are sensational." So sensational that Hayward, despite putting Travilla through the wringer, asked David Weisbart to let her buy two of them, apparently finding them suitable to wear when rubbing elbows with the other "plain people" back in Fort Lauderdale.

Patty Duke, speaking of the "lovely" Hayward, said, "Everyone was thrilled and excited to work with yet another legend." Choreographer Robert Sidney observed the first meeting between Hayward and Duke, noting that the latter "was flip and all that, but the minute she met Susan she knew she was a strong lady and it was no nonsense." He remarked on Hayward's being "the only actress I know who never had any comments about any other actress," and watching on set as the star filmed her first scene with Barbara Parkins, it was clear that she was completely prepared and "absolutely letter-perfect." Parkins admitted that with Hayward, the scenes she'd done earlier with Garland turned out markedly different. Although she was, Parkins has said, "nothing like Judy and couldn't sing," she was "a *movie star.* She was smart, charming, wonderful to work with. Everybody who worked with her on the set liked her." *Almost* everybody, but more about that in a bit.

As Parkins had noted, Hayward wasn't Judy Garland, so accommodations had to be made. Having sung so well in *I'll Cry Tomorrow,* she warned the press that there would be no repeat performance in *Valley of the Dolls.* "I'd love to but time won't permit it," she told a reporter while chain-smoking. "First, I'd have to give up these coffin nails for my voice and second, get back with my singing coach. Instead, my favorite, Maggie Whiting, will be doing the singing for me." Hayward's ghost singer, the warm-voiced Margaret Whiting, had been a constant chart-topper in the 1940s and 1950s with such Capitol Records standards as "That Old Black Magic," "It Might as Well Be Spring," and "Baby, It's Cold Outside" (with composer Johnny Mercer). Whiting was indisputably top-of-the-line pop-music royalty. But her fine and mellow delivery lacks the spine-tingling, larger-than-life, third-balcony Broadway belt for which the Helen Lawson role screams. Still, Whiting's recording session, backed by a full orchestra, pleased the moviemakers, and she sewed it up in a matter of mere hours.

As choreographer Robert Sidney had earlier done with the nimble Judy Garland, he was tasked with helping nondancer Hayward learn gestures and movements for her single song number. Sidney had choreographed Hayward's dance moves eleven years earlier in *The Conqueror.* He told biographer Gene Arceri that when he watched Hayward limbering up for a *Valley of the Dolls* dance rehearsal wearing slacks and a blouse tied at the midriff, he casually mentioned her weight gain: "A little bit of a belly there?" Hayward shot back, "I didn't ask for your anatomical opinion," then exercised virtually nonstop for ninety minutes. Said Sidney, "Every damn day I used to get black and blue because she never stopped."

Then it came time for her to film the "I'll Plant My Own Tree" musical number from Helen's new musical *Hit the Sky.* Manning the orchestra pit was Orrin Tucker, the popular '30s and '40s bandleader. Dominating the stage was a god-awful whirligig mobile in the Alexander Calder style dripping with candy-colored Plexiglas blobs meant to suggest—what, exactly? Tree leaves? Melted gumdrops? Dolls? A production designer's bad acid trip? Everything about the scene is laughably wrong, irresistibly awful—the song, the set, the fit of Hayward's silvery, spangly gown. The visuals don't read as "megastar in her big new Broadway show," they read as "guest star" musical number on any workaday '60s TV variety show trying desperately to be hip and *now.*

And then there's Hayward herself, a star, certainly, but obviously *not* a musical star. She lurches rather than glides, she strikes odd poses, her eyes flash manically and she's forever having to dodge that damn mobile. You almost wonder whether it's going to decapitate her or whether she's going to take one good swat at it and end it. Television producer-writer Stanley Musgrove, an old Hayward pal and associate, watched the shooting alongside Sidney and was struck by something "off" in the star's behavior. He thought she appeared "slightly mad. There was a kind of madness about her." Some wrote off Hayward's odd performance to her real-life grief and depression.

Longtime Hayward intimates have wondered, in retrospect, whether she had begun to manifest early signs of the brain cancer that eventually claimed her life at age fifty-seven; she was one of ninety-one cast and crew members who developed cancer after filming *The Conqueror* less than 150 miles downwind from a Utah A-bomb atmospheric testing zone. What Musgrove called "madness," Barbara Parkins noted, many years later, was a "spastic" quality in her movements. *Valley* crew members also recall an alarming habit of Hayward's at the time. When the spirit moved her, she would let loose with unearthly yelling and screeching. Claiming the screams cleared her throat, she urged raspy-voiced Robert Sidney, "You try it, it's good for you, you need it for your voice."

What hadn't changed about Hayward was a certain frozen, detached quality to her interpersonal interactions. Pretty much from early in her career, once she completed a scene to a director's satisfaction, she would march straight to her dressing room, cutting dead any attempt at small talk. She explained it away by saying that her acting process required her to isolate herself in order to stay in character. But if she happened to encounter any coworkers in her off-hours, she would stare right through them as if they had never met—even if she had worked with them that same day. She was, however, wise (and political) enough to stay clear of apparent rivalry or tension on set. On *Valley*, she refused to supply quotes to writer Betty Rollin, who was on assignment from *Look* magazine to spotlight the three young stars of the movie, already known around Hollywood as "VD." It was probably just as well. She had already told one reporter who'd asked whether she was threatened by the youth and beauty of her costars, "You have your day and then it's somebody else's day. Why try to hang on? I'm not trying to hang on."

Rex Reed observed that Rollin's September 5, 1967, *Look* cover story ("*Valley of the Dolls*—The Dames That Play the Dolls")—a jaw-dropping hit piece, especially for its era—sent the three stars "into a fury" and 20th along with them. It's easy to see why. Rollin led off her story by calling *Valley of the Dolls* "that candy box of vulgarity with something for everyone" and by captioning a photo portrait of the three ingenues posed on the brass bed that graces Neely's boudoir in the movie: "Sporting $1,300 worth of false hair, *Dolls* stars Barbara Parkins, Sharon Tate and Patty Duke loll on the film's most persuasive piece of furniture." Duke refers to her costar as "Barbara Starkins" because of what Duke calls "her obsession with becoming one." Sounding as if she might have been in a manic phase of her psychiatric disorder, Duke sets herself apart from Parkins and Sharon Tate by boasting that she is the only one of the three who *didn't* do a nude scene. "I have too much on the ball," she says. "I don't need to do that." Asked about Neely O'Hara, Duke says, "The other people tested played her like a hard-nosed bitch. I played her loneliness. I understood that. Like when I was 18, I lived alone and I was mean to people. But it was just a defense."

Rollin also describes Duke's sticking two fingers in her mouth, extracting a wad of gum, pushing it back in, cracking it, snorting, uttering some (then) unprintable words, belching, and laughing. "Yesterday's moppet, today's sewer mouth. That's me, 'Old Sewer Mouth.' Why? I dunno. Once, I swore off swearing for a whole year. But I'm at it again." Was she trying to sound like the *new* Patty Duke or Neely O'Hara? Or had she no control over herself? Rollin describes Duke, between bouts of fingernail chewing and popping her gum, expressing her insecurities about her appearance, especially as compared to that of her costars: "I dunno, I guess I gotta act tough. I mean, everyone's bigger than me. Everybody's got a bigger bra size. I'm like a little man. I'll tell you one thing. I'm not doing any more Patty Lanes (her character on *The Patty Duke Show*). The only reason I did that show in the first place was that I had nothing else to do. Boy, was I stuck. Like, I had to turn down *A Patch of Blue*. It would have 'ruined my image.'"

Sharon Tate, opening up herself to Rollin, did herself no favors, either. "People look at me and all they see is a sexy thing," she remarks. "I mean, people see sexy. I mean sexy is all they see. When

I was put under contract, I thought, 'Oh, how nice.' But I was just a piece of merchandise. No one cared about *me*, Sharon." She laments, "People expect so much of an attractive person. I mean, people are very critical on [*sic*] me. It makes me tense. Even when I lay down, I'm tense. I imagine all kinds of things, like that I'm all washed up. I'm finished. I think sometimes that people don't want me around." And she digs herself deeper by observing, "I'm trying to develop myself as a person. Well, like sometimes on weekends, I don't even wear makeup."

As for Parkins, she hardly needed Rollin to burnish her rep for being candid during interviews. Assessed by *Peyton Place* producer Paul Monash as having "a terrible need to be Number One" and someone who "wants to be Elizabeth Taylor overnight," Parkins once described herself as "a volcano in a tight dress." In a single year Parkins had reportedly burned through five of the town's top publicists and several of its most powerful agents. The summer before the release of *Valley of the Dolls*, the Hollywood Women's Press Club nominated her for their "Sour Apple Award" for often failing to show for scheduled interviews or for refusing to answer questions. Was Parkins ruffling feathers because she dared to challenge the status quo or because she was so honest, she was willing to say what others wouldn't? "It's a lonely town," she observed. "To become other than just another pretty lady in pretty clothes, you've got to become a fighter—a fighter for survival. Because that's what it is—survival. But also a fighter to search out your own identity. You have to fight for your independence and not, that dirty word— a starlet. The other day, I heard a producer say he was looking for a 'Barbara Parkins type.' That's the second step. The third is when you become a legend."

Rollin's article sparked a firestorm. Intra–show business rumors of problems on the *Valley* set had by now bled so far beyond Hollywood that even Parkins's usually laudatory hometown newspaper the *Vancouver Sun* mentioned "the well-known fact" of "verbal clashes between Barbara and one of the other Dolls, Patty Duke."

Those who preferred the Barbara Parkins who shot from the hip and refused to be a phony couldn't help but be disappointed when in October 1967, she told reporter Rebecca Morehouse, "I didn't like the story about us in *Look* recently at all. A lot of it wasn't true. . . . They said we were having fights but all of us got along beautifully. I never met girls who got along as well as we did."

But considering how Rollin went in for the kill, and considering the movie's most controversial subjects—sex, plus drug addiction among the rich, famous, and white—it must be attributed to the conventions of Hollywood journalism of the era that neither she nor any other journalist is known to have asked the *Valley* girls even veiled questions about their own exposure to the burgeoning drugs-and-sex culture of a cataclysmically changing Hollywood. More than three decades after the film's release, Barbara Parkins brushed away any speculation of intracast dalliances or self-medicating behaviors: "Nothing like that was happening during the making of *Valley*. We were all just working hard."

Neither Rollin nor any other journalist was invited to observe the filming of what many would view as the film's Main Event: the ladies' powder room smackdown between Susan Hayward's Helen Lawson and Patty Duke's Neely O'Hara. Who doesn't love this notorious highlight of the movie? But really, what exactly is the big shock of the scene? "Oh, my god, it's a wig! Her hair's as phony as she is! Hey, dig me as a redhead!" exults Duke as Neely, grasping Hayward's wig in her hot little hands and making a run for the john. It *is* a wig, and not for nothing, but the Neely character is wearing one, too, as is Hayward throughout the movie. Are we actually supposed to buy a seasoned young showbiz pro's being astounded and thrilled to discover that a Broadway legend's trademark tresses have all these years been—gasp!—a wig? What stage, screen, or TV actress *didn't* sport an array of wigs, especially as does every female character in a '60s epic like *Valley of the Dolls*? And how would *any* savvy performer, like Neely, not immediately spot a wig or a fall on anyone, let alone on a star with whom she's actually worked, however briefly?

About the infamous scene, Duke has said, "Susan was most gracious and professional, except for one thing"—that one thing being how she was willing to look at the lowest point of the climactic catfight. Duke maintained, as highly unlikely as it sounds, that Judy Garland had signaled her willingness to David Weisbart to have her head shaved for the big reveal in the wig-pulling scene. Presented with the same option, Hayward refused. She told choreographer Robert Sidney that she intended to have the studio hairdressers Edith Lindon and Kaye Pownall bleach her own hair white to reveal the character's advanced age and vulnerability. When Sidney advised her to wear a silvery white wig rather than run the risk of letting hairdressers botch her own tresses, Hayward countered that she thought her performance would be less honest were she not to expose her own head of hair.

With the famous on-screen hair-pulling tussle between Rosalind Russell and Paulette Goddard in the 1939 movie version of *The Women* as a yardstick, Sidney might also have done himself a favor by revisiting Susan Hayward versus Marsha Hunt in *Smash-Up, the Story of a Woman*; Martine Beswick versus Aliza Gur in *From Russia with Love*; or Haji versus Lori Williams in *Faster, Pussycat! Kill! Kill!* Sidney initially staged a lengthy tooth-and-claw fight for *Valley of the Dolls*, aimed at conveying maximum impact but minimal actual contact. During rehearsals, Hayward and Duke appeared to be worthy adversaries and more than up for the challenge. Weisbart scheduled the shooting to take place on Stage 15, one of the largest on the lot. There, in past years, Tyrone Power made his last stand in *Jesse James*; Betty Grable in the backstage musical *Diamond Horseshoe* got told, "You are in show business for only two reasons—and you're standing on them"; and governess Julie Andrews calmed a brood of kids rattled by a thunderstorm by trilling "My Favorite Things" in *The Sound of Music*. Subtle and not-so-subtle signs of tension between Hayward and Duke only heightened the cast and crew's anticipation for their confrontation. One actor said, "People expected fireworks. Everybody on the picture wanted to be on Stage 15 to see this fight scene between Susan and Patty. My character wasn't in the scene and neither was Sharon Tate's or Barbara Parkins's, but I'm pretty sure I remember seeing them there."

With everything set to go, Robson put Hayward and Duke through a few rehearsals, during which the actresses initially followed the fight choreography as they had rehearsed with Robert Sidney. Robson, marching to the beat of his own stopwatch, wanted the fight shortened, with Duke grabbing off the wig sooner and running to the toilet cubicle to drop it in and flush. Rehearsing the abbreviated version, Robson noted the actresses being too cautious and safe to be convincing. "They were carefully avoiding contact and Mark was right—he wasn't getting the intensity he was after," said an observer. "But I noticed Susie began spitting fire because Patty was getting pretty aggressive." It wasn't the first time Duke had gotten physically combative with a fellow actor. While the fifteen-year-old Duke was winning raves on Broadway in *The Miracle Worker*, her beloved costar Anne Bancroft decided to take time off before the two were to film director Arthur Penn's 1962 movie version. Suzanne Pleshette, Bancroft's twenty-one-year-old stage replacement, said in a 2006 interview, "Patty Duke thought, *I'm going to be the star of the play now.* Well, hello? No." Pleshette recalled how Duke would "beat the shit out of me." Finally, Pleshette warned Duke not to provoke her because of her "terrible temper." During one particularly strenuous performance, Pleshette recalled, "Something in me snapped, you know?" In the fight scene, when Duke had her legs wrapped around a chair, Pleshette—with superhuman strength—grabbed one of the chair's legs, lifted it into the air, and slammed it down and planted her hands on each chair arm. Pleshette said, "I looked right in her face. And I tell you: Helen Keller saw that night." Although Pleshette conceded hers and Duke's conflicts were "a personal problem," she called her young costar's performance "the most extraordinary thing I have ever, ever seen. What this child brought to this role every single night— new, fresh, alive, brilliant, brilliant, brilliant." After the curtain rang down on Pleshette's final performance, she left the Playhouse Theater with her parents, telling them, "'I will never come down [West Forty-eighth Street] again.' That's how horrible the experience was for me in my soul." For years, Pleshette joked with friends that she would spontaneously break out in black-and-blue marks at the mere mention of Duke's name.

So when Patty Duke (4 feet 11 inches and change) and Susan Hayward (5 feet 3 inches) came out of their corners to go at each other on Stage 15, sparks flew. In the name of art—or something—both gave the scene their all, and then some. Things got the hottest, and most intensely personal for Duke, when the actresses reached the section of dialogue when Neely rides Helen about her new show, and Helen tells her that she turned down the role Neely is playing in her own new show for producer David Merrick. Says Duke as Neely, "Bull! Merrick's not that crazy." Some say goaded by Mark Robson, Hayward hit her next line particularly hard and aimed it right below the belt: "You should know, honey. You just came out of the nuthouse." For the fragile Duke, that one hit uncomfortably close to home.

That's when things went bad. "A terrible thing happened," Duke recalled to her memoir cowriter and friend William J. Jankowski. "As we were doing the struggling with the wig, Susan fell and indeed, she hit her head. That awful man [Robson] said I did it on purpose! What? What could I ever be thinking of to do that to *anyone*, much less Susan Hayward!" Robson suspended the filming, and Hayward was seen by the studio medics. That incident only solidified Duke's persona non grata status among some in the *Valley* company. "Although I am little, I can be a really physically strong person," she recalled. "I got really strong while doing *The Miracle Worker* years before and became even stronger though the years. If nothing else, I am a disciplined actress and there is no way any harm should have come to anyone in that scene. I wouldn't have even let it happen accidentally. Was there water on the floor or something? I don't know, but I do know it was a terrible accident. However, it wasn't nearly as bad as everyone made it out to be. The story made the rounds, and I got a bit of a bad reputation for a while."

Once doctors cleared Hayward, and Robson had rescheduled the filming, old trouper Hayward reported back for duty and won a deserved round of applause from Robson, Weisbart, her fellow actors, and the crew. Anxious to avoid any further incidents, Robson restaged and shortened the action, toning it way down from the more forceful and aggressive approach of the earlier footage. Duke reflected, "I have no idea whether Susan herself thought that I had purposely pushed her, but she did not treat me any differently afterward." But others maintain that Hayward kept an ever-icier, self-protective distance, and was fully prepared and equipped to teach Duke a lesson if need be. Although things ran smoothly during the subsequent round of filming, Duke blamed Hayward's vanity for blunting the impact of what could have been a much more visceral, satisfying scene. "In my opinion, Susan looked better when the wig came off than when the wig was on," Duke said. "Her [real] hair was platinum under that red wig and she looked very beautiful. The whole point of the scene, to me, was completely lost, and it just became silliness about Neely O'Hara throwing Helen Lawson's wig in the toilet. It was supposed to be about how far Neely had fallen as a human being to be able to humiliate Helen in that way who, in the novel, had been going through cancer." [Fact: Helen Lawson has cancer neither in Susann's novel nor in any available draft of the screenplay.] The actress concluded, "It was very disappointing to me. I believe it hurt the character of Neely, and certainly Helen Lawson became more grand. The scene was done, and it was no longer any big deal for me, but it became legendary, and is one of the most famous scenes in the film. Apparently, the loss of Helen Lawson's hair was only important to me."

Hayward wrapped her role on schedule, said her crisp good-byes, and, en route back to Florida in late May, told an interviewer that the whole picture wasn't her cuppa. "It's the way crummy people talk," she said. "Personally, I like to see a nice picture. I think Hollywood more and more is not too healthy an influence. So sue me."

With just weeks of shooting left as the projected end date of May 20 approached, 20th finalized the release date of *Valley of the Dolls* as December 15, during the highly competitive rush of year-end holiday-season movie releases. Robson pressed even harder, making short work of any scene that didn't involve the bigger stars and not spending much more time on those, either. In nothing flat, he dispatched a scene with Duke and a then-struggling young actor named Richard Dreyfuss, whom he had cast as the stage manager of *Tell Me, Darling*, the Neely O'Hara Broadway musical on which he is forced to deal with a leading lady so stoned and messed up that she can't even perform on opening night. In the same year of release as *Valley*, Dreyfuss also had a blink-and-you'll-miss-it moment in *The Graduate*. Looking back on the experience, the Oscar-winning actor has recalled, "I've always said that I was in the best film of 1967 and the worst film of 1967, because I had a part in *Valley of the Dolls*, which I never admitted to for probably 15 years. But then one day I realized that I had never actually seen *Valley of the Dolls*, so I finally did. And I realized that I was in the last 45 seconds of the worst film ever made. And I watched from the beginning with a growing sense of horror. And then I finally heard my line. And I thought, 'I'll never work again.' I actually knew Patty [Duke] at the time, and I told her 'I've never seen the film.' And she said, 'Neither have I.' But I used to make money by betting people about being in the best and worst films of 1967. No one would ever come up with the answer, so I'd make 20 bucks!"

With publicity opportunities dwindling as the end of filming neared, David Weisbart leaned on 20th's publicity department to invite journalists to the set to meet the lesser-known Sharon Tate and Tony Scotti, who had been overshadowed by the press coverage devoted to Garland, Hayward, Parkins, and Duke. Darryl F. Zanuck spurred the publicity push after he viewed Dorothy Spencer's edit of the footage shot to date: "Was very impressed with footage on *Valley of the Dolls*. It has the real smell of success. Sharon Tate comes off much better than expected." Robson, always looking to thank Darryl Zanuck for backing him in ways that Richard Zanuck had not, dutifully spent time on the set with syndicated columnist Harrison Carroll during filming of the nightclub scene involving ringsiders Tate, Duke, and Parkins reacting to Tony Scotti singing "Come Live With Me." Tate remarked that her shimmery, low-cut Travilla-designed evening gown "feels like it weighs a ton and it has a metal frame around the top that almost pulls my shoulders off." Scotti chimed in, "Her own personal frame gets me all upset." "The biggest surprise in the film is Sharon," crowed Robson, who added, "I think it is wonderful to have all these young people. They are not typed. In the minds of the audience they are unpredictable." Weisbart told Harrison Carroll, as well as other columnists: "I venture to say that when the film is all put together, no one is really going to be shocked. It may not be the kind of picture that Walt Disney would have produced, but I just hope it comes out with a feeling of moral honesty."

Discussing actors whom he had demeaned, badgered, and dismissed during filming, Robson was nothing but positive. Of Patty Duke and Barbara Parkins, he said, "TV has been a great help to them—and thus, to me. They are veterans of the business although so young. They are masters of technique. Nothing is a cliché to them. They are always seeking." Robson told reporters he hoped that younger audiences would flock to *Dolls*: "It seems like it's just the beginning. There is a great excitement created also by the audiences of young people in the country who love movies and can't devour enough of them."

Asked by Tony Thomas of the *Toronto Telegram* news service about rumors of conflicts between female cast members, Robson declined to name names, but commented, "Of all the actresses I've worked with, I can't recall one who has come through it without having all kinds of problems—marital, social and psychological. A person with a deep sense of morality in the commercial world is hard to find, and to have an agent who will think not only of your economic welfare but of your welfare as a human being is rare. People are misused in the theatrical business and this causes all kinds of 'hang-ups.' There are, of course, hundreds of varieties of reactions to being an actress but I see repeated over and over again a kind of trend—the difficulty of living a normal family life, great ego problems, great nervousness and an aggressive need for money." He apparently had no comment about the psychological hang-ups or need for money of any of his male cast members.

But the studio publicists' heaviest lifting went into the mounting of an Oscar nomination campaign for Patty Duke. The blitzkrieg launched full force in the spring and battered on relentlessly into the fall, in tandem with the efforts of Duke's agents. Like good little soldiers, newspaper columnists fell in step with the party line: Duke could well be nominated for Best Actress, maybe even go all the way. In the widely read "Just for *Variety*," columnist Army Archerd reported, "[Fox] is predicting confidently that Patty will win another Oscar for this job." "The cast and crew are making bets on it," gushed Alice Pardoe West in her syndicated "Behind the Scenes" column. David Weisbart told reporters that Duke was "the best natural talent I've worked with since Jimmy Dean in *Rebel Without a Cause*," and had been so confident in the actress's performance and star potential that by late summer, he and 20th had exercised an option to make four more films with her. (Weisbart had also penciled in Tony Scotti—and, possibly, Duke—for a campus unrest drama titled *Santa Claus Is Dead*.) Duke told the press that before any 20th assignments, she first wanted to do a couple of movies directed by her husband, Harry Falk, who had directed three episodes of *The Patty Duke Show*. In fact, there were to be no Weisbart-Fox projects after *Valley of the Dolls*. Nor were there to be any Duke-Falk collaborations. Shortly after Duke completed filming, she suffered a miscarriage. She and Falk divorced two years after the release of the film.

On June 24, director Robson and Weisbart called it a wrap on

Valley of the Dolls, with the final production costing $4,926,700, or about $39 million today. International newspapers reported how 20th, Weisbart, and Robson hosted "a swinging party for cast, crew and members of the press" with "music, dancing, libation, much food and gaiety." Travilla could not attend because he was en route from Los Angeles to New York for publicity interviews on the film's behalf—and on his own. He needed to attend to final preparations for the launch of his fashion line for the year, crowing in press interviews that "90 percent of my new line is from the movie." The designer telegrammed Robson: "Dear Mark: Never before have I ever felt so very close to a picture. Perhaps it is because I admire your great artistic ability and find working with you truly an inspiration. Thank you for these pleasant weeks." Similarly, Robson received a charming handwritten letter to "Dearest Mark," signed "Your friend, *always*" by supporting players Pat Becker, Corinna Tsopei, and Linda Peck, who expressed gratitude for the "kindness" and "honor" the director showed them on set while filming their bits as "Telethon Telephone Operators" as background to Patty Duke and guest host Joey Bishop. The letter concluded: "If we ever can be of any help to you—please allow us the privilege of doing so."

Among the invited press at the wrap party was Florabel Muir, who described Sharon Tate wearing "her mini-est of miniskirts by costume designer Travilla" and "little Patty Duke" wearing one of Travilla's short metallic lamé dresses. Duke said that she and her husband now needed to decompress and were "headed to a hideaway with no telephones." Muir gave Barbara Parkins some ink, too, describing her being outfitted in white lace evening pajamas (*not* by Travilla) "and as always displaying a great deal of cool" while she chatted with Tate and Jacqueline Susann, who "looked very much the movie star herself in a stunning beaded cocktail dress."

Robson and Weisbart told reporters that they were so happy with their *Valley* collaboration that they would be continuing their partnership with a 20th Century Fox–financed movie version of Irving Wallace's recently published bestselling thriller *The Plot*, Robson's newest stab at filming a Wallace novel since directing *The Prize* in 1963. Darryl F. Zanuck was all in on *The Plot*, and enthusiastic about the moviemakers' hope of casting Gregory Peck and Paul Newman, Robson's leading man in *From the Terrace* and *The Prize*, to head an all-star ensemble cast.

On July 21, almost exactly one month after the *Valley* wrap party, Weisbart and Robson played an early morning round of golf at the Brentwood Country Club in anticipation of viewing for the first time later that day editor Dorothy Spencer's initial cut of *Valley of the Dolls*, being readied for the long-planned San Francisco sneak preview. With every reason for optimism as they golfed in perfect Southern California weather on the tenth fairway, Weisbart grinned at Robson, said, "This is the life," and toppled to the ground. As Robson administered mouth-to-mouth resuscitation, actors Stephen Boyd and Michael Dunn, playing the same course, rushed over to help. It was too late. Weisbart had succumbed to a massive heart attack at age fifty-two. The gentlemanly producer's early death struck a blow to Hollywood, and an even bigger one to *Valley of the Dolls*.

CHAPTER FOURTEEN

We'll Fix It in Post. Right?

The loss of David Weisbart hit Mark Robson, and many on the *Valley* team, hard. Screenwriter Helen Deutsch wrote the director: "Dear Mark: I have been abroad and therefore unaware until this morning of the sudden and tragic death of David Weisbart. I know you were his friend as well as his co-worker and I want to express my sympathy. Please let me know if there is anything I can do. Sincerely, Helen." Robson replied to Deutsch's Park Avenue address: "I can't tell you how sad the whole occasion was for all of us. David was a wonderful man and his death comes as a blow to so many people who knew him. Thank you again for your note. Best regards, Mark Robson." Jacqueline Susann was especially touched when, at the producer's funeral service, Weisbart's widow presented her with the solid gold pencil with which he annotated screenplays and books.

Still, Robson knew that the movie needed major tinkering, and it obviously wouldn't finish itself. On July 31, the director wrote several detailed drafts for an added scene that would give Barbara Parkins more screen time and might give the movie a stronger sense of the passage of time. The idea was to feature the actress in a *second* lavish, overblown Gillian Girl commercial, to be filmed on a 20th soundstage with Parkins posing and sporting scads of previously unused Travilla finery as well as a succession of fashion-forward makeup styles and over-the-top wigs. The proposed sequence—think of it as *Funny Face* on dolls—would reveal that Anne, though classy and lovely as ever, has begun to betray telltale signs of drug and Lyon damage. Shooting such a scene might have been a relief to Parkins, who has rightly complained that she was asked to spend a good deal of screen time either "standing around" or "wandering around." A lifelong trained dancer and a Martha Graham Dance Company scholarship winner who considered a full-time career in dance, Parkins has said: "Here I am in the film and I'm not moving and I'm dying to move and finally the Gillian Girl scenes came along and I said, 'Oh, please, just let me float through this.'"

On August 1, Robson brought in an unidentified KNBC-TV announcer for a recording session to read the text: "Celebrating the second anniversary of the Gillian Girl, Gillian Products offers a birthday special—Gillian high-fashion makeup. Gillian high-fashion lipstick. And high-fashion hair spray. It helps soothe natural curls as it sets your hair. After your shampoo, just comb, roll up, then brush out. Gillian makeup gives grace and elegance to that high-fashion look. Gillian makeup gives you just enough 'accent' to that flawless complexion. Remember, the beautiful people use Gillian." Despite the delicious promise of the montage, Robson scrapped it for scheduling and budgetary concerns.

To the surprise of many, Darryl F. Zanuck, to help hype *Valley of the Dolls* and other 20th movies, decamped from Paris and swept into 20th to host a flashy annual dog-and-pony-show convention prepared for national and international movie exhibitors. The weekend of special events for the visiting conventioneers, masterminded mostly by both Zanucks and publicity department head James Denton, included a VIP trip to Disneyland, a sneak preview of the company's new Frank Sinatra detective thriller *Tony Rome*, a barbecue on the studio's standing Western set, a show on Stage 15 featuring scenes from *Valley of the Dolls* and the yet to come *Justine* and *Hello, Dolly!* performed by budding stars from the New Talent division, a special viewing of an assemblage of scenes from the studio's upcoming movies held in 20th's biggest screening room, and a *Doctor Dolittle*–themed party at the palatial Mediterranean Revival–style private estate of *Justine* director George Cukor. The exhibitors were also invited to lunch in the studio dining room, where the menu prominently featured a new offering, the *Valley of the Dolls* salad topped with multicolored "pills"—blueberries, cranberries, and golden raisins—and a choice of additions (although, sadly, no cubes of ham).

The charismatic Zanuck Sr. and David Brown held sway over many of the events, effectively reducing Zanuck Jr.—as intended—to a subsidiary role. Top 20th producers like Arthur Jacobs held breakout sessions to discuss their movies individually with the exhibitors and publicity contacts. Richard Zanuck's executive assistant addressed the attendees, emphasizing the studio's slate as being full of "good product . . . [offering] something for everybody." 20th's New York–based domestic sales manager Abe Dickstein said, "A nice picture like *Two for the Road*, you got Audrey Hepburn, you'll win some awards, you give it special attention, you'll turn a little profit. It's nice, sure, but you take a *Tony Rome*, a *Valley of the Dolls*, now those are the pictures you like to sell."

On August 8, after viewing a rough edit, John Williams and Mark Robson discussed placement of music, special audio effects, and vocal issues that needed correction. Robson instructed Williams to set up a small musical combo for a session in which Tony Scotti would re-record "Come Live With Me"; the director wanted the song sung as much more "reflective and romantic" than a previous version. The director also detailed specific notes on how he wanted to overdub Tony Scotti's distorted voice singing "Come Live With Me" over Jennifer North's suicide scene. For a scene set in a San Francisco barroom in which Neely croaks along with her own record on the jukebox, Robson wanted to substitute a different take by ghost singer Gail Heideman, preferring one that she recorded "live" on the set. Jangly hard rock music was prescribed to accompany a scene set in a fleabag San Francisco hotel along the Embarcadero, in which Neely awakens and discovers she's spent the night (or longer) with what the dubbing notes describe as "The Wino." And for Neely's theater alley breakdown scene, Robson debated using distorted church bells, chimes, and trippy reverberating sound effects.

For various reasons, much of the aforementioned were either modified or dropped. For the scene already shot at the Dorothy Chandler Pavilion at the Music Center, theater ushers were meant to throw open the doors as Neely and Ted emerge while the orchestra plays exit music from composer Jerry Herman's smash Broadway musical *Hello, Dolly!* (20th's screen version was in the works). But lines of Patty Duke's dialogue for that same scene needed to be rerecorded from scratch, and her agents reported to Robson that the actress was unavailable. Enter Sherry Alberoni, a show business veteran since age three who, as a nine-year-old, joined the cast of *The Mickey Mouse Club* and as a teen appeared in dozens of episodic TV series, including *The Donna Reed Show*, *The Monkees*, and *Family Affair*, on which she played a recurring role. Casting director Joe Scully was familiar with the voiceover work of Alberoni, who recalled, "They needed five of Patty Duke's lines dubbed for the outdoor scene near the fountain shot at the Dorothy Chandler Pavilion because there was so much extraneous background noise. I don't know if Patty had gone back to New York or she wanted too much money or what. It was my first time dubbing in a session on one of those big soundstages with a sort of circular shape, lined with cloth acoustic padding, and with a big movie screen. We did it in maybe a couple of hours or less, [Mark Robson] just said, *We got it,* and I remember thinking, *This is the easiest $500 I've ever made.*"

Meanwhile, John Williams was impressing Robson and 20th vice president in charge of music Lionel Newman with his transcendent underscoring and orchestral arrangements for the film, notable for a stylistic range that encompassed instrumental variations on the Previns' wistful theme song, a jazzy swing waltz ("Neely's Career Montage"), a Henry Mancini–reminiscent bossa nova ("Chance Meeting"), a lilting Francis Lai–style French *morceau de musique* ("Jennifer's French Movie"), an evocative Mort Lindsey–style up-tempo Judy Garland arrangement ("I'll Plant My Own Tree") replete with bongos (like "Come Rain or Come Shine"), and a dreamlike, spacey, and moving elegy ("Jennifer's Recollection") for the suicide scene. On September 13, Newman conveyed in an intrastudio memo to Richard Zanuck how "delighted" Robson was "with what Johnny Williams has been doing with *Valley of the Dolls* up to now." Zanuck replied, "I couldn't agree more, nor be more pleased. I think Johnny Williams is one of the most talented young composers we have in California. I think it would be to our benefit if we tied Johnny up for two pictures over a period of 18 months. He is tremendously versatile and would be a big asset to our organization." In the same memo, Newman conveyed word that Robson was so pleased with Williams's work for *Valley* that he wanted to reserve his services for his next movie, *The Plot*.

On September 22, casting executive Owen McLean alerted Robson that he had obtained a waiver of recording royalties from Barbara Parkins. Parkins's generosity meant that she had signed away any expectations of further compensation for the use of her "You've got to climb Mount Everest to reach the valley of the dolls . . ." narration on the original soundtrack album; considering how big a hit that record became, the actress's agents may not have provided her the wisest financial advice.

As for the key decision as to which vocalist should record the Previns' theme song for the opening credits, David Weisbart had set the wheels in motion before his passing. The Previns wrote at least a half dozen different sets of lyrics meant to serve as narrative bridges between key sequences throughout the film. That plan was radically simplified, then, later, all but eliminated. Judy Garland had originally been expected to sing the song over the credits, although no evidence has surfaced that she ever recorded it. With Garland's firing, though, the moviemakers began exploring more youthful options, including Barbra Streisand, Petula Clark, Dusty Springfield, Jackie DeShannon, Gloria Loring, Lana Cantrell, Cilla Black, and Nancy Sinatra. Aware of the search for an appropriate "voice" for the movie, Barbara Parkins suggested Dionne Warwick. All the moviemakers needed to hear were Warwick's takes on such Burt Bacharach–Hal David songs as "Message to Michael," "Trains and Boats and Planes," and especially "The Windows of the World," Bacharach and David's Vietnam War protest song, orchestrated with Asian-inflected finger cymbals and plucked strings. Parkins's bright idea gained instant traction. Warwick signed the deal to record what was then known simply as "Anne's Theme." To distinguish her participation from many other singers' routine "theme song" assignments that had already become a cliché by the '50s, the 20th publicity department sent to international newspapers a press release: "Miss Warwick's rendition thus becomes a key adjunct to the continuity and assumes more importance than is usually associated with title tunes."

But Warwick's management team threw up hurdles that prompted Richard Zanuck to fire off a series of telegrams and intrastudio memos on the theme of "What do we do *now*?" Harry McIntyre of 20th's music department learned from Scepter Records consultant George Marek that, because of Warwick's exclusive contract with the label, "under no circumstances would they permit Warwick's recording be used on a movie soundtrack album unless distributed by Scepter. ABC Records [the distributor of 20th Century Fox Records] would probably resist giving up album unless compensated. Therefore, question is whether inclusion in soundtrack album is sufficiently important to justify our paying ABC to transfer album to Scepter." The fractious negotiations stalemated over the percentage of profits 20th would get (2 percent of retail based on

90 percent of records sold) as opposed to how much would go to Warwick's manager and Scepter Records executive Paul Cantor and to Hal David and Burt Bacharach, who derived "a good deal of income from Dionne's record business." Maybe the most vehement opponent of the deal was Florence Greenberg, the firebrand owner of Scepter Records, who placed a series of angry phone calls to 20th in which she made it clear that even if she were going bankrupt and needed a quick $100,000, she wouldn't even entertain a conversation on the subject. The case was thus closed, with lots of finger-pointing as to who was to blame for not checking into Warwick's recording restrictions in the first place.

In the end it was agreed that Warwick would sing "Anne's Theme" in the movie, but her separate recording of the song would not be featured on the 20th Century Fox record label's official movie soundtrack album *Music from the Motion Picture Soundtrack "Valley of the Dolls,"* conducted by Johnny Williams. So who would sing the theme song? The choice was singer-songwriter Shelby Flint, whose disarmingly yearning "Angel on My Shoulder" became a top forty hit in 1961. Flint's pure, whispery soprano—the one that songwriter-singer Joni Mitchell said she most wanted to sound like early in her career—seemed an appropriate vocal analog to Anne Welles's self-doubts about how her life would unfold once she left behind small-town New England for the great, big wicked city. Susan Hayward's "ghost singer" Margaret Whiting is also among the missing on the album, due to her ongoing London Records contract. Instead, "I'll Plant My Own Tree" is (nicely) performed by Eileen Wilson, a former big band singer and cast member of *Your Hit Parade*, and the singing voice of Ava Gardner in *One Touch of Venus*, Jayne Mansfield in *The Girl Can't Help It*, and Barbara Bel Geddes in *The Five Pennies*.

On October 4, more than two months before the movie would debut in theaters, Mark Robson sent Dionne Warwick a personal letter of appreciation; by prior arrangement, the letter was run by 20th as a full-page ad in the major Hollywood trade papers:

Dear Dionne,

All of us connected with *Valley of the Dolls* congratulate you on your wonderful rendition of the title theme by André and Dory Previn.

Since the song is so unusual, with multiple sets of lyrics acting as narrative bridges throughout the picture, there was much discussion as to which artist would be absolutely right.

After hearing the soundtrack, we know you and the song were made for each other. Lionel Newman, the studio's musical director, and John Williams, who contributed a really great scoring job, are leading the chorus of praise for you here at 20th Century-Fox. And we look forward to this month's release of your Scepter single, the "THEME FROM 'VALLEY OF THE DOLLS.'"

Incidentally, the Previns created four more songs for the film. Care to make it a habit?

Cordially,

Mark Robson

Motion picture music promotions specialist Happy Goday deployed his national army of record promotion men to push Warwick's single; additionally, he expected Warwick's manager, Paul Cantor, former William Morris agent and then-current managing director of Warwick's record label, Scepter Music, to match his level of energy. Cantor contacted his Scepter Records distributors and Hollywood-based record promoters, such as George Jay (whom Happy Goday hired for six weeks at $75 per week) and Herbert Lutz, based in St. Louis, Missouri, to urge them to focus on persuading radio program directors and disc jockeys to give airplay to "Theme From *Valley of the Dolls*," the B side of Warwick's current Burt Bacharach and Hal David–written hit single "I Say a Little Prayer." Goday wrote to Jay in his Hollywood offices on West Sunset Boulevard: "I would appreciate it if you could work fast as you can on this one. I would also like you to try, wherever possible, to get program directors, music librarians and disc jockeys to mention that this song is from the new motion picture *Valley of the Dolls*. I know in some places this is impossible but please do what you can." The not-so-subtle pressure worked.

Concurrently, another knotty legal issue arose that required untangling. On October 1, 1967, a 20th legal adviser, Jerome Edwards, had cabled Richard Zanuck, Mark Robson, and the studio's senior legal counsel, Frank H. Ferguson: "Because of comments made about possible authenticity of characters in *Valley of the Dolls* it is my opinion that we should more clearly emphasize that the characters in our film are not intended to resemble any persons living or dead. Accordingly, I have reached the conclusion that for the legal protection of the company our standard clause disavowing such similarities should be more clearly presented in our main title on a separate card in advance of our trademark. I cannot emphasize too strongly that you should issue appropriate instructions accordingly."

On October 16, Zanuck sent an insistent note to Barbara "Bobbie" McLean—the pioneering film editor who had joined 20th in 1935 and had been appointed chief of their editing division since 1949. It read:

Dear Bobbie:

As I have explained to you and Mark, the Legal Department feels that it is an absolute necessity that we run a standard clause disavowing any similarity between the characters we portray in *Valley of the Dolls* and any persons living or dead. This standard clause should be displayed in paid advertising and on the screen in advance of our trademark. On the screen it should appear silently and without any music or background behind it. The clause should read: "The producers wish to state that any similarity between any persons, living or dead, and the characters portrayed in the film you are about to see is purely coincidental."

R.D.Z.

And so the clause read.

In late November and early December, music promoter Happy

Goday proved he was earning his salary by lining up an array of artists to record Dory and André Previn's songs. Soul singer Rhetta Hughes, newly signed by Columbia, recorded "Come Live With Me," and Susan Smith laid down "Theme From *Valley of the Dolls*" for Mercury. Patty Duke, singing for herself this time, recorded *"Patty Duke Sings Songs from* Valley of the Dolls *and Other Selections,"* the United Artists album on which she attacks the title number, "Come Live With Me," "Give a Little More," "I'll Plant My Own Tree," and "It's Impossible." It's a massacre. And yet here in their glorious entirety are the album liner notes penned, apparently straight-faced, by no less than Gene Kelly, Judy Garland's onetime costar who was then preparing to direct two 20th mega–road show pictures, *Hello, Dolly!* and *Tom Swift* (never made): "What you will hear in this superb collection has been hailed as 'the excited voice of Patty Duke,' which is not, as it sounds a misnomer, but which is a deliberate way of suggesting that Patty Duke's lustrous, range-rich and expressive voice displays the very essence of excitement itself. Of course, Patty is an exciting singer, but precisely because her voice is excited and full of action. The songs themselves are diversified, in keeping with Patty Duke's own wide and considerable talents. The numbers demonstrate the subtle nuances of character, of mood and of motivation, of deep human understanding of the troubled soul who sings them. This is the personality of 'Neely O'Hara' in *Valley of the Dolls*, the destroying and self destructive [sic], self-centered and eruptive singer which Patty Duke portrays with such power and verisimilitude. One detects the magic of her talents in the warm modulations of her voice, in the heart-touching airs, the nostalgic themes, and, above all, the deeply moving arias which come through. What impresses above all is the diversity and range of Patty Duke's performance. Here gathered together are different songs which express the gamut of emotions which charge through vibrant and dynamic Neely O'Hara. And different they are, for they exhibit the changing moods of a woman alternately in ecstasy and anguish, self-pity, romance, bitter cynicism and bright hope, yielding softness and brassy harshness. There are few performers who can offer this gamut of human emotions with such clarity and controlled power." *Whew.* Talk about "princess fire and music." As if Gene Kelly's effusive endorsement were not enough, Duke's album photos were shot by "Curtis Lee Hansen," who, years later, won fame as Curtis Hanson, the Oscar-winning coscreenwriter and director of *L.A. Confidential.*

Fellow *Valley* star Tony Scotti also tossed his hat into the ring with a Liberty Records album, *Starring Tony Scotti Featuring Theme from "Valley of the Dolls."* Like Duke, Scotti let loose on the title song as well as a ballad version of "I'll Plant My Own Tree." To coincide with the movie's theatrical release, Gladys Knight & the Pips (on the album *Silk N' Soul*), Andy Williams (on his album *Honey*), Jack Jones (on his *Where Is Love?* album), and the Pleasure Seekers had a go at the theme song. So did Tony Bennett, back phrasing like crazy, but the cut didn't surface until his *I've Gotta Be Me* album, released in 1969. Meanwhile, arranger-conductor-record-producer and frequent Frank Sinatra collaborator Don Costa's orchestral version for Verve won lots of airplay; so did a version by the Clebanoff Strings on Decca Records. Catering to the cocktails and mood music set, the Hollywood Sound Stage Orchestra released the easy-listening album *Theme from "Valley of the Dolls"* on Somerset Records; the Ray Conniff Singers warbled the theme on their *Honey* album; the Golden Strings Orchestra schmaltzed it up on their *Grandes Temas do Cinema* collection; the Music City Orchestra made it sound like karaoke; and 101 Strings made the tune the opening number of their overoptimistically titled album *"Valley of the Dolls" and Other Academy Award Hits.* Gifted harpist Dorothy Ashby took a more adventurous approach to the theme song on her jazzy album *Afro-Harping*, while popular pianist Floyd Cramer took a predictably more tried-and-true route on his *Class of '68* disc. Orchestra leader and soundtrack composer Hugo Montenegro featured the theme on his RCA album, *Hang 'Em High*, tracks for which were recorded earlier but only released in 1968. Even champagne bubbly

Lawrence Welk got into the act by producing (with Randy Wood and George Cates) a session starring accordionist Myron Floren squeezing out his take, arranged and conducted by Richard Maltby, before Maltby went on to become a Tony Award–winning and Laurence Olivier Award–winning director and composer.

Aimed at a groovier crowd, fabulous jazz pianist Ahmad Jamal worked the theme on his *But Not for Me* album, and saxophone maestro King Curtis, backed by his Kingpins, laced into something more soulful with his earthy rhythm-and-blues version on *Sweet Soul*, arranged and produced by Arif Mardin, for Atco Records. On Philips Records, folk rock group Natty Bumppo slayed the theme song in a distinctively psychedelic attack all their own. On the November 30 episode of TV's *The Dean Martin Show*, the great Lena Horne sang "I'll Plant My Own Tree." Even moored on a bleak set of dead trees straight out of *Halloweentown*, Horne sank her teeth into the song as if it were sirloin, delivering the best-sung version of the number that anyone could reasonably expect.

Jacqueline Susann, not surprisingly, horned her way into the act. "Who the hell writes a theme song for a movie called *Valley of the Dolls* without getting the title into the lyrics?" she complained to everyone within earshot. Who indeed? To rectify what she saw as a missed promotional opportunity, Susann collaborated with Bob Gaudio, a member of the Four Seasons and the songwriter (with Bob Crewe) of most of the pop singing group's biggest hits, including "Big Girls Don't Cry" and their masterwork, "Rag Doll." The lyrics of their brainchild ballad titled, of course, "Valley of the Dolls," hammered the title relentlessly: "Little children never play in the Valley of the Dolls/But grownup children sometimes stray in the Valley of the Dolls/It's so easy to get lost on that road without an end. . . . I need someone who can take me from the Valley of the Dolls." The pop quartet the Arbors ("A Symphony for Susan") released on Date Records their Susann-endorsed album *The Arbors Sing "Valley of the Dolls,"* the cover of which features the book jacket art for "The most sensational bestselling novel of our time!" Then there was a version by singer Kathy Keegan, whose big Judy Garland/Gogi Grant belt made her a regular on *The Ed Sullivan Show* and in nightclubs. When Compass Records stamped Keegan's single version "The Only Authorized Title Song," Dionne Warwick's recording got retitled "(Theme From) *Valley of the Dolls.*" And when Susann agreed to be the centerpiece and occasional narrator of 20th's 1967 fifty-minute nationally syndicated TV vanity documentary *Jacqueline Susann and the "Valley of the Dolls"*—first broadcast on WABC-TV New York on January 27, 1968, to triple the average ratings for the time slot— she strong-armed the studio into bookending it with the Arbors' version. The TV show, which features such talking heads as Rona Jaffe, Cleveland Amory, Helen Gurley Brown, David Brown, James Aubrey, Sharon Tate, and Barbara Parkins, includes music composed by the future two-time Oscar-winning duo of Al Kasha and Joel Hirschhorn.

But the might and money were behind Warwick's superior talent and song, and that buried the Susann-Gaudio effort. In her 1987 biography *Lovely Me: The Life of Jacqueline Susann*, Barbara Seaman writes that songwriter–movie critic Ruth Batchelor also wrote lyrics for the theme song—or at least *a* theme song, anyway—but the labels on both the Arbors' and Kathy Keegan's work credit only Susann and Gaudio.

Record promoter Happy Goday helped broker the deal for Vic Damone, Sinatra's favorite singer, to record "Come Live With Me" and "I'll Plant My Own Tree" for RCA Victor. Goday cheered Damone on, telling him, "I honestly think you can make these into a hit record. . . . Vic, I can't begin to tell you how grateful we are here at Fox about this." Damone got John Williams to both arrange the charts and conduct the sessions recorded on the evening of October 17. Both "turned out absolutely great," according to Goday, but only "Come Live With Me" won release on November 21 as the B-side of a single; the A-side was a medley of Billy Hill's 1936 pop standard "The Glory of Love" and the "Theme from *Guess Who's Coming to Dinner.*" Some record labels list the producer-arranger of both sides as Neely (yes, really) Plumb, who worked, at times uncredited, as an instrumentalist and/or music producer on several films, including *The Sound of Music*. Other pressings, however, correctly list John T. (for "Towner") Williams as the arranger and conductor. While Damone fulfilled an October 25 singing engagement at the Riviera Hotel in Las Vegas, he received a Western Union telegram: "Hap just ran the recordings for me. They are simply wonderful. I can't thank you enough for your help and the magnificent rendition of both. Best regards, as always, Mark Robson."

In case the totality of those recorded versions were not enough for late '60s dolls-loving moderns, "(Theme From) *Valley of the Dolls*" was available for purchase on sheet music and on player piano rolls distributed by Q. R. S. Meanwhile, 20th shipped thousands of free promotional copies of Dionne Warwick's "(Theme From) *Valley of the Dolls*" to local and national entertainment journalists, TV show hosts, and movie critics, including Ed Sullivan, Earl Wilson, Sheilah Graham, Bob Thomas, Joyce Haber, Vernon Scott, and Bosley Crowther. Each record came with a printed note from Mark Robson reading, in part: "I believe, as do André and Dory Previn, who wrote this lovely theme, that Dionne has done a beautiful job both on the soundtrack and on the Scepter record. We hope you will enjoy listening to it and will play it often. VALLEY OF THE DOLLS will be ready for viewing in the near future. Geography permitting, it will be my pleasure to show it to you personally. Cordially, Mark Robson."

But before he could show it to them personally, *Valley of the Dolls* had to face its first public preview audience.

CHAPTER FIFTEEN

La Publicité—
Sell It, Sister

With just over two months remaining before the targeted release date of December 15, 1967, 20th, Robson, and Zanuck arranged their first public sneak preview. On Friday, October 6, the marquee of the G. Albert Lansburgh–designed Warfield Theater on Market Street in San Francisco read: "Hollywood Sneak Preview Tonight—Movie Version of the Biggest Book of the Year." The film's identity was a secret to virtually no self-respecting book or movie fan, so the line for tickets stretched for blocks down Market Street, and moviegoers jammed to the rafters the 2,250-seat theater. Among the 20th contingent flown in from LA were Richard Zanuck, Mark and Sara Robson, producer David Brown and Helen Gurley Brown, assistant director Stan Hough, film editor Dorothy Spencer, casting director Owen McLean, production manager L. B. "Doc" Merman, publicists Regina Gruss and Don Prince, and soundmen James Corcoran and Dave Dockendorf. Darryl F. Zanuck sat out the event.

The preview didn't go as hoped. Instead of sweeping up audiences in glam, romance, and melodrama, instead of titillating them with scenes of wild, abandoned sex and drug abuse, instead of moving viewers to empathize with the tragic trials and tribulations of the characters, producer Brown recalled, "The film was so campy, everyone roared with laughter." As the moviemakers chatted in the lobby after the screening, one audience member was so irate that he made straight for Dick Zanuck and dumped a cup of Coke all over him.

Zanuck dried himself off and convened his colleagues in the theater manager's office to read the audience reaction cards. Well, you can *imagine*. After dining at Ernie's, the fabled Montgomery Street restaurant immortalized in Alfred Hitchcock's *Vertigo*, the 20th contingent conducted the post mortem at their hotel, the Fairmont. Robson looked ashen, but Brown was so unshakable in his certainty that they had a hit on their hands that he calmed down his colleagues. One clue? The size of the preview audience. Another? The number of ticket buyers who had to be turned away. Still another good omen? Audience curiosity about *How did they ever make a movie of "Valley of the Dolls"?* would sell lots and lots of tickets.

In Darryl F. Zanuck's heyday, the executive might have rewritten problem scenes, recast certain roles, reshot the worst of the movie, and worked closely with the editors. This lot merely licked their wounds and trekked back to Hollywood, where they promptly "leaked" to columnists exactly what they wanted them to print. The Louella Parsons–trained Dorothy Manners told her readers: "Reports out of San Francisco on the sneak preview of *Valley of the Dolls* are boffo. Raves for the 'Dolls': Barbara Parkins, Sharon Tate, Patty Duke, Susan Hayward (in the role inherited from Judy Garland), and a new romantic killer, Tony Scotti." But there was pushback. Far less boffo were the stories filed by other journalists—such as the *Daily News*'s and *Daily Variety*'s Florabel Muir—who reported that the movie was headed "back to the cutting room" after the audience laughed at all the wrong times—especially during Patty Duke's and Tony Scotti's sanitarium scene. But Muir also reported how Patty Duke "does an excellent job," and that although "beautiful," Barbara Parkins's role "doesn't give her much chance for any histrionics."

On October 24 the *Valley* troupe received big news: the movie was officially confirmed to debut at two of Manhattan's choicest movie houses, the arty, 600-seat Festival at 6 West Fifty-seventh Street and the previously set Criterion, the 1,700-seat *Streamline Moderne*–style showplace at Broadway and Forty-fourth Street, previous home to reserved-seat, two-performances-daily road show engagements of such prestigious widescreen hits as *South Pacific*, *Lawrence of Arabia*, and *My Fair Lady*. The bookings only further encouraged 20th Century Fox to proceed with a full-throttle promotional campaign. Posters and magazine and newspaper ads were designed to hit the obvious selling points—the notoriety of the novel, the sex, the addictive, multicolored "dolls," and the lovely Dolls.

The advertising copy went for the hard sell: "The motion picture that shows what America's all-time #1 bestseller first put into words!" "America's all-time bestseller is now a film you will never dare forget!" and "The nation's most startling and hotly discussed bestseller now on the screen with every shock and sensation intact!" Some of the posters and print ads describe the Helen Lawson character as "a gut, fingernail and claw fighter—[who] went down swinging. She took the yellow pills." Catchy prose, except for the small detail that Helen Lawson makes it a point of honor not to rely on pills and is never seen taking one during the entire running time. Nearly all the advertisements feature the disclaimer "Any similarity between any person living or dead and the characters portrayed in this film is purely coincidental and not intended."

To shoot special promotional art, 20th expensively hired Hollywood Golden Age glamour photographer extraordinaire George Hurrell. His images of Sharon Tate, Patty Duke, and Barbara Parkins—along with those shot by the equally expensive Pierluigi Praturlon—became visual key elements in the advertising effort. For various other newspaper, magazine, and theatrical key art images, 20th also hired photographer Stanley Tretick for a special session during which he captured photos of Sharon Tate, Patty Duke, and Barbara Parkins striking fashion model–style poses meant to convey surrender and passion; these were used in the newspaper ads and as key art on the movie posters. (A debate rages among Hollywood glamour photography aficionados as to whether Hurrell or Tretick is responsible for the iconic image of the three young stars posed on a brass bed; a September 1967 *Look* magazine cover story on *Valley of the Dolls* credits Tretick.) During the shoots for these images, the actresses were paired with male partners who are clearly *not* Paul Burke, Tony Scotti, or Martin Milner. According to an obscure handwritten note in the studio records, one of the shadowy, all-purpose studs in the advertising was listed as "T. Selleck." At the time, twenty-two-year-old Tom Selleck was a 20th contract player and student in the New Talent School. None of the other male models were identified.

The 20th advertising team sent to movie theater exhibitors this letter on 20th Century Fox Film Corporation stationery detailing a tie-in "sweepstakes" between the studio and Bantam Books meant to entice ticket buyers:

> The Promotion is two-fold:
> Lucky Name Game Bookmark Promotion Sweepstakes
> Window Poster Promotion Sweepstakes
> Each phase of this Promotion affords you the chance to enter *many* times, thus making you eligible to win fantastic gifts each time.
> The rules for entering the game are simple to follow!
> In this Sweepstakes, upon your request, you will be sent:
> a bookmark mat and proof
> a window decal
> a 40 x 60" theater lobby poster.
> *Don't delay!*

To participate in the contest called the "*Valley of the Dolls* Lucky Name Game," theater owners were instructed to stamp the name of their theater on the bookmarks and partner with the managers of local bookstores, drugstores, and grocery stores to distribute the bookmarks free to customers. Each bookmark displayed the photo and name of one of the "dolls" from the movie. If a customer presented a bookmark that matched the name of the "doll" displayed on the forty-by-sixty-inch poster in the theater lobby, that person got in free. "Thus, you must predetermine how many winners there will be!" Theater owners could send a photo of the lobby display along with the winning bookmarks (self-signed and also signed by the theater managers) to qualify to win prizes of their own from 20th.

Theater owners also received a paper foldout *Valley of the Dolls* promotional item in the shape of a can of film along with a tiny strip of six film frames showing Susan Hayward. It read: "Mr. Exhibitor—Get ready for the biggest 'Read the Book—See the Motion Picture' Promotion in Motion Picture History, backed by All-Out Music Promotion. Top recording artist Dionne Warwick sings 'Anne's Theme' [the title later got changed to "(Theme From) *Valley of the Dolls*"] on Septor [*sic*] Records. Frankie Valli and the Four Seasons sing *Valley of the Dolls* (words and music by Robert Gaudio and Jacqueline Susann)—a Philips single set to hit the airwaves soon. [Note: More like set to hit the airwaves *never.*] 'Valley' Fashion Promotion—Fall and Resort wear by the distinguished couturier Travilla with an in-person coast-to-coast tour in leading department stores by the famed designer already in progress. $50,000 Sweepstakes Co-sponsored by 20th Century-Fox and Bantam Books."

The Bantam Books paperback edition had already begun hitting bookstores in 1966. But Bantam's movie tie-in edition was the splashiest of them all. Its cover design featured four-color still photos from the movie—"Now a scorching 20th Century-Fox Motion Picture—Everything You Knew It Had to Be!"—as well as a shamelessly flattering, leggy illustration of Jacqueline Susann by Robert K. Abbett, well known for his work for Ballantine, Pyramid, and Ace Books. Bantam, which would continue printing new paperback editions for decades, also rushed out a second movie-related headline reading "Now a smash Twentieth Century-Fox Motion Picture!"

Robson and David Weisbart had planned to hit the interview

circuit as a team. Now the director had to do so on his own. Robson knew from the pros—like Jackie Susann—that the way to get people talking about him and *Valley of the Dolls* was to spend time with any reporter willing to listen. For a December 10 story in the *Philadelphia Inquirer*, the reporter mentioned Susan Hayward's comment about the movie's dialogue sounding like how "crummy people" talk. Robson said, "Well, you won't find the film crummy. I didn't shoot it for the excitement of shocking people. Actually, I think you will find it quite beautiful. The style of the film is very lovely." Admitting that he didn't think Susann had written "a very good book," he said he undertook the challenge because he thought it had the potential of being made "into a good movie, with the possibilities for character development. When we started to peel off the excesses and got down to the core of the characters, we found some pretty interesting people. I think we have improved on some of the characters because I felt it necessary to make some of them more honest, but in all due respect to Jackie Susann's work, our Neely O'Hara and Helen Lawson are very much the same as they were in the book." Robson remarked in another interview, "It's a true picture of how some women in Hollywood behave today and we are not trying to smooth the scene over."

The director went out of his way to praise "the kids" in the movie. "Barbara is marvelous," he crowed to Hollywood newsman Dick Kleiner. "Nobody has seen her except on TV, but *Peyton Place* is the equivalent of years of repertory theater. Patty is an old pro at twenty. And Sharon seems to be a great natural actress." To reporter Rebecca Morehouse, he predicted that Parkins would become "a bright, wonderful star. To me, she is reminiscent of early Ingrid Bergman and Liz Taylor." (Could any two actresses possibly be less alike than Bergman and Taylor?) According to a number of Hollywood columnists, 20th was "determined to turn Barbara Parkins into a star," and with Robson echoing the rosy predictions, the studio used *Valley* to publicize Parkins's next assignment, costarring with Michael Caine in the movie version of John Fowles's novel

The Magus, director Michael Cacoyannis's follow-up to his Oscar-nominated *Zorba the Greek*. (Candice Bergen, a top choice for Parkins's *Valley of the Dolls* role, got the role instead; the muddled movie that resulted was no *Zorba*.)

Of Sharon Tate, Robson told Baltimore's *Evening Sun* columnist Lou Cedrone, "She has a special quality. It's a quality the stars of yesterday had. I think she'll make it." But to no one's greater surprise than Patty Duke's, in the same feature article, he doled out especially fulsome praise to her: "Patty could very well likely be, for her age, one of the best young actresses in the world today. She has energy, vitality, authority. Imagine at that age—to be a veteran."

Asked about Judy Garland, he was more candid, telling *Boston Globe* film critic Marjory Adams, "We all loved Judy. But Judy didn't seem to want to go in front of the cameras. She felt that as long as she showed up in her dressing room, that was all we required. We worked ten days with her and finished just one page and a quarter of her role. The rest of the cast teased, flattered and cajoled Judy in an attempt to get her on the set. It didn't work. Everybody was heartbroken when we called the deal off. We just had to let her go. After ample warning." Chatting with Clifford Terry in a *Chicago Tribune* feature, Robson elaborated, "I think Judy is so beset with financial problems, men problems . . . a fading youth . . . all these things . . . she just can't function all the time. And she doesn't do it on purpose. She would appear in the morning on time, and get made up and talk, and didn't realize there was a whole team of people waiting for her. She also seems to have the problem of control. Maybe in the theater performances it's easier for her, since she isn't restricted by motion."

When asked to weigh in on the film's potential for being a cautionary tale for women aspiring to show business careers, Robson told *Toronto Telegram* reporter Tony Thomas, "The need for expression comes out of some other psychological need, the personality is upset before the decision to perform. All you can do is to tell women that if they go into this business, they can expect a marvelous, miserable, exciting, terrible, confining and expansive way of life. [Actresses] have enormous pressures put on them by the public, the press, their studios and their agents. They are bombarded. And it takes the most level-headed person not to change. It's not a happy life. You seldom find a great artist in any field who is well adjusted. In fact, the maladjustment is part of the artistry. They see things obliquely because of their problem."

Meanwhile, elaborate preparations were under way for what would turn out to be that series of trouble-ridden prerelease screenings in Venice, Nassau, Jamaica, Colombia, Miami, and Mexico aboard the *Princess Italia*. Before each screening, passengers and invitees were promised the chance to "dine on a sumptuous buffet, while being treated to a fashion show of $175,000 worth of Travilla dresses created for the film." Even the backdrop to the nautical premieres was fraught with backstage tension. Robson wrote Susan Hayward on October 20, inviting her to see the movie in Miami aboard the *Princess Italia* on the evening of November 27. Hayward, hearing that Travilla had gifted Sharon Tate, Barbara Parkins, and Patty Duke with gowns especially designed for the sailings, asked through her agent, Jack Gordean, for similar treatment; so did Jacqueline Susann. When Susann heard about Hayward's request, both of them upped the ante by requesting an additional free evening gown *and* cocktail dress above and beyond what the designer had given the young stars. Mark Robson conveyed to marketing executive Jonas Rosenfield that the designer "does not feel that he should do this for the other two ladies." And he didn't.

Even aboard ship, members of the press picked up telltale signs of animosity among the cast members. One Florida-based reporter commented how the "usually scintillating, sparkling Susan Hayward strode briskly right past Patty Duke as though she were a stranger, yet they share the movie's sure to be most-talked-about showdown scene. Still, our Susie (who looked sensational) has a secret and an excuse: she's nearsighted and wasn't wearing her specs."

She may not have been wearing her "specs," but her vision was acute enough to spot what evening wear Duke had chosen for what she knew would be her first encounter with Hayward since their last encounter: the white Travilla gown Duke wore in the wig-yanking scene, the one that had sent Hayward sprawling onto the floor and hitting her head.

During the Colombia to Miami, Florida, leg of the voyage, Sharon Tate, Paul Burke, Travilla, and other notables endured seas so turbulent that many of them became violently ill. After everything that could possibly go wrong did, notably technical mishaps and overwhelmingly negative response to the movie, the cast members remained obligated to sit for press interviews. "Most of us did the best we could to hide out from the press," Patty Duke wrote decades later, and said that she and Sharon Tate would avoid reporters by hiding under empty casino tables playing cards, scheming ways to get out of talking about the movie. Still, she said, "I was better than most allowing myself to be interviewed, and I was still very loyal to my character." Wisely dodging any loose talk of a possible Oscar nomination, she instead told reporters that her primary focus was a happy home with husband Harry Falk. "If [producers] realize that I'm versatile, I'll be considered for more vehicles and I can decide whether a given offer fits in with our plans. I wanted a strong, memorable role so that if I decide to relax and be a housewife for a year or two, I won't be entirely forgotten." In subsequent decades, Duke confessed that, like most of the other *Valley* survivors, she could hardly wait to leave that boat: "Once we docked, I licked my wounds and prayed that I could get another job."

Working the shipboard press, Paul Burke said, "I've been so involved for so long with stark super-realism in 'Twelve O'Clock High' and 'Naked City' that it was delightful to find myself in the world of glamour—beautiful clothes, beautiful settings, beautiful people. Yet the drama is never sacrificed for lavish mounting." Jacqueline Susann, rejoining the voyage after previously seeing the movie in Venice and declaring it *merda*, valiantly spun her negative reactions when talking to Jeanne Miller for the *San Francisco Examiner.* The novelist invoked the advice of Ernest Hemingway, who encouraged all novelists to sell their work to Hollywood so long as they avoid the theater when the film is released. "I think that the movie is very well done," Susann said, adhering to the old advertising doctrine "Sell It, Don't Smell It." "I also think it proves conclusively that Hollywood is coming of age because the film depicts the cut-throat life behind the scenes in show biz with relentless honesty—something that would have been played down in the past."

In private, Susann met with Mark Robson and conveyed her ideas for voiceovers that she hoped would be recorded before the movie's release. The director took notes during their conversation and sent them to Richard Zanuck:

INT. TONY POLARS [*sic*] NIGHT CLUB
SEQUENCE

ANN [*sic*]: When I first saw Jennifer, I thought she was the most beautiful girl in the world. Later, when we became friends, I learned that she just thought of herself as a body—her mother had convinced her of that.

NEELY'S MONTAGE

NEELY [variously spelled Neeli and Neel]: To be spotted somewhere during her exercises: I couldn't have gotten through it without pills. They were "*dolls*" · · · pills to keep me going—and those beautiful red dolls to put me to sleep. [Robson elaborated in his note to Zanuck: Jackie felt it necessary to explain to audience members who hadn't read the book that dolls = pills.]

JENNIFER AND TONY PARK SEQUENCE: AT THE
END OF THE SCENE WHERE THEY EMBRACE

JENNIFER: It was the first time I really
was happy. . . . I was with somebody who
cared about *me*.
[Jackie felt it was necessary to tell
the audience that the mercenary Jennifer
was on the level when it came to being
attracted to Tony.]

OVER SCENE OF AIR CRAFT [*sic*] AND JENNIFER
RETURNING TO L.A. FROM PARIS

JENNIFER: Claude sold my contract to Fox.
The studio wanted me as a sex
symbol. . . . But at least I was going
home. Thank God, I've kept doing my
breast exercises. . . . That lump . . .
couldn't mean anything. . . . It is so
small. . . . Oh God, make it go away.
[Jackie feels this necessary for the
following scene in the hotel where
Jennifer explains she is going to have a
breast operation; she wants to take the
audience in on this fact so that it won't
appear later that we are piling on more
trouble. Also, she feels that the above
line helps prepare Jennifer's
suicide . . . that it motivates it. In
any event, the scene was cut]

INTERIOR BEDROOM LYON'S BEACH HOUSE. OVER
THE SILLOETTE [*sic*] SHOT OF LYON LETTING
DOWN ANN'S [*sic*] HAIR

ANN [*sic*]: Suddenly it didn't matter to me
if we were married or not. . . . Just
that we were together.
[Jackie thinks it necessary to tell why
Ann (*sic*) who has rejected Lyon before at
her home in Lawrenceville is now willing
to accept him after a few years, on his
terms.]

Included with Jacqueline Susann's voiceover suggestions was Robson's November 19 cover note to Zanuck: "All is going very well although the sea is rough. With this letter are some changes that Jacqueline Susann has suggested after her first viewing of the picture. Naturally the running was traumatic for her. She never once has become contentious or difficult about anything. She was very aware of the necessity to abridge and change her novel as it became a film. There are a number of places where she has suggested voiceover technique in order to clarify in her mind certain moves and relationships in the film. I think this is a very natural and normal reaction on her part . . . she is still trying to help. However, because of my knowledge of the film and my desire to remove as much of the soap opera as possible, it is extremely difficult for me to pass judgments on the merits of her case. I naturally feel that it is all there but then I may be too close to the film. I wish you would make a judgment and a decision in these matters for me. As we all know it would be almost impossible to get these things done, recorded and shipped to New York for the early openings of *Valley*. If Jackie's ideas have merit in your mind it could be accomplished for some of our later dates. Fondest Regards, Mark."

Zanuck quickly responded in a Western Union telegram: "I have studied your letter and the suggestions made by Jacqueline Susann and while every one of Jackie's suggestions make sense, I honestly do not believe that any of them are necessary to the telling of our story. I think that everything Jackie worries about is implicit in the film without the necessity of voiceover. While there is no doubt that her suggested voiceover could be used to more fully explain thoughts, motivations I tend to feel that this would be hitting everything on the head too strongly and would tip off many things which I believe evolve naturally through the film itself. Even if I did not have any of these objections it is as you know too late to do anything even if we wanted to. Give my best to everyone. Best Always, Dick."

CHAPTER SIXTEEN

Nobody Digs the Valley but the Public

On December 15, 1967, *Valley of the Dolls* debuted in Manhattan, opening later that month throughout the rest of the country. The movie faced a challenging marketplace, a changing world. The U.S. population stood at 200,706,052, the minimum wage was $1.60, a dozen eggs cost $0.53, and a gallon of milk could be had for $1.07. At the beginning of the 1960s, America appeared to be on the brink of a golden age, as typified by the New Frontier of the dynamic new president, John F. Kennedy, and his introduction of the most ambitious and all-inclusive social agenda to combat inequality and injustice since the New Deal. By the time of the movie's release, race riots and protests had become increasingly commonplace across the country as blacks and other allies demanded fair treatment of minorities. The 1963 publication of *The Feminine Mystique* by Betty Friedan was a watershed event in feminism's second wave, with ever-increasing numbers of women taking to the streets to demand equal rights on every playing field. A 1962 march in front of Independence Hall in Philadelphia lit the fuse on the modern gay rights movement. Turmoil and conflict were in the air as the Vietnam War raged, draft cards and flags got burned, families were torn apart by differing political beliefs, 200,000 people marched around the world in protest of the war, and support for it eventually fell to 37 percent from 52 percent.

One might expect that upheaval and change to be reflected in America's favorite books, movies, TV shows, Broadway offerings, and pop music. Yet the top spots on the December 11 *New York Times* bestseller list were held down by *The Secret of Santa Vittoria*, *Valley of the Dolls*, *Capable of Honor*, *The Birds Fall Down*, *The Mask of Apollo*, *The Fixer*, *Tai-Pan*, *All in the Family*, *The Adventurers*, and *A Dream of Kings*. With the average movie ticket costing roughly $1.30, Hollywood's Christmas fare was slightly more in step with the times what with *The Graduate*, *Guess Who's Coming to Dinner*, and *In Cold Blood* on the way in a year that had already included zeitgeist films like *Cool Hand Luke*, *In the Heat of the Night*, *Titicut Follies*, and *Bonnie and Clyde*, alongside more escapist fare like *Barefoot in the Park*, *Wait Until Dark*, *Camelot*, *You Only Live Twice*, *Thoroughly Modern Millie*, *The Dirty Dozen*, and *In Like Flint*. TV's most-watched shows were the comforting, reassuring *The Andy Griffith Show*, *The Lucy Show*, *Gomer Pyle, U.S.M.C.*, *Gunsmoke*, *Family Affair*, *Bonanza*, *The Red Skelton Show*, *The Dean Martin Show*, *The Jackie Gleason Show*, *Bewitched*, and *The Beverly Hillbillies*. Theater audiences were being challenged by *Everything in the Garden*, *Galileo*, *The Birthday Party*, and even the racial equality–minded musical *Hallelujah, Baby!* along with straight old-fashioned comedies like *There's a Girl in My Soup*. On the Billboard charts, for every "Light My Fire," "For What It's Worth," "Respect," "I Was Made to Love Her," "Soul Man," and "Incense and Peppermints"—let alone "Sgt. Pepper's Lonely Hearts Club Band" or "Are You Experienced"—there was a "Somethin' Stupid," "Windy," "To Sir, With Love," and *The Sound of Music* and *Doctor Zhivago* original soundtracks.

Going into the first release of *Valley of the Dolls*, 20th executives remained confident that the movie would make lots of noise at the box office, even without being shown on a reserved-seat road show, with advanced ticket prices and on a twice-daily basis. The Zanucks had, in fact, briefly considered a road show release strategy before rejecting it for a number of reasons, not the least of which was that they wanted to book many of the best theaters for the release of the wildly overbudget $18 million musical *Doctor Dolittle*. To spread the word, Herb Lyon's "Tower Ticker" *Chicago Tribune* column for November 29 reported, "The hot [*Valley of the Dolls*] preem-ing at the State Lake Dec. 20, will run on a grind [continuous] basis, no reserved seats, etc.—and looms large as a record buster."

Well, not if the top national magazine critics had anything to say about it. *Time* magazine's reviewer wrote, "The story is about girls who take all sorts of pills, but *Valley of the Dolls* offers only bromides. . . . Viewers are likely not to feel anything—except numbness." Likewise, Arthur Knight in *Saturday Review*: "Ten years ago, its putative stars—Barbara Parkins, Patty Duke, Sharon Tate—would more likely have been playing hat-check girls than movie queens. They are totally lacking in style, authority, or charm. The men opposite them—Paul Burke, Tony Scotti, Martin Milner, and Charles Drake—are given little to do but cluck sympathetically from time to time. Susan Hayward, the only 'pro' of the lot, sports makeup that makes her look more like Katisha than an aging Broadway queen. Ineptitude, inadequacy, and downright dishonesty characterize every aspect." Opined the *New Yorker* critic: "A thoroughly maladroit soap opera, whose innumerable iridescent soap suds are blown up ten times bigger than life and therefore become comic, even when they are meant to be tragic, laughable." *Cue* magazine warned, "Sometimes you'll laugh in the wrong places at the script. There's a lot of talk about taking pills (dolls). But what kind of pills do you take to sit through a film like this?" *Newsweek*'s critic called it "one of the most stupefying and clumsy films ever made by alleged professionals, [it] has no more sense of its own ludicrousness than a village idiot stumbling in manure." Although he thought "Jennifer is played quite nicely by Sharon Tate," the only scene more unintentionally funny than Jennifer's suicide scene was Patty Duke and Scotti's asylum duet on "Come Live With Me." He wrote, "The song has ended but the lunacy maunders on." Said acerbic *New York Herald Tribune* and *Today* TV critic Judith Crist: "There's sad news for the smuts today: *Valley of the Dolls* has finally arrived on the screen and it's not a dirty movie . . . [it's] badly acted, sleazily made, with a cheapjack production underlining the near-idiot level of the script. . . . Jacqueline Susann acts as well as she writes. Patty Duke . . . scores high in the repulsive bracket. . . . Susan Hayward can count this as *her* horror movie (all middle-aged stars have their monster roles these days)."

Newspaper critics showed just as little mercy. This from Kathleen Carroll's star-and-a-half (out of four) review in the *Daily News*: "There was an outside chance director Mark Robson could rise above the material, not, although it's hard to believe, sink below it." She called it a "sleazy production" featuring "attractive but vapid" Parkins and Tate and then Duke who "isn't vapid. She's just too much." Hayward's "few embarrassing moments" paled against the inadequacies of the male cast, "hardly the types that drive women to the dolls." Gerald Nachman's "Stage and Screen" column called the newcomers "terrible," with Tate coming off "sensuous and vacuous as her role" and Scotti "a flat-faced male starlet"—"scraps of merchandise stuck onto a gigantic piece of junk sculpture." The *Chicago Tribune*'s Clifford Terry called it "a motion picture that would make *The Best of Everything* look like *Citizen Kane*," while Barbara Parkins "comes off as interesting as a Madame Tussaud reproduction of Suzy Parker" and Patty Duke about as convincing as "a Northwestern cheerleader who has sneaked out behind the fieldhouse for a smoke . . . creating what has to be the most inadvertently hilarious performance since Carroll Baker played a prostitute in *Sylvia*." The critic thought Tony Scotti looked like "a delivery boy" and that Hayward's brief screen time and one song gave her "plenty of time to establish her impersonation of a Bowery Girl gone legit." The *Atlanta Constitution* critic called the movie "monumentally bad . . . trite, vulgar, overblown, overdone, over-everything." He thought Barbara Parkins "could be a very fine actress and could be a big star," but Patty Duke's performance was "the worst anyone has done since Carroll Baker as Harlow . . . [demonstrating] almost no insight into her character." The *San Francisco Examiner* critic Jeanne Miller called the movie "an unbelievably clumsy, old-fashioned and uninspired soap opera" with "choppy, disjointed" direction and a "banal" script reducing to the level of "absurd annoyances" tragedies like cancer, alcoholism, drug addiction, and Huntington's chorea "by virtue of the ludicrous dialogue which makes these disasters unintentionally laughable." She assessed the performances as ranging from "undistinguished to atrocious" with Burke and Scotti "totally unimpressive," Duke "shrill, hysterical . . . embarrassing," and Tate "faring no better than Duke"; Parkins possesses "a remarkably alluring and very distinctive voice which might compensate, with the proper script and direction, for her pronounced lack of acting ability," while Susan Hayward "stands head and shoulders above the others."

Don Morrison in the *Minneapolis Star* trashed the movie as just "one big pill," and, noting how the book detailed addiction to red, yellow, and blue "dolls," remarked on how red pills were used almost exclusively in the movie, "conceivably because they photograph better in 'Color by Deluxe' . . . though I suspect they are a medication especially compounded for the cast—namely, bubble gum." The *Evening Sun*'s critic, calling it "hilariously bad," wrote of Duke's and Scotti's psychiatric hospital musical duet, "That, man, is the funniest serious scene I have seen since Lizabeth Scott stared long and hard at Humphrey Bogart in *Dead Reckoning*." The critic for Vancouver, British Columbia's the *Province*—one of Barbara Parkins's birthplace newspapers—complained of Duke's being "presented to us as the reincarnation of Judy Garland, with a little of Barbra Streisand and Fannie [*sic*] Brice thrown in," but yet like "any stage struck high school kid and bears no resemblance to the pros, even to those unfortunate singers who will always be playing the second-rate clubs." He thought Barbara Parkins fit the bill in a role calling for stunning beauty, but when it came time for her to emote? "Nothing. She has one of the deadest beautiful pans since Virginia O'Brien." In summary, "Every cliché in the show biz movie handbook is there, short of that scene where John Payne tells Betty Grable the act would be better without him." *Variety*'s reviewer called Tate "particularly good," and although Duke's performance was "erratic," it would "command greater casting attention."

Meanwhile, New Jersey's *Herald-News* staff writer Leslie Davis thought Patty Duke's "the one good performance" and that although she might have been too young to be believable in her final breakdown, "she manages . . . to make the scene quite effective." Barbara Parkins "wears incredible clothes during the film . . . but never changes her expression." Kevin Thomas positively gushed in his *Los Angeles Times* review, calling the movie an "absorbing melodrama of pertinence and wide appeal," sure to be a favorite for its "shop girl fantasies of fame and fortune" and graced with "sumptuous" sets, "much beautiful New England scenery," and its four leading ladies "handsomely gowned in $150,000 worth of Travilla costumes." Susann's "fevered, splotchy prose" had been superseded by the "tautly-structured, well-shaped (and very salty) screenplay," while André and Dory Previn's "poignant songs" underscored Robson's "astute direction." Then, going completely gaga, he cited "Duke's gutsy, all-the-stops-out performance, the kind that gets Academy Award." Barbara Parkins and Sharon Tate "do very well in less flamboyant roles," Susan Hayward was "terrific in an all-too-brief performance," Paul Burke "suavely played," Tony Scotti "impresses," and Lee Grant made a "thankless role" seem "vital and sympathetic." We'll have what he's having.

Easily one of the more knowing reviews came from Andrew Sarris in the *Village Voice*, even if he predicted the movie would never become a camp classic. He wrote of Jacqueline Susann's work as resembling that of "Grace Metalious in the stern moral tone she adopts to expose hypocrisy by exploiting vice." The novel is "the daughter of *Peyton Place* and *The Carpetbaggers*" and is populated by characters "patched together from dirty stories about a multitude of Broadway and Hollywood stars." Sarris, a preeminent American proponent of the *auteur* theory, also complained of Robson's direction ("as always, mechanical and impersonal") and the movie as a long way down from the "delights" and dizzy excesses of Delmer Daves in, say, *A Summer Place, Susan Slade,* and *Youngblood Hawke.* He found Parkins "dully competent . . . in the Fox good-looking brunette tradition of Gene Tierney, Linda Darnell, Jean Peters, down to the ladylike dregs of Dana Wynter." Meanwhile, "Sharon Tate is luscious enough to be gift-wrapped at the Playboy Club Candy Concession, but kinetically speaking, she belongs to the beautiful, expressionless school of acting frequented in the past by Tina Louise, Suzy Parker and Jean Shrimpton." Patty Duke "reminded me of nothing so much as Peggy Ryan pretending to be Judy Garland. By contrast, Susan Hayward reminded me less of that old pro Ethel Merman than that old pro Susan Hayward." As for Paul Burke, Tony Scotti, and the rest, Sarris wrote them off as "Elmer Fuddish male foils who deserve all the anonymity a merciful career can provide." *The Hollywood Citizen-News* critic Nadine Edward asserted that despite the movie's "hauntingly beautiful score" and Travilla's "breathtaking fashions," the "strangely miscast" Patty Duke was "obviously struggling with her ponderous and pivotal role—but never quite mastering it," and the movie's ineptness would "undoubtedly be a disappointment to many."

The most intriguing review of all appeared in *Films and Filming* from iconoclastic British film critic and author Raymond Durgnat, who championed the work of Michael Powell, Douglas Sirk, and Alfred Hitchcock long before it was fashionable. Durgnat crowned *Valley* "Hollywood's first auto-satirical soap opera," one that delivered "louder laughs than Jerry Lewis's last four comedies put together." He insisted that Robson and his screenwriters subversively brought "Dada to Hollywood," "slip[ping] in naughty words like 'fag,' 'butt,' and 'son-of-a-bitch' with the death-defying casualness of children daring to utter 'pee,' 'bum,' and 'poo.' The net effect is to make utter nonsense, not only of soap opera sentiment, but of every conceivable convention of, in a sense, life itself." The critic even went so far as to compare Robson's sense of irony, social satire, and premeta *meta* to that of melodrama maestro Douglas Sirk in *Magnificent Obsession*, *All That Heaven Allows*, and *Imitation of Life* made for producer Ross Hunter, the gloss and glamour monger extraordinaire of Universal Pictures. Declaring that Robson and company at times succeeded in "out Sirk-ing Sirk," Durgnat wrote: "Take my advice and go see it, preferably with a discriminating friend, and see if you don't agree that it's the most weirdly satisfying evening you've spent at the movies since Yoko Ono's *No. 4* [eighty minutes composed entirely of human posteriors], then write to me and I'll send you your money back."

The poor reviews floored Robson. He chalked up some of the unflattering notices to the challenges of filming a vastly popular book. "It's something of a disappointment to do things you think are interesting and have it reviewed badly," he said. "But I realized the reviewers were waiting for *Valley*. They made their minds up long before they saw the film." Trying to put on the bravest face possible, he observed, "There's always the problem of fighting the preconceived notions of those who read the book. The larger the number, the greater the preconceived notions. Audiences tend to disagree with the casting, with that portion of the book being covered by the film, with the emphasis of the adaptation—with so many different aspects. You just can't please everybody. Another problem—and one which is ever present—is that the film critic invariably reviews the book rather than the picture. If he really liked the book, then the picture doesn't measure up. If he hated the book, you can be sure he'll hate the picture. You're damned if you do and damned if you don't." He announced that he was moving forward with two projects, one the long-gestating World War II escape thriller by Jon Cleary, *The Long Pursuit*, to star Paul Newman, and the earlier-announced *The Plot*, adapted by screenwriter John Michael Hayes (*Rear Window, To Catch a Thief*). Neither came to fruition.

After those savage reviews, many in Hollywood circles—hostile or not—were curious whether or not the public would swallow the pills. Jacqueline Susann was gutted, but not surprised, by the bad notices. To help lift her spirits, on the night of the movie's opening she and Irving took a long stroll and wound up on Broadway near the Criterion Theater. The line for *Valley of the Dolls*—a heady mix of well-dressed Manhattanites, housewives, drag queens, hustlers, teens, East Village artists, druggies, and leather boys—stretched for blocks. Jackie exulted, "Irving, these are my *people!*"

The world was full of Jackie's people, as things turned out. Richard Zanuck telegrammed the director: "Am sure that you have been brought up to date on the fantastic business that *Valley of the Dolls* is doing here in New York. This is sensational and I want to congratulate you and you know how exhilarated we all are. This is the worst week-end for New York films as it is the last chance for Christmas shopping. But despite this we are only a couple of thousand dollars behind the [Who's Afraid of] Virginia Woolf? record which opened in June. Congratulations." City after city reported fantastic box-office earnings. *Variety* called the opening week's grosses at Grauman's Chinese Theatre "boffo," topped by an even bigger second week reported as "gigantic" at $76,000. The picture went on to a nine-week run at Grauman's. 20th bought ads in the Hollywood trade papers reading: "First 5 days *Valley* sets all-time record for any 20th Century-Fox picture playing Los Angeles."

But not everyone was happy. One disgruntled letter writer, fresh from "spending a hard-earned $2.50" on seeing *Valley* at Grauman's Chinese Theatre, wrote Robson calling herself "sick with disappointment" and, for two handwritten pages, berating the director and "so-called authoress" Susann for being out of their "cotton-pickin' minds" and "from the funny farm" for having the "audacity" to change the ending of such a well-known novel. How could they leave "Paul Burke (who is *so* super!) standing in that doorway?" let alone utterly ignore the novel's time period, characters, and action. She also criticized the film's use of exteriors of a hotel other than the actual Martha Washington, where, she said, she'd lived for four years. The letter was signed "Not Cordially" and, underneath the woman's name, "A movie fan (usually)."

Long before the internet made such "fan" letters common, moviemakers usually ignored them. But Robson took the bait and in a lengthy, bristly typed response, he admitted that although he "seldom answer[ed] letters of this sort, I felt that in your particular case, I wanted to very much." He explained that the ending of Susann's novel (almost to the bitter end, Anne sticks with philandering husband and absent father Lyon) was "non-constructive" and he wanted at least one character—Anne for certain, and Lyon, too, if possible—to have learned something by the final fadeout. He thought it was better dramatically "to leave up in the air" the possibility of their eventual reunion; the unspoken word "sequel" hung in the air. Robson continued: "I know it's difficult for you to understand that a book is a book and a film is a film. They are two different mediums." And "regardless of your opinion of Jacqueline Susann's novel, she did write some very interesting characters." Had he filmed the entire novel, the movie would have run four or five hours and would have required "a phoney [*sic*] make-up [ending] for which I believe you would have criticized me even further." For his windup punch, Robson added that "while you say [the Martha Washington Hotel] never looked like that . . . we photographed it without changing a thing." He invited her to write again "in rebuttal," adding he would be "very glad to hear from you." There is no evidence that she ever responded.

Week after week, the movie continued to break records nation-wide. From January through May of 1968, *Valley of the Dolls* opened across the world. Not surprisingly, it inspired lampoons and paro-dies. *Mad* magazine had a field day with their September 1968 fea-ture "Valley of the Dollars," illustrated by the great Mort Drucker. The Larry Siegel script featured author "Jackpot Susann," "Neely O'Horror, who is really Judy Garland—or maybe the Lennon Sis-ters," "Anne Welts," "Mel Nebbish," "Tony Dullard," and was chock full of snark. "You read the book! You saw the movie! Now enjoy this *Mad* satire. . . . It's almost as funny!" "Any similarity between characters in this film and actual persons, living or dead, is rather remote—but try to guess who they're supposed to be anyway! It'll take your mind off the ridiculous plot." On February 19 of the same year, on *The Carol Burnett Show*, a comically deadpan Burnett, Vicki Lawrence, and guest star singer Gloria Loring—bewigged and costumed by Bob Mackie—knelt and lounged like Parkins, Duke, and Tate on the very same brass bed used for *Valley of the Dolls* publicity shots. The parody sketch, also titled "Valley of the Dollars," began with the narration: "Once upon a time, there was a book called *Valley of the Dolls*. It was all about show business, sex, alcohol, pills, scandals—and sex. Naturally, it became a best-seller. It also became a motion picture. And for those of you lucky enough to miss it, here is our version." When Lawrence's zombielike Neely murmurs, "I'm fed up with Hollywood. I'd like to just quit," Bur-nett's Anne says, "You can't quit now. You're a big star, a big talent, a big lush." "Thanks, Anne, you're my only real friend," Lawrence says, then hiccups.

Weekly, 20th sent Robson charts showing the massive box-office haul for each and every theater in the United States and Canada where the movie played. Robson had at least some reason to be proud and happy. On that final, modest $4,690,000 budget, *Valley of the Dolls* grossed $50,000,000 ($351,327,586 today) worldwide, before home video. By comparison, the production costs on 20th's Frank

Sinatra detective movie *Tony Rome* ran $3,480,000, but in the United States and Canada combined, it took in only $4,000,000. The studio fared better with *Planet of the Apes*, taking in $32,589,624 in North America alone, on a $5.8 million budget. But then there was *Doctor Dolittle*. Expensively touted as the next *Sound of Music* and playing some of the nation's best theaters at advanced ticket prices, it took in only $3.5 million at the box office on a $17 million production budget. When the dust settled, the makers of *Valley of the Dolls* laughed all the way to the bank. Rancid reviews and all, it was more profitable than *Bullitt* ($42,300,873), *Oliver!* ($37,402,877), *Romeo and Juliet* ($38,901,218), and *Rosemary's Baby* ($33,395,426) and made roughly the same amount as *The Odd Couple* ($44,527,234).

In Hollywood, that kind of money can forgive a multitude of sins, so 20th renewed its drive to get the movie some love from the People Who Mattered—Oscar voters. At 8:00 p.m. on Saturday, January 20, Fox hosted an invitation-only screening for members of the Academy of Motion Picture Arts and Sciences in advance of the 40th Academy Awards ceremony scheduled to be held on April 10, 1968, at the Santa Monica Civic Auditorium. Several *Valley* participants tossed their hats in the ring and launched costly Oscar nomination campaigns. Patty Duke's team bought ads in *Variety* and the *Hollywood Reporter* illustrated with a wistful/sexy black-and-white photo of Duke accompanied by a quote from critic Kevin Thomas's infamous *Los Angeles Times* review: "Patty Duke as Neely O'Hara gives a gutsy all-stops-out performance. The kind that gets Academy Awards." Beneath that was a list of impressive box-office earnings, labeled "Wham," "Gigantic," "Boffola," "Amazing," and "Giant" because, especially back then, what said Academy Awards–worthy louder than big money in the bank? Designer Travilla's awards ads featured pull quotes from various outlets—"an arresting showcase for Travilla," "a stupendous collection . . . exciting, appropriate, shows great skill in depiction of character," and "fabulous fashions." But when the 1968 Oscar nominations were announced, John Williams was the movie's only participant to be recognized, in the category of Best Music, Scoring of

Music, Adaptation or Treatment. (Alfred Newman and Ken Darby won for *Camelot*.)

Despite a production riddled with infighting, feuding, tension, tragedies, missteps, and double-dealing, the box office pointed to the inevitable. The Zanucks convened the major players and suggested the patently obvious. *Let's do it all over again.*

CHAPTER SEVENTEEN

Over, Under, Sideways, Down, and *Beyond the Valley*

The Hollywood Machine feeds on success, repetition, rinse, repeat. 20th's cash coffers overflowed with *Valley* profits, so naturally the studio bosses wanted to stay in the Jacqueline Susann business—especially when they were drowning in a sea of red ink from recent Richard Zanuck–sanctioned calamities and underperformers, including *Doctor Dolittle, The Sweet Ride, Prudence and the Pill, The Secret Life of an American Wife, A Guide for the Married Man, Caprice, Fathom,* and *Bandolero!* Meanwhile, in the studio pipeline were other Zanuck Jr.–greenlit underachievers and write-offs-to-be, among them *Star!, Che! The Magus, Justine, Staircase, The Only Game in Town, Hard Contract, Deadfall, The Day the Fish Came Out, The Bible . . . In the Beginning,* and *Lady in Cement.*

Veteran movie publicist Jet Fore confided in friends and colleagues, including *Chicago Sun-Times* journalist Roger Ebert, that Darryl F. Zanuck was on the warpath over his son's backing such a string of financial losers. Richard Zanuck, said Fore, was "desperate" to save the studio from irrelevancy, embarrassment, and potential insolvency—and equally desperate to redeem himself in the eyes of his ferociously competitive and indisputably brilliant father. To try and save his job and the studio, Zanuck Jr. scrambled to line up what he thought could be a slate of likely financial winners, especially ones with the potential to click with young, hip ticket buyers and, whenever possible, critics. Said Fore of Fox's product at the time, "Every producer in town has his nephew up in the [Hollywood] Hills trying to remake *Easy Rider* and what have we got in the can? Nothing but a Western and two war movies." (That Western turned out to be *Butch Cassidy and the Sundance Kid* and the war movies were *Patton* and *M*A*S*H*—both major hits with audiences and critics.)

In the face of potential financial ruin, a return to *Valley of the Dolls* seemed like a good bet—to some, anyway. So in late January 1968, with *Valley* fever running hot, David Brown initiated communication with the Zanucks on the topic of exercising their contractual options with Susann and Mansfield's corporation, Sujac Productions. In advance of a February 21 West Coast meeting between Richard Zanuck and the Mansfields, Brown wined, dined, and sweet-talked Jacqueline and Irving in New York. Certain that they had been shortchanged on their *Valley of the Dolls* deal, the Mansfields came armed with legal advice from their Manhattan-based attorney, Arthur A. Hershkowitz, and their agent, George Chasin, the latter of whom looked after the business affairs of top-tier moviemaking talent, including Marilyn Monroe, Alfred Hitchcock, and Cary Grant.

During a formal meeting with Jackie and Irving, Brown pushed hardest for a "sequel" in the form of a *Valley of the Dolls* nighttime TV series meant to duplicate the runaway success of *Peyton Place*. The Mansfields declared themselves unopposed—so long as production began no earlier than 1972, as stipulated in their contract. (By the end of the negotiations, Fox and Sujac would agree that neither party could launch a series version before 1977.)

More immediately, though, Brown asked if Susann was interested in creating a hundred-page (minimum) detailed story treatment for a big-screen *Valley* sequel. The author's main priority at the time was the completion of her potential blockbuster novel *The Love Machine*, for which she helped herself to the juicy inside dish on the rise and fall of rapacious, cutthroat, bed-hopping CBS TV network executive James Aubrey, aka "The Smiling Cobra." "Make me mean, Jackie, a real son of a bitch," Aubrey reportedly advised Susann. By contract, Fox had first look at Susann's sophomore novel—set by Simon & Schuster for 1969 publication—as well as her subsequent effort. Fox had also reserved the right to get a first look at any *Valley of the Dolls* follow-up novel if and when Susann wrote one. During the meeting Susann impressed Brown by presenting a vivid, well-thought-out description of a general plotline, incidents, and characters for a *Valley* motion picture sequel. She even had her title all picked out: *Beyond the Valley of the Dolls.*

As Barbara Parkins has recalled, "Jackie was happy about the sequel idea, at first, and I was excited about it. I was to play the starring role of Anne Welles again and Paul Burke was to play Lyon and it was supposed to be the further adventures of Anne." As suggested by intrastudio memos, some of the further adventures Susann discussed during her meeting with Brown were never-filmed carryovers from the original novel. Anne suffers through more of Lyon Burke's humiliating infidelities with various female clients, clashes with him over his absentee parenting of their increasingly rebellious (Neely-like?) teenage daughter, and eventually she learns to navigate her life as a single mother. The sudden death of her cosmetics baron benefactor, Kevin Gillmore, leaving Anne a fabulously wealthy young widow, propels her to build (and crash) her personal life and career before she pulls herself up by her bootstraps and becomes a respected, celebrated TV news reporter.

Susann had, in *Valley of the Dolls*, played off Jennifer North, played out Helen Lawson, and left Neely O'Hara's future looking mighty grim. But why, apart from Susann's personal identification with Anne, coupled with the novelist's great fondness for Barbara Parkins, would such a born storyteller focus her follow-up on the least dynamic character in the novel? Opinions differ on whether Susann's original sequel ideas included resurrecting Helen Lawson (probably not) and/or Neely O'Hara (at least a cameo appearance?). But some of the author's earliest musings may likely have contributed to *Shadow of the Dolls*, Rae Lawrence's authorized sequel novel, published in 2001.

Early the morning immediately after Brown's meeting with the Mansfields, he was authorized to propose that Fox pay Susann $75,000 for the hundred-page "Sequel to *Valley of the Dolls*" with an additional $25,000 due on the first day of principal photography, with Susann retaining the book publishing rights. The writer's original contract required Fox to pay her $50,000 for *any* produced movie sequel, whether or not she was involved. To further sweeten the deal, the studio agreed to shell out $125,000 to merely get first look at even an *outline* for *The Love Machine*; that nonrefundable fee would set up Mansfield as producer on one future Fox film project to be mutually agreed upon by Mansfield and the studio brass. If Brown and Richard Zanuck liked *The Love Machine* enough to spring for the film rights, then Sujac Productions would receive another $125,000, and Mansfield would make his big-screen bow as the movie's producer. Indicative of how badly 20th wanted, *needed* to cut the deal, Brown told Chasin that the final *Love Machine* purchase price—the asking price was already hinted at upward of $1 million—would be separate from the previous $250,000 set aside for Mansfield and Susann. And the cherry on top? Well aware of Susann's and Mansfield's residual rancor over the lowball original contract, Fox committed to kick back to them 5 percent of the *Valley* profits. (Chasin would presumably have insisted on gross points, not net; after all, thanks to Hollywood's infamously byzantine system of accounting, Eddie Murphy is credited with calling net points "monkey points" because only a *naïf* or monkey would ever expect to get them.)

After his discussion with Chasin, Brown called the Mansfields at the Beverly Hills Hotel, informed them of what he called his "little proposal," wished Irving and Jacqueline a pleasant return flight to Manhattan, and made plans for the two couples to rendezvous there soon. Brown assured them that the negotiations were not strictly business: "Friends, Irving, friends; it transcends friendship." Friends, sure, but the Mansfields and their legal eagles scoured the offer for loopholes and landmines. But by late February, Susann's deal, Mansfield's deal, and the first-look *The Love Machine* negotiations were sealed.

20th announced in *Variety* and other trade publications that production on the *Valley* sequel would begin within one year. With the original movie continuing to shatter box-office records and defy expectations and based on Susann's conversations with David Brown, it is not surprising that she imagined Fox expecting a high-budget, classy follow-up—one that would fly in the face of the studio's usual rushed, penny-pinching cash-ins like *Return of the Fly* or *Return to Peyton Place*. Mansfield, meanwhile, was puffed up at the thought of producing that sequel and having himself billed over the title and over his wife: "An Irving Mansfield Production of Jacqueline Susann's *Beyond the Valley of the Dolls*." After signing the deal, Mansfield also envisioned himself directing the movie. Hey, if the first film was the best a veteran like Mark Robson could do, then why not give Mansfield a shot?

Except that 20th initially wanted to give Robson first crack. In 1957, when Robson's glossy, sanitized *Peyton Place* became a money machine for the studio, Darryl F. Zanuck lavished $500,000 on the prepublication screen rights—without having seen a page—to Grace Metalious's slapdash 1959 *Return to Peyton Place*. The deal also included the rights to a third Metalious novel, *The Tight White Collar*. On the publication of *Return to Peyton Place*, *Time* magazine's book critic opined that it read like something that had been "whacked together during a long weekend." Hoping somehow that lightning might strike twice, Zanuck and producer Jerry Wald had naturally asked Mark Robson to slip back into the director's chair. He flatly refused, as did many others, and the thankless job fell to José Ferrer. None of the original cast members came back, either. *Return to Peyton Place*, despite some delicious contributions from Mary Astor and Tuesday Weld, had crept in and out of theaters in the spring of 1961.

Robson may have been heartened by the mighty *Valley* box-office returns but he was still smarting from the lacerating reviews. He told Zanuck that he next wanted to do something "more substantial and a complete change of pace . . . I've never made a sequel to one of my pictures and I don't intend to start now." He repeated the quote for the press. In secret, some months after the tail end of the theatrical release of *Valley of the Dolls*, Robson and his attorneys set in motion plans to demand an audit of the worldwide box-office receipts. The director believed that he had been substantially shortchanged on his profit participation deal. He vowed he would not make another movie for 20th and didn't. The audits, cross-accusations, and legal action dragged on for years. On January 22, 1970, Robson received a detailed report from a London-based accounting firm after they had examined the distribution accounting records of 20th pertaining to *Valley of the Dolls* from November 1967 to that present date. Although the investigation had not concluded at that time, the firm reported evidence of omission of film receipts, incorrect charging of items of expenditure to film, inclusion of "trailer" costs in film costs and omission of trailer receipts, and nonreconciliation of box-office figures quoted by U.K. distributors versus those reported by 20th Century Fox Ltd.

Robson's turn-down encouraged Irving Mansfield that Fox would eventually view him as a most viable director for *Beyond the Valley of the Dolls*. Meanwhile, he took out Hollywood trade paper ads announcing his production deal with Fox, one that might lead to at least one other film if—*big* if—the studio approved of the property choices Mansfield presented within the first year of the contract. Obviously, David Brown expected those properties would be *The Love*

Machine and a new contender, *Five Foot Two*, Susann's proposed take on the exploits of scrappy, finagling theatrical showman-lyricist Billy Rose, described by longtime friend, the playwright-screenwriter Ben Hecht, as "a kind of slum poet and Jack the Ripper rolled into one." On first hearing of the novels, Darryl F. Zanuck was sold on neither *The Love Machine* nor *Five Foot Two*. As his memo detailed to his son and Brown: "Could anybody possibly be interested in a story dealing with 'The Smiling Cobra'? Won't it turn out to be another dull thing like [the 1954 three-Oscar-winning all-star boardroom drama] *Executive Suite*? For ten years, Billy Rose tried to promote me on his life story. Of course, if the authoress has some spectacular new slant then there might be something worthwhile; but it looks to me right now that, because of her phenomenal success, she is searching frantically for a follow-up in the theatrical world."

Susann filed her draft titled, as promised, *Beyond the Valley of the Dolls* on May 13. Studio notes describe the writer as putting characters Anne Welles, Lyon Burke, and their turbulent, beautiful, sixteen-year-old Julie through heartbreak, suffering, and redemption, all unfurling against a big international canvas. To flesh out and deepen Susann's material into a full screenplay, Zanuck asked Brown to look into the soonest availability for *Valley of the Dolls* survivor Dorothy Kingsley; the writer was too busy working on the NBC TV series *Bracken's World*, shot on the Fox lot. Instead, the gig went to Gabrielle Upton (billed sometimes as Gillian Houghton), the prolific forty-six-year-old head writer for the TV soaps *Guiding Light* and *The Secret Storm*, as well as screenwriter of the original *Gidget* movie. Upton's first-draft screenplay sparked unanimous agreement among Brown, Zanuck, and the Mansfields that she be replaced.

Next up was Jean Holloway, a fifty-one-year-old pro who had spent what she called "three miserable years" in the 1940s under MGM contract struggling with scripts, trying to make something out of *Till the Clouds Roll By* and *Summer Holiday*. Through the '50s, she had subsequently found greener pastures, awards and nonstop employment writing for TV. Her career prospered well into the 1960s on episodic TV hits, including *Wagon Train*, *Dr. Kildare*, and *The Ghost & Mrs. Muir*, the latter of which she developed for the small screen from one of Fox's best-loved films of the 1940s. At the time of her signing to write the new *Valley* movie, Holloway had returned to the big screen for producer Ross Hunter's remake of the creaky old weepie *Madame X*, in which Hunter tried and failed to interest director Douglas Sirk. At 20th's expense, Holloway relocated to Manhattan, the better to be available for consultations with Mansfield and Susann. It was a bad marriage. Susann complained to Fox of the screenwriter's peculiarities, such as her firing several secretaries who refused to walk her dog. Susann described Holloway as "a little princess" who would recline for hours like a dying swan "when she said she had an abscess on her can." And when the scriptwriter purportedly refused to pen one of Susann's important obligatory scenes, the writer told a Fox story department executive: "She won't even write a scene with a girl at dinner; listen, you can't work with a woman like that." Holloway, she declared, "can't write." Meanwhile, Mansfield found the screenwriter so intransigent that he avoided meeting with her and sent her packing back to California.

The long wait for a viable screenplay, first from Gabrielle Upton, and then from Holloway, who turned in her first-draft script on May 15, 1969, further tightened the screws. Zanuck Sr. pressed his son to get the project in gear. But although David Brown thought Holloway's script "a great improvement over the previous version," it still lacked the special hot sauce that seasoned the Susann brand. He advised further developing the project but to hedge their bets by now budgeting the movie version "at a rock bottom minimum" and having it shepherded by "a television writer-director."

Meanwhile, Susann pitched in by secretly rewriting (gratis) Holloway's script, almost exclusively in dialogue. Although Brown found the dialogue "impossible" and the writing "hopelessly corny," he reported that "the girls in the office can't get their hands off the material and they think it's 'sensational': these are the same girls that were clutching *Valley of the Dolls*. . . . I am certain that Jackie could get three or four hundred thousand dollars for the paperback rights alone . . . and I am going to encourage her to do so." Brown opined that, with a quick polish, the script would contain the ingredients needed to be the basis for a "highly successful" movie ready for production as soon as September or October.

Richard Zanuck read the script and on June 6 strongly disagreed, asking his father and Brown where was "the human and personal tragedy, [the] tremendous amount of sex, drug addiction, alcoholism, homosexuality, suicide, breast cancer, insane asylum, underground movies" of *Valley of the Dolls*? He complained that the script read "like a Disney picture" and was centered on an Anne Welles "so good-goody that she makes me want to vomit." He concluded: "We all know that the original picture was corny soap opera at its very worst but still it satisfied the thrill-seekers because of its suggestion of depravity . . . unless we throw in an equal amount of lowdown sex and perversion of one kind or another, we will be making a grave error." By mid-June, David Brown caved and began to push for a radically different "exploitation flick" approach: "I hate to say this, [but] the ideal writer-director would be an American-International (*The Trip, Wild in the Streets*) team of picture makers. . . . [We should] consider doing it in an intentional 'put-on' style so that it will be an intentional 'camp' version of a soap opera."

By this time, Richard Zanuck had tired of the egos and demands of what Fox insiders had taken to calling the Susann-Mansfield "menage." He also sparked to the idea of a sequel that could be shot quickly and cheaply, a movie Brown described to him as "rougher and lower in taste, if that's possible, than the original" and one calculated to appeal "to a much younger audience in addition to retaining the shock value of the original." Still, Zanuck set his story department assistants on the task of arranging a last-ditch effort office meeting with Irving Mansfield, Jean Holloway, and Brown. Could the marriage be saved?

The Zanucks concurrently pushed David Brown to get his hands on the thirty-one-page *Love Machine* synopsis from Susann or her publisher. After reading it, Darryl F. Zanuck wrote his son and Brown, calling the synopsis "one of the outstanding commercial properties I have read in a long while. It held me gripped, interested, amused and it proves that the author's writing of *Valley of the Dolls* was no accident. . . . It is [potentially] a smash film with great casting possibilities . . . cannot praise the possibilities any more."

Not surprisingly, with DFZ's rave review, the younger Zanuck's response was entirely negative. Even if the book should become the biggest bestseller of all time, Zanuck opined that "the absence of the pill device" and the fact that "guessing games as to the identity of television characters is not nearly as fascinating as the same games about Hollywood personalities" made it "a much lesser motion picture possibility" than *Valley of the Dolls*.

Nevertheless, Zanuck and Brown met George Chasin at the studio to hear the financial terms for *The Love Machine* screen rights—a staggering $1.5 million plus 7.5 percent of Fox's gross from the first box-office dollar earned. Irving Mansfield also insisted on attaching a rider to the deal that would cut him in for a retroactive share of Fox's sizable profits from the record sales and music publishing rights for *Valley of the Dolls*. It was a very short meeting.

Darryl Zanuck warned: "We would be lunatics to accept such a deal that would set an outlandish precedent. No established star has ever been paid this much and only Broadway hits have ever received this much and that is after they have proven that they are legitimate hits." Brown concurred and revealed inside information to the Zanucks that explained some of the motivation behind Susann's and Mansfield's financial brinkmanship. First, their long-festering resentment of Mark Robson's profit-sharing on *Valley of the Dolls*. Second, Susann's obsession with overtaking Harold Robbins as the world's highest-paid novelist—an idée fixe of Susann's so rabid that Brown reported witnessing her having to be restrained from coming to blows with a Christmas dinner guest who dared to debate whether Susann or Robbins was worth more.

The Hollywood press gleefully reported that Fox's competitors for *The Love Machine* included producer Joseph E. Levine ("an idiot," according to Fox executives, who paid big for the screen rights to Harold Robbins's *The Carpetbaggers*, *Where Love Has Gone*, and *The Adventurers*); Dean Martin (willing to buy the rights at his own expense); Paramount boss Charles Bluhdorn; and Columbia Pictures producer Mike (M. J.) Frankovich (*Bob & Carol & Ted & Alice*), eager to acquire the property for writer-director Richard Brooks (*Elmer Gantry*, *In Cold Blood*), who wanted to make *The Love Machine* his next project. When several bidders found the Mansfields' terms too rich and fell out, Chasin circled back to Fox, offering the movie rights at a reduced $1 million against 10 percent of the gross. Fox relented, but before the deal could close, Frankovich and Columbia swooped in with the full $1.5 million, promising to make Mansfield the film's "executive producer." But not director and *not* listed over the title.

Then came a coup de grâce. In a *Los Angeles Times* story by Wayne Warga, Richard Zanuck answered why he had found it relatively painless to lose to Columbia the movie rights to the soon-to-be-published *The Love Machine*, saying the book's "ingredients are not nearly as good as they were in *Valley of the Dolls*," calling the book's leading character, Robin Stone, "old stuff, particularly in films," and that the plot was "all in *Executive Suite*," before concluding "that and the price made it easy to pass up."

Through studio story executive Jim Fisher, Zanuck summoned Mansfield and screenwriter Jean Holloway for that do-or-die meeting to save their version of *Beyond the Valley of the Dolls* with a quick, focused rewrite. The Mansfields flew to the coast, but after reading Zanuck's comments in the *Los Angeles Times*, when Fisher telephoned them to confirm Mansfield's attendance at the meeting, Susann and Mansfield blasted him with both barrels. Susann berated Zanuck for not calling to personally welcome them, for not sending his customary note with flowers, and, she added, he had "hurt himself" and his reputation as "a bright young guy" by publicly throwing Susann and her new novel under the bus. She commented: "Not a word that he offered a million dollars for the book? He tried to make it look like he'd turned *me* down."

Mansfield affirmed his willingness to keep his morning appointment with Zanuck but not if Jean Holloway was present. Informed that the screenwriter's attendance was nonnegotiable—Zanuck claimed he wanted to determine whether or not the writer should be kept on or cut loose—the conversation devolved into a shouting match. Susann accused Zanuck of treating her husband "like a contract employee," "a chain gang employee." Warned that Fox was likely to view Mansfield's refusal to meet with Holloway and Zanuck as a breach of his producer's contract, Mansfield advised that any threatened litigation should be taken up with his legal team. Soon after, Fox telegrammed Mansfield informing him that he had violated the terms of his producer agreement and was officially off *Beyond the Valley of the Dolls.*

Meanwhile, Darryl F. Zanuck was unrelenting in applying the thumbscrews to Zanuck Jr. to make 20th profitable and relevant—or face the consequences. Roger Ebert characterized the 20th brass as "absolutely desperate to come up with a sequel." But in which direction to go *now* with *Beyond the Valley of the Dolls*? Not, Zanuck decided, backward; the acrimonious falling-out with the Mansfields had made that impossible anyway.

In late June, at the suggestion of David Brown, along came an out-of-left-field new candidate—one-of-a-kind exploitation director-producer-writer-photographer Russ Meyer, a freewheeling, iconoclastic maverick known for casting lavishly endowed women and lantern-jawed, hapless male leads, as well as for his sharp sense of satire, outrageous camp, and social criticism.

Brown sent Zanuck a selection of national magazine and newspaper features on Meyer who, after acidic *New York Herald Tribune* critic Judith Crist praised aspects of his most recent movie *Vixen!,* he advised, "is looking for an opportunity to do something for a major company and is available." Brown floated the possibility of 20th funding a Meyer-directed *Valley* sequel but farming out the release to a smaller, less prestigious company.

Signed by 20th at a salary of $60,000 (about $462,000 today), Meyer chose as his writing partner in crime the untried Roger Ebert, whom Brown described as "a very young, exceedingly groovy film buff." Their combined writing fee was set at $2,500 per week (about $57,000 today), which Meyer kicked over to Ebert. Neither Meyer nor Ebert bothered to read the original novel, but Meyer read the most recent *Beyond the Valley of the Dolls* script draft as well as Jacqueline Susann's original treatment. The writer-director and Ebert screened a studio print of *Valley of the Dolls* on July 16 and then spent three weeks monkeying with Holloway's draft—until they gave up. Instead, they concocted a new script involving young female hopefuls struggling to make it in the L.A. pop music scene. To further sever ties with Susann and the first movie, they initially minimized the Anne and Lyon characters, then renamed them, and, later still, shuffled them off to the sidelines. Out went Barbara Parkins and Paul Burke; this cost-cutting gambit would easily permit Meyer to recast the film with unknowns. It would also potentially allow them to duck paying the $50,000 owed to Susann for a sequel. The studio could now argue—and *did* later argue in court—that the movie was not a sequel. Privately, Brown crowed, "The entire movie will cost us less than Columbia paid for the story rights to *The Love Machine*. Naturally, we will have not only the title going for us but we will also be able to exploit it as being 'By the author of *The Love Machine*.' The cast will be loaded with girls—black and white and yellow as well as every conceivable type of young man." The studio budgeted *Beyond the Valley of the Dolls* at a paltry $900,000 and scheduled a lean shooting schedule with a bare-bones crew.

Then, on the nights of August 8 and 9, psychotic cult leader Charles Manson sent his crazed acolytes Tex Watson, Susan Atkins, Linda Kasabian, and Patricia Krenwinkel to the Benedict

Canyon home at 10050 Cielo Drive, rented from music producer Terry Melcher by director Roman Polanski (then filming in England) and his wife, Sharon Tate. Melcher, who had apparently rejected Manson's musical aspirations, was the target, but Manson's instructions to his followers were to "totally destroy everyone in [it], as gruesome as you can." Back at El Cielo Drive after their return from dinner at the classic El Coyote Mexican Café on Beverly Boulevard, Sharon Tate (eight-and-a-half months pregnant) and several friends, including celebrity hairstylist Jay Sebring (an ex of hers with whom she remained friends), budding screenwriter Wojciech Frykowski, and coffee heiress Abigail Folger, were ritualistically and barbarically slaughtered; the next night, supermarket owner Leno LaBianca and his wife, Rosemary, were similarly murdered. Tate's friend Barbara Parkins has said that she would have been there, too, had she not been traveling in England; Jacqueline Susann had also been invited, but when the author's friend, critic Rex Reed, visited her at the Beverly Hills Hotel, they chose to stay in instead. Susann told friends that when she learned about the murders the following day, she wept by the hotel pool. (Years later, when doctors delivered Susann the grim news that her cancer had recurred, she quipped that she could have sped up her death if only she'd attended Tate's party.)

The unthinkable events paralyzed Hollywood with fear and dread—some would say that it changed the town forever. But Meyer and Ebert decided to use tragedy as grist for their mill, speedily rewriting *Beyond the Valley of the Dolls* as a parody of the first movie, filtered through the gruesome aftermath of the Tate-LaBianca massacres. Without being specific about the movie's resemblance to the recent murders, Meyer announced to reporters that, like *Valley of the Dolls*, his movie would be "big and slick," but unlike *Valley of the Dolls*, it would be "what's happening now." On October 14, David Brown brought Darryl Zanuck up to speed on the project, having just read Meyer and Ebert's new script: "Dick and I are very impressed . . . in terms of its being a wild exploitation film which lives up to the title." In a *Los Angeles Times* piece Aljean Harmetz quoted an unnamed 20th executive saying, "What we are hoping for with *Beyond the Valley of the Dolls* is an X film with an R rating"; Harmetz quoted another unidentified studio source as saying, "Meyer, at least, makes absolutely no pretense about what he does." As the director himself told Harmetz, "The name of the game is box-office. Getting as many fannies on the seats as possible. All I have to sell is my name. People see it and know what to expect."

Rated X and dumped in theaters on June 17, 1970, *Beyond the Valley of the Dolls* began with an introductory title card reading: "The film you are about to see is not a sequel to *Valley of the Dolls*. It is wholly original and bears no relationship to real persons, living or dead. It does, like *Valley of the Dolls*, deal with the oft-times nightmare world of show biz but in a different time and context."

The movie deeply offended such establishment film critics as the *Los Angeles Times*'s estimable Charles Champlin, who called it "a treat for the emotionally retarded, sexually inadequate and dim-witted." The *Washington Post*'s Gary Arnold wrote it off as "the most wretched of movies . . . witless, hysterical, gratuitous, technically inept, needlessly brutal." Other reviews were worse.

Before the film's release, a lawsuit—*Sujac Productions, Ltd. v. Twentieth Century-Fox Film Corporation*—was filed with the Superior Court of the State of California. In it, Susann and Mansfield claimed $10 million in damages, positing that, as a "sex exploitation film, [that] employs total nudity and is scandalous of content," it misled moviegoers and fans of her books, sullied her reputation, and damaged the *Valley of the Dolls* franchise. Yet, the low-budget slasher/musical/parody/hellzapoppin' flick earned $9 million at theaters and eventually, with revival showings and video sales, $40 million. Decades later it attained a level of gonzo cult status that landed it on the *Village Voice*'s 2001 list of the "100 Greatest Films of the Century."

If *Beyond* thwarted Jacqueline Susann's, Barbara Parkins's, and Paul Burke's aspirations for a true *Valley of the Dolls* successor, at least Susann won a vindication of sorts. After the writer's death in September 1974, the court ordered 20th Century Fox to pay her estate $2 million in damages. Barbara Parkins declared herself relieved that she hadn't gotten stuck in "a piece of trash, garbage. It got an 'X' rating. I was better than that."

There may be evidence to suggest that Parkins paid a cost for the months 20th committed her to the possibility of reprising her role in the sequel. She turned down *Goodbye, Columbus* (Ali McGraw did it) and a plum part in *They Shoot Horses, Don't They?* (the one that earned Susannah York an Oscar nomination). Her talent representatives also advised her to reject playing the terminally ill working-class Radcliffe music scholarship heroine in the box-office smash *Love Story*. Parkins has said about those and other missed opportunities, "I must have had my head in the sand. Where were my agents' heads? What were they thinking? I would have become a big star but I have no regrets." Still, when *Beyond the Valley of the Dolls* went sideways, because of Parkins's multipicture deal, "Fox had to give me something." The studio executives' idea of "something" was the role of a sexy glamour girl who cracks safes with her toes in the John Huston–directed spy thriller *The Kremlin Letter*, after which she played a Satanist in the occult horror movie *The Mephisto Waltz*.

CHAPTER EIGHTEEN

Doll Parts

Patty Duke, Sharon Tate, and Barbara Parkins climbed out of the valley and found that after the big buildup, battles, friendships, letdowns, anger, heartbreak, and ridicule, there was redemption—for two of them. Duke admitted that she "shrank, withered, and flew away. I was embarrassed by my work. I'd like to tell you I knew I was doing camp, but I didn't know. I was being serious." Despite her own high ambitions and the faith David Weisbart and 20th had shown in her, major movie stardom slipped through her fingers. Still, she found lots of TV work for which she earned eleven Emmy nominations and three wins—for *My Sweet Charlie*, *Captains and the Kings*, and a redo of *The Miracle Worker* (this time playing Annie Sullivan). Her rambling, troubling 1970 *My Sweet Charlie* Emmy Award acceptance speech offered a national audience a brief window into the harrowing psychological struggles that she had begun to experience during *The Patty Duke Show* and that emerged more dramatically during *Valley of the Dolls*. Her mania, depression, mood swings, violent tendencies, sexual acting out, and alcohol and drug use reached a tipping point, and at thirty-five, she was finally diagnosed and treated for what was then known as manic depression but what we now call bipolar disorder.

Despite Duke's formidable challenges, she rarely stopped working and, from 1985 to 1988, served as president of the Screen Actors Guild. In 2002, she starred in a limited-run revival of Stephen Sondheim's melancholy musical *Follies* and also joined the Broadway revival cast of *Oklahoma!*; in 2009, she joined the national company of *Wicked* during its San Francisco stop. Topping all of those, though, was her tireless work as a champion of civil rights and gay rights and her groundbreaking mental health advocacy. She wrote candidly about her life and challenges in two *New York Times* bestsellers, *Call Me Anna: The Autobiography of Patty Duke* (cowritten with Kenneth Turan) and (with Gloria Hochman) *A Brilliant Madness: Living with Manic-Depressive Illness*. She spoke all over the country in her mission to help destigmatize mental illness. "I've survived. I've beaten my own bad system and, on some days, on most days, that feels like a miracle," she wrote on her website. Happily married since 1986 to Michael Pearce, she died at age sixty-nine in 2016.

Before the unimaginable loss of Sharon Tate in 1969, she married director Roman Polanski in 1968, with Barbara Parkins as her bridesmaid. She followed up *Valley of the Dolls* by stealing the show from Dean Martin and his costars in *The Wrecking Crew*, the Matt Helm spy spoof in which Tate showed comedic promise as a maladroit redheaded spy. Her final film, the frantic Italian-made comedy chase *12 + 1*, paired her with the great Vittorio Gassman and Orson Welles. Since her murder, Tate's look and style have been celebrated on-screen by Sharon Stone in *Casino*, and she has been portrayed by Margot Robbie (as a soulful free spirit in Quentin Tarantino's period revisionist history fantasia *Once Upon a Time . . . in Hollywood*) and Hilary Duff (in the dire and exploitative *The Haunting of Sharon Tate*). Her sister, Debra Tate, a staunch advocate for lifetime incarceration of Manson's followers, created a loving tribute in her 2014 book, *Sharon Tate: Recollection* with a foreword by Roman Polanski. It is nearly impossible to watch Tate in *Valley of the Dolls* and not be moved by her guilelessness, her beauty, and the tragedy of a life cut so short.

In 1968, just after the release of *Valley*, Barbara Parkins relocated to England to live with her lover, actor Omar Sharif. The relationship didn't last, for like Lyon Burke, Sharif liked women very much and at this point in his life, anyway, he might have said what Lyon said: "I'm not looking for a wife." Parkins later characterized Sharif as a man who proposed marriage to every woman he loved. She posed for *Playboy* in 1970 and 1976 and appeared throughout the '70s and '80s in movies and TV shows, including *Lady Randolph Churchill* and *Captains and the Kings*, though never again at the white-heat level of *Peyton Place*. Mostly retired from the public eye since the 1990s, she has made a life beyond Hollywood, pursuing photography, constant world travel, and advocacy for rescued wildlife. Parkins has observed of herself and her *Valley* costars: "There are very eerie but fascinating parallels to our own personal lives and the destinies of the characters of Neely, Jennifer, and Anne as told in the film. Patty's life was eventually plagued with mental problems and addiction and her career as a star falling apart. Sharon, like her character, dies so young—only in life, horrifically murdered at the hands of the Manson family. So sad. Sharon had invited me to the house on that night but I was in England. Had I been in Los Angeles, though, there's no question that I would have been there. I miss Sharon to this day and I think often of that horrible night. And me? I eventually left Hollywood and went home, so to speak, to carry on my life and do what I felt was important. It's kind of amazing and bizarre when you think about it."

Susan Hayward fled back to Florida, but in 1972, five years after *Valley*, she starred in two TV movies, playing a lawyer in *Heat of Anger* and an inner-city doctor in the much better *Say Goodbye, Maggie Cole*. She also played a small role in a William Holden feature-film Western, *The Revengers*. As for Susan Hayward's post-*Valley* personal life, she took up briefly with a southern politician and, though she temporarily curbed her smoking and drinking, health issues forced her to pull out of a sold-out engagement of Jerry Herman's musical *Mame* after seventeen weeks of performances at Caesar's Palace. But she remained the old Hayward. When the temperamental and difficult Celeste Holm was announced as her replacement and rudely crashed Hayward's farewell cast-and-crew gala—shades of Neely O'Hara bulldozing her way into Helen Lawson's after-party—Hayward slashed in lipstick across the powder room mirror: "CELESTE WHO???" and signed it: "SUSAN HAYWARD."

In 1972, after Hayward received a diagnosis of metastatic lung and brain cancer, she began suffering frequent and debilitating epileptic seizures. But she was asked to be an Oscar presenter and she would not be dissuaded. "This will be the last time the public ever sees me, so I want to look beautiful," she told costume designer Nolan Miller. And so, on April 2, 1974, at the 46th Academy Awards ceremony, Hayward was injected backstage with Dilantin to prevent a seizure on camera. Wearing a thirty-pound shimmering Nolan Miller creation and what the designer called "the damnedest Susan Hayward wig ever made," the star made that gallant final public appearance with Charlton Heston, her costar in *The President's Lady*, released twenty-one years earlier. Fifteen minutes after leaving the Dorothy Chandler Pavilion stage, she suffered another major seizure. After enjoying a brief remission, on March 14, 1975, Hayward lost the final battle in a life filled with them.

It's ironic that after decades of attempting to put *Valley of the Dolls* behind them, Lee Grant, Patty Duke, and Barbara Parkins eventually allowed themselves to get swept up in the movie's slow and steady resurgence as a beloved icon of camp, '60s high style, endearing ineptness, wretched excess, and, yes, even early feminism. In many ways, *Valley of the Dolls* was the last gasp of a certain brand of Hollywood glam, shameless melodrama, and irresistible kitsch, which since then has been saluted everywhere from fashion runways to TV shows like *Mad Men*. Harbingers of the movie's resonance, power, and enduring popularity had begun surfacing even by the '70s, when, for instance, Kurt Vonnegut Jr. satirically

consigned to Billy Pilgrim, the hero of *Slaughterhouse-Five*, one single book in English—*Valley of the Dolls*—to pass the time on his
long voyage to Planet Tralfamadore. Meanwhile, the movie's title
became so etched into the pop culture consciousness that the
Jamaican reggae artists Roy & Dizzy, the Fabulous Shoemakers, released the 1971 single "Valley of the Dolls" (a tribute to the version
by King Curtis), and eight years later, the London punk rock band
Generation X (with lead singer Billy Idol) released their song about
fame, "Valley of the Dolls," on a Chrysalis Records album with the
same title.

The *Dolls* renaissance reared its head in the '90s. In 1993's *Bad
Movies We Love*, this writer and Edward Margulies canonized the
hell out of the movie in our book's "The Hall of Shame" chapter.
Sold-out revival house showings around the country were joyously
raucous and participatory—drag queens turned up dressed as the
various characters and audiences ritualistically shouted out the
ripest lines, such as "Ted Casablanca is not a fag, and I'm the dame
who can prove it!" and the deathless "They drummed you right out
of Hollywood, so you come crawling back to Broadway. Well,
Broadway doesn't go for booze and dope." No wonder the movie
became known as "the gay *Rocky Horror Picture Show*."

The film became the embodiment of camp; in other words, at
some point, it became congealed *canned* camp. Performer John
"Lypsinka" Epperson observes, "At one point in *Valley of the Dolls*,
Patty Duke talks about the weekly dance at the sanitarium where
she's trying to rehab, and she says of the dance, 'It's really camp.'
Well, when 'camp' is brought up in a movie that *is* 'camp,' then perhaps 'camp' died at that very moment." Nevertheless, a deliberately
arch 1995 Theater-A-Go-Go! stage parody, featuring Jackie Beat
(the drag persona of actor-singer-screenwriter Kent Fuher) as Helen
Lawson and Kate Flannery (*The Office*), proved such a favorite with
Los Angeles audiences that the production transferred the following year to Greenwich Village's Circle in the Square Downtown.
The Los Angeles County Museum of Art film department hosted a

gala 1997 *"Valley of the Dolls* Weekend" featuring two sold-out screenings of the movie as well as a return performance of the Theater-a-Go-Go! stage version. During that celebration, Courtney Love was seen doing Jennifer North's bust-firming exercises while rocking a beaded gown once owned by Jacqueline Susann, and *E!* online columnist Bruce Bibby (aka Ted Casablanca) asked good-sport special guest Barbara Parkins what she'd been doing with herself for the past thirty years. On k.d. lang's 1997 *Drag* album, the singer sensitively revisited "(Theme From) *Valley of the Dolls*," and in 2015, the R&R Soul Orchestra—retitling it "Why" (Theme from *Valley of the Dolls*)—made the song sound relevant all over again.

Parkins, Grant, and Duke reunited for a *Valley* lovefest on the January 11, 2000, episode of *The View*. Parkins recorded a 2006 audio commentary for the DVD release and showed her capacity for self-deprecating humor during the June 13 release party; Duke had been scheduled to be part of that recording session but, for unspecified reasons, withdrew. Despite time, distance, and the vastly different directions they took in their post-*Valley* lives, the lack of warmth between Patty Duke and Barbara Parkins seemed to persist. When in September of 2010, Parkins was quoted during a fan event as calling Duke "cold and reserved" during the making of the movie, Duke took to Facebook to hold out an olive branch: "Dear Barbara Parkins, I hope this will reach you thru electronic magic. I learned yesterday that you were quoted in a Chicago publication, as saying, you feel that I have been cold and reserved to you. I apologize for what I may have done to give you this impression. It is far from what I really feel. Hope you are well and happy, and . . . that the holidays, bring you great joy. Anna Patty Duke."

In 2014, *Valley* addict Courtney Love saluted her obsession with her animated video (with Michael Mouris) *Valley of the Doll Parts*, spoofing the movie, herself, *and* Lindsay Lohan, Paula Deen, Miley Cyrus, Chloë Sevigny, and James Franco. And in the ongoing triumphant march of the *Dolls*, the prestigious Criterion Collection produced a deluxe 2016 double DVD set, packed with extras. Parkins discovered that her own daughter, Christina, had become a *Valley of the Dolls* cultist when she would repeatedly invite friends over for *Valley* nights. Parkins would hear her daughter and friends "laughing and hooting" until she'd go in and say, "'It's not that funny! It's about dealing with drugs and sex and three women spiraling out of control and it's a sad story.' And she'd say, 'Oh, but it's sooo funny, Mommy, look at you.'"

Jacqueline Susann's financial haul from the Hollywood sale of the rights to her second novel, *The Love Machine*, made her $1.5 million richer in 1969. The film version flopped with audiences, but the book sold well, despite many critics complaining it lacked the punch, the sweep, the sexiness, the va-voom of *Valley of the Dolls*. Susann came back stronger in 1973 with *Once Is Not Enough*, another novel that also earned terrible reviews but became the year's second biggest publishing success. Robert Evans championed the film version of the book at Paramount, with Irving Mansfield serving as its executive producer, and it turned out to be a decent moneymaker but no *Valley*.

Troubled by a racking cough, Susann, a heavy smoker, was diagnosed in 1973 with lung cancer and underwent cobalt and chemotherapy sessions. The cancer metastasized, and after being admitted on her fifty-sixth birthday to Doctors Hospital at 170 East End Avenue, opposite Gracie Mansion (known as the treatment center of choice for the rich and famous), she died on September 21, 1974. Her last words to her husband were: "Come on, doll, let's get the hell out of here." What a dame!

After her death came the 1976 publication of her novella *Dolores*, a Jackie Kennedy roman à clef that became a big bestseller. Her science fiction romance, *Yargo*, a trunk item from the 1950s that should have stayed there, hit the original paperback market in 1979. Among the announced projects Susann never got the chance to write was one that would have focused on the son of Neely O'Hara (so would that have been based on Joey Luft or . . . ?) and *The Comedy Twins*, another roman à clef show business novel about a pair of warring brothers, believed to be inspired by the miserable and abusive relationship between major star Milton Berle and his never-was-a-star brother Frank.

The Oedipal rivalry between Darryl F. Zanuck and his son, Richard, nearly destroyed them both. In 1970, Zanuck Sr. seemed mostly devoted to the futile effort of making a star out of his latest mistress, Genevieve Gilles, and to the removal of his son from the top production post at 20th. When Zanuck orchestrated the ouster of his son, Richard's mother, Virginia, signed over her hundred thousand 20th shares to shareholders outraged by Zanuck Sr.'s poor business decisions and philandering. The stockholders voted out the senior Zanuck in a bloodless coup. After Darryl F. Zanuck was deposed from the studio he helped make into one of Hollywood's most envied, his health declined. He suffered a stroke and returned to the United States, where he and his son reconciled. Zanuck also returned to Virginia, and they lived together until his death in 1979 at age seventy-seven.

Zanuck Jr. and David Brown created the Zanuck/Brown Company and went on to produce *The Sting, Jaws, Cocoon*, and *Driving Miss Daisy*. David Brown's last movie was *Along Came a Spider* in 2001; he died in 2010 at ninety-three. Richard D. Zanuck ended his movie career with Tim Burton's 2012 *Dark Shadows*, though others produced his projects after his death. He succumbed to a heart attack in 2012 at seventy-seven, the same age as his father.

As for other key figures involved in the making of *Valley of the Dolls*, costume designer William Travilla and actor Paul Burke worked again with Mark Robson on *Daddy's Gone A-Hunting*, released in 1969; later in his career, the designer moved into TV with long-term commitments on *Knots Landing* and *Dallas* before he died in 1990 at age seventy. Cinematographer William Daniels shot his final feature films, *Marlowe* in 1969 and *Move* in 1970, and died that year at age sixty-eight. Editor Dorothy Spencer cut Mark Robson's *Daddy's Gone-A-Hunting*; *Happy Birthday, Wanda June*; *Limbo*;

and *Earthquake* before retiring in 1979 with *The Concorde . . . Airport '79*; she died in 2002 at ninety-three.

John Williams reunited with Mark Robson, composing the *Earthquake* score, and went on to honor and renown for his work on the *Star Wars*, *Raiders of the Lost Ark*, *Jurassic Park*, and *Harry Potter* franchises, as well as *E.T. the Extra-Terrestrial* and *Schindler's List*. Mark Robson made five more movies after *Valley of the Dolls*, including the hugely profitable *Earthquake*, before a heart attack claimed his life in 1978, just days before he would have completed production on the troubled and contentious *Avalanche Express*.

In the years marking the ascendance of *Valley of the Dolls*, some in Hollywood have badly wanted to have another shot at it—or, at the very least, a way to celebrate it. 1981 brought a dreary, fun-free CBS *Valley of the Dolls* miniseries, and in 1994, for a single season, there came a loosely adapted late-night nudity-friendly soap opera worth seeing mostly for Sally Kirkland's out-there performance as Helen Lawson. In *Scandalous Me: The Jacqueline Susann Story*, the 1998 USA Network TV movie, Michele Lee played Jackie, and Barbara Parkins played Annie Laurie Williams, the agent who sold *Valley of the Dolls* to 20th. The same year, news about two *Valley* movie projects surfaced. Rhino Films (*Fear and Loathing in Las Vegas*, *Why Do Fools Fall in Love*) executives began talking about a *Beyond the Valley of the Dolls* remake, and at Fox, actress-director Betty Thomas (*The Brady Bunch Movie*) was in line to produce and (possibly) direct what was reported as a "wicked, *Brady Bunch*–like spin" contemporary remake for 20th Century Fox; four years later, the project was in preproduction stage—then it wasn't any longer. In 2000, Bette Midler (a Razzie nominee for Worst Actress) and Nathan Lane played Jackie and Irving for laughs for director Andrew Bergman (*The Freshman*) and screenwriter Paul Rudnick (*In & Out*). Roger Ebert, who, after all, scripted *Beyond the Valley of the Dolls*, wrote of *Isn't She Great*: "Jackie Susann deserved better." Indeed, she did.

The estate of Jacqueline Susann chose Rae Lawrence to continue the *Dolls* saga. Although Lawrence was given access to Susann's early work on the *Valley of the Dolls* sequel, in its 2001 publication, *Shadow of the Dolls* was dismissed by *Kirkus Reviews* as a "capable but unexciting rehash." Late that same year, Marlo Thomas (who had been a candidate to play both Neely *and* Anne in the 1967 movie) portrayed Jacqueline Susann opposite F. Murray Abraham's Irving Mansfield in Barbara Zitwer and Mark Hampton's play *Paper Doll*; Pittsburgh Public Theater audiences were more enthusiastic than the critics. Leonard Foglia (*Master Class*) directed a revised version of *Paper Doll* that February and March at Duke University in North Carolina, and though the show was scheduled for a spring 2002 Broadway opening with Fran Drescher replacing Thomas and Abraham remaining in the role, it never happened. A one-woman play by Paul Minx, *See How Beautiful I Am: The Return of Jackie Susann*, debuted at the 2001 Edinburgh Festival and was performed again in 2008.

Things sounded a bit more solid in 2011, when Lee Daniels (*Empire*) announced plans to write and direct a *Valley of the Dolls* TV pilot set in the 1960s for 20th Century Fox and Chernin Entertainment; it is believed that legal hiccups and the failure of two other post–*Mad Men* '60s period dramas cooled Hollywood toward the project. Asked how *Valley* influenced Daniels's 20th television musical drama TV series *Star*, which ran from 2016 to 2019, he said, "Because it lived in me a little bit longer about women and their struggles for fame in Hollywood. For me, it was about women and fame and people taking advantage of them, and also what these three girls would do to get to the top." Which explains why Queen Latifah even utters, "Sparkle, Neely, Sparkle!" on the show's 2017 episode titled "Code of Silence."

But no true *Valley of the Dolls* addict will be satisfied with such temporary, transitory fixes. That's why, ever since 2014, the pulses of *Doll*-aholics have quickened with any rumor that a potential big-screen version, documentary, or limited series is on the way. At one point, playwright and screenwriter Paul Rudnick, who scripted *Isn't She Great* and 2004's *The Stepford Wives* redo, had reportedly polished off a *Dolls* remake screenplay. The starry names most often tossed around as potential Dolls have included Anne Hathaway, Emmy Rossum, and Lily Collins as Anne Welles; Jennifer Lawrence, Blake Lively, or Gal Gadot as Jennifer North; Madonna, Glenn Close, Cate Blanchett, Patti Lupone, and Meryl Streep as Helen Lawson; and Lily James, Emma Stone, and Juno Temple as Neely. But someone slammed on the brakes, and the movie never got made.

Still, hope springs eternal. Movie critic, author, and podcaster Alonso Duralde says, "I dream that one day Todd Haynes will do for *Valley* what he did for *Mildred Pierce*—an exhaustively faithful adaptation that includes the novel's passage of time, the fiancés who didn't make it to the big screen, and the tumult of Anne and Lyon's marriage. But what I'd most like to see restored from the book is the friendship between the three women. In Susann's novel, Anne and Neely are supportive neighbors as they're both starting out in New York City, and they eventually share an apartment with Jennifer, the three of them backing each other up and helping each other out (until Neely betrays Anne, of course, and it stings all the more in the book because their friendship has been so well cemented). Say what you will about the 1967 feature (and I've said plenty, admittedly), one of its biggest failings is that the three heroines are on-screen together only once—the still photo of Neely and Mel's wedding. The book is ripe for a screen version that goes deep, and I hope someone makes it in my lifetime."

Valley of the Dolls fever is such a thing that, in fact, Red Cherry Eyelashes has launched a special collection—"Inspired by Jacqueline Susann's *Valley of the Dolls*"—with a choice of lashes of various lengths and thicknesses dubbed "Molly," "Mary Jane," and "Xannie." In the past decade, the movie's retro-glam appeal has been saluted in dozens of international magazines, including everything from *Harper's Bazaar* to *People*, featuring work by designers Tom Ford, Issey Miyake, Lanvin, and Yves St. Laurent. Deal with it. The longer the jones for another *Valley of the Dolls* gets denied, the more ravenous it grows. And here's why. . . .

CODA

Valley of the Dolls has left its lipstick traces all over pop culture. Jacqueline Susann's book—with its depictions of female solidarity, of women asserting their sexuality, of women ascending to positions of power—was way ahead of the curve. She wrote about prescription drug addiction when it seemed like an anomaly confined to the beautiful and the damned who lived their lives upon the wicked stage. In 2019, statistics tell us that 5 million people are chronic abusers of sedatives and tranquilizers, 3.3 million people abuse painkillers, and 1.7 million are hooked on stimulants. In 2017, more than 70,200 Americans died from drug overdoses.

In many ways Susann flew in the face of the confines and strictures of the era in which she lived. She refused to "know her place," to pretend to be a contented housewife, or to stay in her lane. She insisted she had valuable things to say to and about women. Mocked as mawkish, sensationalistic, and inept, when Susann wrote, she laid her cards on the table about relationships, addiction, marriage, loss, infidelity, ambition, depression, careerism, the emptiness of fame and success, aging, and the beauty trap. Those subjects had always been fair game before, of course, so long as the writer was male.

Valley of the Dolls casts a spell because it feels real and lived-in. Susann was no prose stylist, but she was a born storyteller. She creates memorable, funny, sexy, messed-up, foolish, relatable, brave characters who become dependent on pills to sleep, to forget, to get slim, to work harder and faster, to get happy, to sparkle. She writes about them with unshakable sincerity and conviction. No winking, no irony, no tongue in cheek. The novel is bleak and unsparing. In Susann's universe, rich, handsome white knights may come along, but they're almost invariably fallible, unreliable, ineffectual. No one gets a happy ending. *Time will take you on,* Susann warns, *and it will claim your youth, your looks, your desirability, your health, your intellect, your value in the eyes of society. All you've got, if you're lucky, is your talent and maybe some self-esteem and a good friend or two.*

That message didn't always go down so well in the mid-60s, especially among feminists. Today, though, Susann has about as many champions as she does critics. Feminist culture critic Camille Paglia views *Valley of the Dolls* as "one of the great books of the postwar era. The kind of language that [Susann] uses and the kind of imagination she has are totally contemporary." Brooke Hauser (author of *Enter Helen: The Invention of Helen Gurley Brown and the Rise of the Modern Single Woman*) rightly called *Valley of the Dolls* "a very angry book" that "showed the ugly, seedy side of womanhood. It showed what happens when women age and lose their beauty and what kind of double standard exists in society."

There is far less rage, sincerity, or authenticity in the work of novelists directly influenced by Susann's money-sex-power, "blind item"–driven dynamic. But that didn't hinder the extraordinary publishing success of imitators, including Judith Krantz (*Scruples, Princess Daisy,* and *Mistral's Daughter*), Sidney Sheldon (*The Patty Duke Show* and *I Dream of Jeannie* creator who wrote *A Stranger in the Mirror* and *The Other Side of Midnight*), Jackie Collins (*The World Is Full of Married Men, The Stud,* et al.), and more. 1993 saw the publication of a curio called *Just This Once,* the brainchild of Scott French, who reportedly spent eight years and lots of cash concocting an artificial intelligence program meant to emulate Jacqueline Susann's writing style, plotting, characters, and dialogue— as if it were that easy. On publication, few critics went easy on the novel. Susann's estate raised legal objections that, in this brave new world of ever-mutating technical innovation, went straight to the heart of copyright laws. In the end, the Carol Publishing Group and the Susann estate agreed to split the profits of a print run of thirty-five thousand copies.

Other Susann successors and admirers have invaded television. From 1998 to 2004, for instance, millions of viewers got hopelessly hooked on HBO's boundary-nudging, catty, moving, and wise zeitgeist series *Sex and the City*, the creator of which, Candace Bushnell, wrote of *Valley of the Dolls*, "It's always been a bit of an inspiration for me." When that series ran its course, *Girls* took up the cause from 2011 to 2017. In 2016, Lena Dunham, the show's creator, posted on Instagram a *Valley of the Dolls* publicity photo of Patty Duke reaching toward a giant bottle of red pills along with this missive: "Lately I've been noticing that nearly every pop cultural image we see of a woman on psychiatric medication is that of an out-of-control, exhausting and exhausted girl who needs help. But guess what? Most women on meds are women who have been brave enough to help themselves. It's important that we see normalizing portrayals of people, women, choosing to take action when it comes to their mental health. Meds didn't make me a hollowed out version of my former self or a messy bar patron with a bad bleach job. They allowed me to really meet myself. I wish that for every lady who has ever struggled. There's really no shame. Night, dolls." In November of 2018, Dunham stepped forward to acknowledge that she, a survivor of sexual assault and coping with multiple surgeries to treat a serious medical condition, had been sober for six months after "misusing" the anti-anxiety drug Klonopin.

Even in death, Susann has the last laugh. Today, who reads Harold Robbins and Sidney Sheldon, whose novels feel past their prime? Lots and lots of people read Jacqueline Susann, whose work gets constantly rediscovered, talked about, and enjoyed. When, in July of 2016, Grove Atlantic published a fiftieth anniversary edition, sales figures totaled over 300,000 copies, adding to the book's earlier total sale of over 31 million copies in thirty languages. Transgender actress Laverne Cox (*Orange Is the New Black*) narrated the audio version. As for the film version of *Valley of the Dolls*, well, that is a clotheshorse of a different color. Of course the film gains some of its tailwind by carrying over the virtues of Susann's work—the big characters, the outsized melodrama—but on the big screen, unlike in the novel, we experience it all at an emotional distance. The film is a chilly, weirdly zombified, hollowed-out thing, oddly edited, disjointed, underpopulated, cheaply appointed, and without a drop of Susann's full-steam and damn-the-torpedoes authenticity, commitment, or sincerity. It pulls its punches. So we revere it instead for its sometimes screamingly '60s, sometimes timeless fashions, its stabs at glamour, its deeply terrible, endlessly quotable dialogue, ridiculous songs, thousands and thousands of dollars in full wigs and falls, and its acting. There's the hallucinatory, machine-polished perfection of Barbara Parkins's coiffures, makeup, furs, voice, world-class hair, and impenetrable *hauteur*. We revel in Lee Grant's fascinating, slightly sapphic, spidery weirdness.

But time has also caught up with the movie in certain unforeseen ways. Sure, Patty Duke's endearing, disquieting, and untethered too-muchness remains a hoot, but less so when one becomes aware of the addiction and mental health challenges she suffered before, during, and after shooting. As for Susan Hayward, she ranges from radiating full-on movie stardom to looking just plain out of it, which makes much more sense when one knows of her alcoholism, her 1955 attempt at suicide with an overdose of sleeping pills, and the possibility that she had begun to show the effects of the brain cancer that would claim her life in 1975. And then, there's the presence of Sharon Tate, who is so immediate, raw, and unguarded that your heart goes out to her. That she suffered an unimaginably ghastly and cruel demise makes watching her exquisitely touching and makes her character's death scene, accompanied by John Williams's lovely score, almost unbearably poignant.

A number of *Dolls* companion-piece films have been almost as campy—try keeping a straight face watching Pia Zadora accept a screenwriting Oscar in *The Lonely Lady*, saying, "I don't suppose I'm the only one who's had to fuck her way to the top," and what is *Showgirls* but the unholy union of *Valley of the Dolls* and *All About*

Eve, sleazed up with stripper poles, lap dances, and screenwriter Joe Eszterhas's jaw-droppingly antiwoman dialogue? But as the world grows steadily grimmer, stranger, and slower to laugh, *Valley of the Dolls* is likely to remain unchallenged in its position at the peak of the Mount Everest of brilliant, irresistible, life-transforming badness.

Acknowledgments

So many people graciously shared intense and candid personal memories of Hollywood in the '60s, of Jacqueline Susann, of 20th Century Fox, of the making of *Valley of the Dolls*. Over the years, those who were *there*—Sherry Alberoni, Army Archerd, Jack Arnold, Brendon Boone, Scotty Bowers, Suze Lanier-Bramlett, Sue Cameron, Mimi Craven, Herbert Diamond, Nina Foch, Sydney Guilaroff, Ernest Harada, Ross Hunter, Martin Kearns, Karen Jensen, Ernest Lehman, Janet Leigh, Eva Marie Saint, Lara Lindsay, John Martin, Jeff Maxwell, Leslie McRay, Marilyn Michaels, Terry Moore, Kim Novak, Letty Cottin Pogrebin, Johanna Ray, Christopher Riordan, Joan Rivers, Nat Segaloff, Connie Stevens, Venetia Stevenson, Lurene Tuttle, Raquel Welch, Albert Whitlock, Patricia Winters—told me the most extraordinary (sometimes unprintable) things, providing me with the closest possible experience to *being there* without actually having been. Not all of you are cited in the book but, believe me, you're in there. All of it, all of you are deeply appreciated. For their smarts, good humor, generosity, and patience with even the most micro of questions (*Valley* superfan) Alonso Duralde, Howard Green, William J. Jankowski (such a talented author and loving friend to Patty Duke), Tom Lisanti, Albert Poland, Don Romano, Matt Tyrnauer, and Andy Zambella (that adoring fan and friend of Barbara Parkins) just couldn't be beat. I am deeply and permanently indebted to *Dolls*-aholic Carlton Stovall, whose generosity, knowledge, and kindness are boundless. At the Cinematic Arts Library at the University of Southern California, Edward Sykes Comstock, the great Ned, made my access to the David Weisbart Collection a joy. Even when I thought I'd exhausted every possible resource there, Ned came back with even more. My gratitude to Peggy Alexander, curator, Performing Arts at the UCLA Library Special Collections, where I spent long joyful hours absorbing the trove of materials in the Mark Robson Collection and its fascinating items pertaining to *Valley of the Dolls*, *Von Ryan's Express*, and other Robson projects. Every visit to the Margaret Herrick Library of the Academy of Motion Picture Arts and Sciences yielded more puzzle pieces, most especially when Howard Prouty and Louise Hilton gave me the earliest possible access to the pertinent documents in the Richard Zanuck Collection. Although my loving, boisterous, complicated, one-of-a-kind family is not as large as it once was, the memories loom large in my storehouse of peak, formative experiences; even when I bewildered them, the deep affection never waned. I wish all of you were still here to laugh and cry with. My impossible, brilliant colleague, cowriter, and friend Ed Margulies, that goes for you, too. As for the friends and colleagues who instantly *got* what this book is, I can never thank you enough for the feeling I got watching your eyes light up; Robin Aiello, Alan Barnette, Suze Lanier-Bramlett, Deborah Corday, Barry Gray, Kevin O'Brien, Eileen O'Farrell, and Shane Zade. I love that your passion and enthusiasm reads so easily. My love to the adored purr brigade Rudolph, Jack "Frosty" Frost, Magnus, and Callie, who (along with the departed, acutely missed Gustav and Benjamin Button) were always nearby to give me a lift and to insist that I remember my priorities. Without Gary, of course, none of it would be half as much fun. And I will be eternally grateful to my literary agent Mary Evans for her rock-steady belief that this was one story I was meant to tell. You persevered and triumphed in getting it to the editor for whom it was always meant. And to my brilliant, funny, gifted editor Rick Kot, it was more than worth the long, long wait.

Selected Bibliography

Andersen, Christopher P. *A Star, Is A Star, Is A Star! The Lives and Loves of Susan Hayward*. Doubleday, 1980.

Arceri, Gene. *Brooklyn's Scarlett—Susan Hayward: Fire in the Wind*. BearManor Media, 2010.

Behlmer, Rudy, Richard D. Zanuck, et al. *Memo from Darryl F. Zanuck: The Golden Years at Twentieth Century-Fox*. Grove Press, 1993.

Biskind, Peter. *Easy Riders, Raging Bulls: How the Sex-Drugs-and-Rock 'N' Roll Generation Saved Hollywood*. Simon & Schuster, 1998.

Brown, David. *Let Me Entertain You*. William Morrow & Company, 1990.

Bugliosi, Vincent, with Curt Gentry. *Helter Skelter: The True Story of the Manson Murders*. W. W. Norton & Company, 1994.

Clarke, Gerald. *Get Happy: The Life of Judy Garland*. Delta, 2001.

Core, Philip. *Camp: The Lie That Tells the Truth*. Delilah Books, 1984.

Custen, George F. *Twentieth Century's Fox: Darryl F. Zanuck and the Culture of Hollywood*. Basic Books, 1998.

Duke, Patty, and Kenneth Turan. *Call Me Anna: The Autobiography of Patty Duke*. Bantam, 1988.

Duke, Patty, and Gloria Hochman. *A Brilliant Madness: Living with Manic-Depressive Illness*. Bantam, 1997.

Duke, Patty, and William J. Jankowski. *In the Presence of Greatness: My Sixty-Year Journey as an Actress*. BearManor Media, 2018.

Dunne, John Gregory. *The Studio*. Vintage Books, 1998.

Edwards, Anne. *Judy Garland: A Biography*. Taylor Trade Publishing, 2013.

Evans, Robert. *The Kid Stays in the Picture.* It Books, 2013.

———. *The Fat Lady Sang.* It Books, 2013.

Finch, Christopher. *Rainbow: The Stormy Life of Judy Garland.* Grosset & Dunlap, 1975.

Grant, Lee. *I Said Yes to Everything*: *A Memoir.* Blue Rider Press, 2014.

Guinn, Jeff. *Manson: The Life and Times of Charles Manson.* Simon & Schuster, 2014.

Gussow, Mel. *Don't Say Yes Until I Finish Talking: A Biography of Darryl F. Zanuck.* Doubleday & Company, 1971.

Harris, Mark. *Pictures at a Revolution: Five Movies and the Birth of the New Hollywood.* Penguin Books, 2009.

Harris, Marlys J. *The Zanucks of Hollywood: The Dark Legacy of an American Dynasty.* Crown, 1989.

Holston, Kim R. *Susan Hayward: Her Films and Life.* McFarland & Company, 2015.

Jaffe, Rona. *The Best of Everything.* Penguin Books, 2005.

Kellow, Brian. *Ethel Merman: A Life.* Penguin Books, 2008.

Korda, Michael. *Another Life: A Memoir of Older People.* Delta, 2000.

Koster, Bob. *Adventures in Hollywood.* BearManor Media, 2013.

Levy, Emmanuel. *Vincente Minnelli: Hollywood's Dark Dreamer.* St. Martin's Press, 2009.

Linet, Beverly. *Susan Hayward: Portrait of a Survivor.* Atheneum Books, 1980.

Lisanti, Tom. *Fantasy Femmes of Sixties Cinema: Interviews with 20 Actresses from Biker, Beach, and Elvis Movies.* McFarland & Company, 2015.

Lisanti, Tom. *Glamour Girls of Sixties Hollywood: Seventy-Five Profiles.* McFarland & Company, 2015.

———. *Drive-in Dream Girls: A Galaxy of B-Movie Starlets of the Sixties.* BearManor Media, 2017.

Margulies, Edward, and Stephen Rebello. *Bad Movies We Love.* Plume, 1993.

Mosley, Leonard. *Zanuck: The Rise and Fall of Hollywood's Last Tycoon.* Little Brown & Co., 1984.

Rebello, Stephen. *Alfred Hitchcock and the Making of* Psycho. Dembner Books, 1990.

Sanders, Ed. *The Family: The Story of Charles Manson's Dune Buggy Attack Battalion.* Dutton, 1971.

——. *Sharon Tate: A Life*. Da Capo Press, 2016.

Seaman, Barbara. *Lovely Me: The Life of Jacqueline Susann*. William Morrow & Company, 1987.

Segaloff, Nat, and David G. Grubbs. *A Lit Fuse: The Provocative Life of Harlan Ellison*. NESFA Press, 2017.

Shipman, David. *Judy Garland: The Secret Life of an American Legend*. Hyperion, 1993.

Statman, Alisa, and Brie Tate. *Restless Souls: The Sharon Tate Family's Account of Stardom, the Manson Murders, and a Crusade for Justice*. It Books, 2012.

Susann, Jaqueline. *Valley of the Dolls*. Bernard Geis Associates, 1966.

Tate, Debra. *Sharon Tate: Recollection*. Running Press, 2014.

Thomas, Tony, and Aubrey Solomon. *The Films of 20th Century Fox*. Citadel Press, 1979.

Photo Credits

Insert page 1: (*top*): Collection of the author; (*bottom*): Courtesy of Letty Cottin Pogrebin

Page 2: (*top*): Curt Johnson; (*bottom left and right*): Collection of the author

Page 3: (*top and center*): 1967, 20th Century Fox, 2020, The Walt Disney Company, photo courtesy of Alonso Duralde; (*bottom*): Collection of the author

Page 4: (*top left*): 1967, 20th Century Fox, 2020, The Walt Disney Company

Pages 4 and 5: (Travilla sketches): The Jason Merrin Collection

Pages 6 and 7: 1967, 20th Century Fox, 2020, The Walt Disney Company, courtesy of The Jason Merrin Collection

Page 8: (*top*): 1967, 20th Century Fox, 2020, The Walt Disney Company, courtesy of The Jason Merrin Collection; (*bottom*): 1967, 20th Century Fox, 2020, The Walt Disney Company, from the collection of the author

Page 9: 1967, 20th Century Fox, 2020, The Walt Disney Company

Page 10: (*top*): 1967, 20th Century Fox, 2020, The Walt Disney Company; (*center*): 1967, 20th Century Fox, 2020, The Walt Disney Company, courtesy of Alonso Duralde; (*bottom*): 1967, 20th Century Fox, 2020, The Walt Disney Company

Page 11: (*top*): The Jason Merrin Collection; (*bottom left and right*): 1967, 20th Century Fox, 2020, The Walt Disney Company

Index of Names